HUMAN BEHAVIOR
FOR SOCIAL WORK PRACTICE
A Developmental-Ecological Framework

HUMAN BEHAVIOR
FOR SOCIAL WORK PRACTICE
A Developmental-Ecological Framework

Wendy L. Haight
University of Illinois

Edward H. Taylor
University of Minnesota

LYCEUM
BOOKS, INC.

5758 South Blackstone Avenue
Chicago, Illinois 60637

© Lyceum Books, Inc., 2007

Published by

LYCEUM BOOKS, INC.
5758 S. Blackstone Ave.
Chicago, Illinois 60637
773+643-1903 (Fax)
773+643-1902 (Phone)
lyceum@lyceumbooks.com
http://www.lyceumbooks.com

10 9 8 7 6 5 4 3 2 1

ISBN 0-925065-91-9

ISBN-13 978-0-925065-91-9

We are grateful to Mary Whalen and Dawn D'Amico for permission to use their
photographs.

Haight, Wendy L., 1958-
    Human behavior for social work practice : a developmental-ecological framework /
Wendy Haight, Edward H. Taylor.
        p. cm.
    Includes bibliographical references.
    ISBN 0-925065-91-9 (alk. paper)
        1. Social service–Philosophy. 2. Social service–Methodology. 3. Social service–
Research. I. Taylor, Edward H. II. Title.
HV40.H22 2006
361.3'2–dc22   2005037290

For my parents, Richard L. Haight and Donna V. Biotano Haight

For my children, Dominique and Marisa Taylor

About the Authors

Wendy L. Haight is associate professor and PhD program director at the University of Illinois School of Social Work at Urbana-Champaign. Her BA is from Reed College, and her PhD is from the University of Chicago where she studied developmental psychology. Her research focuses on vulnerable families involved with the public child welfare system. Most recently, she and her colleagues have described the psychological development, experiences, and perceptions of rural children who live in foster care because of parent methamphetamine abuse. Based on this descriptive data, they developed and are currently evaluating a mental health intervention for rural foster children from methamphetamine-involved families who are experiencing trauma symptoms. She is the author of *Africian American Children at Church: A Sociopolitical Perspective* and co-author of *Raise Up A Child*, and *Pretending at Home: Development in a Sociocultural Context*.

Edward H. Taylor is associate professor in the School of Social Work at the University of Minnesota, Twin Cities Campus. Previously he served as chief of social work for the Department of Psychiatry, University of North Carolina, and he spent ten years as a clinical social worker and researcher with the National Institute of Mental Health, Intramural Research Program. Throughout his career, Professor Taylor has specialized in assessing, treating, and researching children and young adults with severe mental disorders. He is co-author of *Schizophrenia and Manic Depressive Disorder* and author of the *Atlas of Bipolar Disorders*.

Contents

Preface

1. **A Developmental-Ecological Framework** 1
   Developmental-Ecological Analysis of Social Work Issues 4
   Developmental Theories 5
   Integrating Ecological-Systems Perspectives with
   Developmental Perspectives 18
   Building the Knowledge Base Through Applied Social
   Science Research 24
   Summary 26

2. **Social Work with Infants and Young Children**
   *Attachment Relations in the Family** 34
   Child Welfare with Infants and Young Children 37
   Highlights of Development During Infancy and Early
   Childhood 40
   Development and Organization of Attachment
   Relationships 47
   Implications for Child Welfare 58
   Summary 66

3. **Social Work with Children in Middle Childhood**
   Spiritual Development in the Community 76
   Highlights of Development During Middle Childhood 79
   Developmental-Ecological Analysis of Spiritual
   Development in Middle Childhood 88
   Implications for Social Work with School-Age Children
   and Their Families 98
   Summary 103

4. **Social Work with Adolescents**
   *Mentoring in Schools** 108
   School Social Work with Adolescents 110
   Highlights of Development During Adolescence 114
   The Development of Mentoring Relationships 124
   Implications for School Social Work with Adolescents 130
   Summary 134

5. **Social Work with Young Adults**
    Professional Development and Multicultural
    Education in Schools of Social Work. **143**
    Social Work Education with Young Adults 145
    Highlights of Development in Early Adulthood 146
    Facilitating the Professional Development of Social
    Work Students 152
    Implications for Social Work Education 157
    Summary 163

6. **Social Work with Midlife Adults in Mental**
    Health Contexts:
    Understanding and Treating Depression **169**
    Mental Health Care with Midlife Adults 170
    Highlights of Development in Middle Adulthood 177
    Developmental-Ecological Analysis of Depression in
    Middle Adulthood 183
    Implications for Social Work 191
    Summary 192

7. **Medical Social Work with Older Adults**
    Alzheimer's Disease **199**
    Medical Social Work with Older Adults 204
    Overview of Development in Late Adulthood 208
    Alzheimer's Disease: Developmental-Ecological Analysis . . . 215
    Intervention 218
    Summary 226

8. **Conclusion.** **235**
    Developmental-Ecological Framework Guides Problem
    Solving in Social Work 237
    Modern Social Work is Evidence-Based 238
    Social Work Issues Affect Multiple Interacting Systems 240
    Social Work Issues Affect Individuals Across the Life Span . 241
    A Global Perspective is Necessary to Social Work in
    the Twenty-First Century 242

Glossary. **243**

Index **251**

Chapters 2 and 4 are coauthored with Susan A. Cole.

Preface

This book grew from a series of conversations about the complexities of teaching the social work foundation course, Human Behavior in the Social Environment (HBSE I). HBSE is a broad curriculum area that provides the basic foundation knowledge for understanding how humans respond and adapt to life challenges such as illness, interpersonal violence, poverty, war, and natural disaster. We felt a responsibility to introduce students to the broad range of social science theory and research that undergirds the responses of modern social workers to challenges faced by clients, but also to provide a coherent problem-solving framework for applying social science content to social work. We strived to avoid a superficial listing of findings, and to provide students with analytic strategies for approaching the many evolving social problems they will face in the twenty-first century. This book is an outgrowth of our attempts over the past decade to introduce HBSE I students to social science research as interpreted through the goals and values of social work.

The goal of our text is to communicate a strategy for critical thinking and problem solving. The goal is not to provide a traditional, comprehensive overview of HBSE. Such breadth would necessarily sacrifice the depth necessary to adequately illustrate the use of social science to address complex social work issues. We recommend that our text be used in conjunction with a series of selected readings chosen by the instructor. To aid students and instructors, each chapter provides a comprehensive list of references, as well as text and Web-based resources.

Our text begins with an in-depth presentation of the developmental-ecological framework as an analytic strategy for understanding complex, contemporary social issues. This framework is compatible with the bio-psycho-social-spiritual perspective of the social work curriculum but elaborates on this model with a focus on the complexity and diversity of developmental change. The presentation of developmental change does not focus on traditional stage theories, but on more contemporary cultural-historical concepts of development as a loosely coordinated ensemble of change embedded within particular contexts and individual lives.

Throughout the text, we illustrate a developmental-ecological framework through in-depth presentation of issues relevant to twenty-first-century social workers. We have selected a range of current issues relevant for clients throughout the life span, and in various contexts of social work practice. These issues include supporting the attachment relationships of infants and young children in the child welfare system; development of children through community organizations; adjustment and achievement of at-risk adolescents through school-based mentoring; professional socialization of young adults through social work education; mental health of individuals in middle adulthood; and functioning of older adults living with Alzheimer's disease.

For the purposes of discussion, we take as our unit of analysis the individual. This is not because we believe that individual pathology is the root of complex societal problems such as poverty, or that the individual is necessarily the appropriate level of intervention. Rather, we choose to focus on the individual level of analysis because many social workers on the front lines confront complex social problems as manifested in the lives of individual clients. Furthermore, those social workers focused on social policy need to understand the various ways in which complex social problems affect the daily lives of diverse individuals.

In addition to in-depth examples of contemporary social work issues, we also present a set of perennial issues encountered by social workers that affect individuals at all points of the life span and that are likely to persist into the twenty-first century and beyond. Across the chapters, text boxes discuss main topics such as "Violence across the Life Span," "Poverty across the Life Span," and "Substance Abuse across the Life Span." Other boxes introduce selected topics such as "International Perspectives" including social work research in India, Japan, and Taiwan.

A number of pedagogical features will help students learn from the text. An introduction to each chapter provides a framework for understanding that chapter, a concise summary at the end of each chapter highlights the chapter's main points, and key terms are set in italic type in the text and are defined in a glossary at the end of the text. Each chapter provides study and discussion questions about important issues and problems that students can work through individually as well as in class.

In our experience, social work students are eager not only to apply HBSE content to real-life social work issues such as poverty, violence, and substance abuse, but to learn more about the experiences of practicing social workers. We also have included end-of-chapter text boxes, "Practice Stories and Advice from the Field," derived from our interviews with experienced social workers in a variety of practice (schools, mental health, health, and child welfare) and policy contexts.

Acknowledgements

Many people had a hand bringing this book to fruition and it is a pleasure to acknowledge them here. The social work students in Wendy's HBSE 1 class, Spring 2006, energetically provided thoughtful and comprehensive critiques. Cathleen Lewandowski (Wichita State University), Barbara Turnage (University of Central Florida), Hope Haslam Straughan (Wheelock College), Terri Combes Orme (University of Tennessee), Joanne Levine (Wichita State University), Eleanor Downey (Colorado State University), Michael Hayes (Providence College), Carol Dorr (Regis College), Ted Watkins (Texas State University, San Marcos), Mary Ann Clute (Eastern Washington University), Sydney Hans (University of Chicago), Jolyn Mikow (University of Texas, San Antonio), Marilyn Lewis (The Ohio State University), Patricia O'Brien (University of Illinois, Chicago), Michaela Farber (The Catholic University of America), Barbara Rittner (SUNY, University at Buffalo), and Tim Page (Louisiana State University) reviewed the manuscript and their commentary was invaluable.

We greatly appreciate Susan Cole's help in writing chapters of this book. She has been a true co-author.

Our family members, Susan Wells, and James, Matthew, and Camilla Black provided support and advice. Susan was particularly helpful with the sections on child welfare, and Jim advised on brain development. We also thank Susan and Scotty Daniels for reading, offering insightful suggestions, and editing large sections of this book. Finally, we thank David Follmer for his innovative and interdisciplinary approach to publishing social work texts.

Figure 1.1.
In the United States, African Americans and the elderly are at increased risk of living in poverty. This older man is purchasing used winter clothing.

1

A Developmental-Ecological Framework

Social workers are committed to enhancing the welfare of vulnerable people through direct services to individuals in need and through social and political action. These commitments to social justice are a legacy from the nineteenth-century progressive era including the "friendly visitors," volunteers, and paraprofessionals who provided assistance to those who were impoverished. Today, social work is a profession requiring undergraduate and, increasingly, graduate social work degrees. Modern social workers practice in the public schools, child welfare agencies, health and mental health settings, and at colleges and universities. Given the complexity of modern social problems, the challenges facing social workers are enormous. As a student of social work you may wonder: How do social workers approach complex and diverse issues such as child maltreatment, poverty, unemployment, oppression, domestic violence, mental illness, and end-of-life care? What unifies social work interventions across varied contexts such as inner-city schools and rural nursing homes with individuals ranging widely in age, ethnicity, and socioeconomic status? How do social workers assess whether their efforts have been helpful, harmful, or inconsequential?

Clearly, there are no simple answers. Social work draws upon a rich knowledge base built primarily upon the social and biological sciences and interpreted from the perspective of social work values and ethics. Such an interdisciplinary stance may be one of social work's greatest strengths. It also may be its greatest challenge as social workers struggle to formulate and apply a consistent analytic framework for approaching diverse social problems. The goal of this book is to present and illustrate a coherent interdisciplinary framework for social work practice using a developmental-ecological perspective.* This perspective is compatible with the bio-psycho-social-spiritual perspective common in social work texts. It elaborates on this approach through a focus on developmental change within particular cultural and historical contexts, and individual lives. An example of a nineteenth-century forbearer of modern social work, Clara Brown, illustrates the developmental-ecological framework.

---

* In this book, the terms perspective and framework are used interchangeably.

In the 1800s Central City was the capital of the Colorado Territory and a growing, wealthy mining town. Discovery of gold and silver had helped turn a miner's camp into an economic and cultural center. An elegant opera house and East Coast-style hotel were built. Operas and stage productions were routinely brought in from New York and the West Coast. The town was also the home of several stone churches with colorful stained-glass windows. As in many towns and cities, the wealthy and upper-middle class of Central City lived on one side of a mountain stream, and the working-class people and poor lived on the other side. Racial segregation existed in both law and practice, but slavery was not allowed, and a free African American could find gainful employment. Voting rights for women had not yet been seriously considered, and laws and customs impeded women's acquisition of wealth or power.

Within this historical and cultural context, an African American woman, Mrs. Clara Brown, won financial stability and exercised considerable leadership for approximately twenty years. Clara Brown spent her first 50 years of life as a slave in Kentucky, suffering not only physical hardship but, most significantly, the loss of her four children and husband, who were sold away from her. Upon the death of her owner, she was granted her freedom and, because the laws of Kentucky required that freed slaves leave the state within a year, she eventually joined a wagon train headed for the Colorado gold rush. After settling in Central City Mrs. Brown began taking in laundry and doing odd jobs for wealthy miners and land owners. Within a short period of time, she began investing in land and developed considerable wealth, which she used to give back to her community. Mrs. Brown started the first Sunday school in Central City and nurtured it into the city's first permanent church. In addition, she opened her home as an informal settlement house for people of all races. At 60 years of age, Mrs. Brown organized a wagon train to rescue approximately thirty-four African Americans endangered by racial violence in Kentucky and Tennessee at the end of the Civil War. For the remainder of her life, Mrs. Brown gave financial help to every church in Central City, supported antipoverty causes, and worked to end segregation in public schools. When she was in her late 70s, the governor appointed Mrs. Brown to represent Colorado in assisting former slaves fleeing the South's brutality and racism. Following her death, dignitaries from across the state attended Mrs. Brown's funeral. Today, people visiting Colorado's state capital in Denver will see a stained-glass window honoring this courageous pioneer who overcame so many odds, traveled so far, and gave so much (Baker, 2003).

How can we account for the remarkable leadership of Mrs. Clara Brown, who lived during a time when African Americans were regarded by the larger society as subhuman, and women as both intellectually and morally inferior to men? What role might biology, psychology, social context, and cultural-historical factors have played in shaping her into a leader who influenced public policy, won the confidence of powerful male politicians, and became a recognized spiritual and ethical leader for a predominantly white community? The developmental-ecological framework presented in this text will provide you with an analytic framework, or set of intellectual problem-solving tools, to systematically consider the development of complex individuals such as Clara Brown, their families, communities, and times, as well as to address challenging issues facing social workers in the twenty-first century.

A developmental-ecological framework draws upon the fields of *human development* and *ecology* to consider the ways in which human beings shape and are shaped within complex and dynamic cultural and historical contexts. Human development examines the loosely coordinated ensemble of biological, psychological, and social changes that humans undergo throughout the life span, as well as the process (or causes) of change (Cole & Cole, 2001). Such changes may be universal to all humans, or they may vary in content and timing across cultural and historical contexts. Ecology is a branch of science that deals with the interrelationships of organisms with their environment. Thus, a developmental-ecological analysis of Clara Brown would consider her biological, psychological, and social characteristics as they change over time in relation to her particular cultural and historical context. This analysis of Clara Brown might consider:

- The strength provided by lifelong physical and mental health
- An ability to learn without formal training
- Persistence and commitment to hard work and service
- Kentucky's law forcing freed slaves to leave the state
- The lack of organization and need for leadership in America's frontier
- The existence of a community where one could prosper financially and socially
- The problems of racism, sexism, and poverty within nineteenth-century American society

Thus, to understand Clara Brown, we must consider not only her resiliencey, talent, and drive, but also the social systems, culture, and group needs within nineteenth-century Central City. Together, health, skill, and ecological factors created a unique set of opportunities and challenges. Clara Brown thrived, in part, because she successfully created a fit within the particular social context of Central City. Without her internal personal strengths interacting within a particular ecological context, Mrs. Brown's story would have unfolded differently. Much of human development is profoundly intertwined with social systems, time, place, and space. It is impossible to understand human actions removed from their cultural and historical contexts. Had Mrs. Brown arrived earlier or later in Colorado, or not gone to Colorado, her development and destiny, and perhaps, also, the destiny of Central City, would have been different.

DEVELOPMENTAL-ECOLOGICAL ANALYSIS
OF SOCIAL WORK ISSUES

An adequate understanding of the life of Clara Brown clearly requires consideration of a large amount of complex information. Similarly, practicing social workers must respond to an enormous volume of complex information on a daily basis as they advocate for and support their clients. Systematic consideration of biological, psychological, and social factors as they change over time within particular cultural-historical contexts is critical to adequate assessment and effective intervention.

One way in which human beings deal with complex social information is through informal *folk theories* of human behavior and development including values, beliefs, and explanations for how the social world works within our families and communities. In general, folk theories are effective for dealing with everyday life within our particular families and communities, for example, interacting with our neighbors and parenting our children. Folk theories are less useful, however, when we are confronted with problems that are difficult or unusual for us, or that occur within cultural communities with which we are not familiar. Implementing an effective intervention for a child struggling in school may be especially challenging when that child comes from an immigrant family with folk theories of child development divergent from the social workers' folk theories. Reliance on folk theories in such situations can result in misunderstandings and poor communication because they often are implicit and unexamined and may include stereotypes, superstitions, and inaccuracies.

Like folk theories, *social science theories* are frameworks that help us to understand, explain, and predict the social world. In contrast to folk theories, social science theories are explicit regarding, for example, the nature of human development and must be supported by logic and empirical research. Social science theories are open to critical evaluation and may be challenged on the basis of their accuracy, breadth, and coherence. Most importantly, they may be revised as new knowledge and perspectives emerge.

According to the philosopher of science Karl Popper, scientific theories are attempted explanations, approximations to the "truth." By treating theories as intellectual objects separate from ourselves, we can put them on the table for scrutiny. By vigorously and actively criticizing our theories, we uncover incorrect assumptions, inconsistencies, narrowness, and errors, thereby moving closer and closer to the truth (Popper, 1999).

Social work draws upon a wide variety of social science theories from those exploring individual development to those focusing on community development (Payne, 2005). In this chapter we focus on social science theories that address the developmental processes that support adaptive functioning. There is no single comprehensive theory that adequately portrays the complexities of human development.There are a variety of different theories that contribute to our understanding of the complex interaction of biological, psychological, and social factors that shape human development within particular historical and cultural contexts. For the purposes of analysis in this book, biological, psychological, social, and cultural-historical aspects of development will be discussed separately. In reality, however, these aspects of development interact in mutually influential and complex ways; for example, as infants develop the physical strength and coordination necessary to crawl and toddle independently, their knowledge of the physical world expands.Their social relationships also change; for example, babies may be physically capable of independent locomotion before they have the judgment necessary to do so safely, thus provoking restrictions from, and conflict with, caregivers. Thus, changes in one area of development have ramifications for other areas of development, and development may be uneven. Furthermore, social and cultural contexts vary in the ways in which development is supported; for example, the extent to which babies are allowed to move about independently varies. Some families in the United States allow babies to careen around in baby walkers, while in some hunter-gatherer groups, older infants are carried attached to the mother for much of the day. These different experiences may shape not just early physical development, but social and emotional development as well.

DEVELOPMENTAL THEORIES

Biological Theories

Biology plays an important role in the developmental process. Biological theories in human development traditionally have focused on genetic factors underlying developmental change—changes in behavior were seen as resulting primarily from changes in biology.The major cause of development was viewed as maturation, that is, genetically determined patterns of change that unfolded with age. Individual differences in human development were attributed primarily to differences in genetic inheritance (Cole & Cole, 2001). In the early part of the twentieth century, relatively little attention was given to the role of environment in human development.Arnold Gesell (1880-1961), an influential pediatrician, attributed children's behavioral development primarily to inherent maturational mechanisms and attributed only a weak role to the environment (Gesell, 1940).

Recent research from a biological perspective, relevant to social work, addresses the myriad and complex ways in which biology and environment interact and particulary how the environment affects brain development throughout life. A classic experimental paradigm involves the postmortem comparison of the biological development of young rats raised in a complex, or "enriched," environment, with that of rats raised under standard laboratory conditions, an "impoverished" environment. The rats raised in the enriched environment have many other rats with which to interact and objects to explore. The rats raised in the impoverished conditions are reared in social isolation in standard laboratory cages. Growing up in a socially and intellectually enriched environment has dramatic effects on rats' brain anatomy, endocrine systems, and physical growth and behavior. Complex social and cognitive experiences result in greater control over stress responses and improved social skills (Black, Jones, Nelson, & Greenough, 1998). Brain changes are distributed over several neural systems and involve a gross enlargement of the brain, as well as the formation of new neurons (brain cells) and synapses (connections between neurons) (Wallace, Kilman, Withers, & Greenough, 1992).

In addition to illustrating the flexibility of the mammalian brain, modern neurodevelopmental research illustrates that there are limits to the influence of environment. Older rats do display neural plasticity, but even when placed in enriched environments they do not display the same degree of plasticity as young rats (Greenough, Black, & Wallace, 1987). The development of the mammalian brain appears to be shaped at the cellular level by environment and experience throughout the life span, but particularly in early life. (Because of ethical considerations, some developmental research uses animal models. Findings may be relevant to humans to the extent that systems [e.g., mammalian brains] share relevant characteristics.)

Modern biological research is important to social work, in part, because it draws our attention to the complex ways in which our genetic and cultural heritages interact. For example, the use of mood- and mind-altering substances has a long history in human cultures, but some genetically predisposed individuals may become dependent (see boxes 1.1–1.3). Modern research into the biological bases of behavior and development also addresses a variety of issues central to social work policy and practice including *learning differences, disabilities,* or *disorders; autism;* and serious neuropsychiatric disorders such as *schizophrenia* or *bipolar disorder* (e.g., Gottesman, 1991; Goodwin & Jamison, 1990; McNeil, Cantor-Graae, Torrey, Sjostrom, Bowler, Taylor, et al., 1994; Taylor, 1987, 1997, 2005; Torrey, Bowler, Taylor, & Gottesman, 1994). Understanding the biological origins of behavior disorder and how it interacts within particular cultural-historical contexts can have profound implications for the development of effective social work interventions. For example, understanding the neurological bases of autism as a developmental disability, as well as the ways in which early intervention can and cannot affect its course, has shifted the focus of interventions. In the first half of the twentieth century, interventions focused on modifying presumably pathological family interactions. Today, social workers recognize autism as a developmental disability, provide support to families of autistic children, and identify appropriate early intervention resources within the community (Schreibman & Koegel, 1996).

BOX 1.1 SUBSTANCE ABUSE ACROSS THE LIFE SPAN
Defining Substance Dependence

- Substance dependence has been viewed from moral, cultural, public health, and scientific perspectives. For a scientific perspective, the National Institute of Drug Abuse identifies substance dependence as present if three or more of the following have been experienced or exhibited during the previous year:
- Difficulties in controlling substance-taking behavior in terms of its onset, termination, or levels of use
- A strong desire or sense of compulsion to take the substance
- Progressive neglect of alternative pleasures or interests because of psychoactive substance use
- Increased amount of time necessary to obtain or take the substance or to recover from its effects
- Persisting with substance use despite clear evidence of overtly harmful consequences, depressing mood states consequent to heavy use, or drug impairment of cognitive functioning
- Evidence of tolerance, such that increased doses of the psychoactive substance are required in order to achieve effects originally produced by lower doses
- A physiological withdrawal state when substance use has ceased or been reduced, as evidenced by the characteristic withdrawal syndrome for the substance, or use of the same (or closely related) substance with the intention of relieving or avoiding withdrawal symptoms

Source: Barlow, D. H. & Durand, V. M. (2005). *Abnormal psychology: An integrative approach*. Belmont, CA: Thomson Wadsworth. Retrieved April 2006 from http://www.nida.nih.gov/Drugpages/DSR.hym1.

Psychological and Social Theories

Psychological and social factors also play important roles in human development. Psychodynamic theory, based on the work of Sigmund Freud and his followers, heavily influenced psychological and social theories of development throughout the twentieth century. Until the end of the 1960s, it was the dominant theory in social work practice. Psychodynamic theory assumes that behavior emerges as a result of movement and interaction in the mind (psychic determinism) and that some of these thought processes are hidden from conscious awareness (the unconscious) (Wood, 1971; Yelloly, 1980). Development occurs as individuals progress through a series of stages. Mental pressures (drives) to relieve physical needs such as hunger

··

BOX 1.2 SUBSTANCE ABUSE ACROSS THE LIFE SPAN

Substance Use in the United States

Alcohol and other substances are widely used throughout the United States. Studies indicate that:

- forty percent of the general population report having used an illegal substance in their lifetime (Sadock & Sadock);
- approximately 15% of the general population claim to have used an illegal drug in the past 12 months (Sadock & Sadock);
- lifetime prevalence of substance abuse is about 20% (Sadock & Sadock);
- approximately 9 million Americans meet the DSM-IV-TR criteria for being alcohol dependent (Mack, Franklin, & Frances);
- another 6 million Americans abuse alcohol (Mack, Franklin, & Frances);
- approximately 10.4 million youths between the ages of 12–20 consume alcoholic beverages (Mack, Franklin, & Frances);
- about 6.8 million of the youths who use alcohol are involved in binge drinking, and 2.1 million are considered heavy drinkers (Mack, Franklin, & Frances);
- approximately half of all alcohol sold in the United States is consumed by 10% of the people who drink (Mack, Franklin, & Frances).

Sources: Mack, A. H., Franklin, Jr., J. E., & Frances, R. J. (2003). Substance use disorders. In R. E. Hales & S. C. Yudofsky (Eds.), *The American psychiatric publishing textbook of clinical psychiatry* (4th ed., pp. 309–378). Washington, DC: American Psychiatric Publishing; Sadock, B. J., & Sadock, V. A. (2003) *Synopsis of psychiatry behavioral science/clinical psychiatry* (9th ed., pp. 383–384). Philadelphia: Lippincott Williams & Wilkins.

··

and sex create the tension (libido) that propels development. Social work has drawn upon the rich and complex developmental ideas of psychodynamic theory to consider how emotion from past relationships and experiences affect individuals' present behavior (Irvine, 1956). Although psychodynamic theory has left an important legacy in social work, for example, an emphasis on feelings and an open listening relationship (Wallen, 1982), today it is a widely contested developmental theory. The often-unconscious thought processes that undergird psychodynamic approaches are difficult to assess empirically. An increasing reliance on empirical research in social work as well as pressure from managed care in the United States have directed models of explanation away from the interpretive and metaphorical accounts of behavior provided by psychodynamic theory.

In part as a reaction against psychodynamic approaches, some early psychological theories focused on observable environmental factors underlying

```
BOX 1.3 SUBSTANCE ABUSE ACROSS THE LIFE SPAN
Risk Factors for Substance Dependence
```

- Race, ethnicity, and living in city/urban environments are not good predictors of who will become dependent or abuse a substance.
- Higher rates of addiction are found in people who have lower levels of education and income.
- Men are at greater risk for developing dependency of alcohol than women.
- Lifetime alcohol dependence for men is 21.4%.
- Lifetime alcohol dependence for women is 9.2%.

Source: Barlow, D. H., & Durand, V. M. (2005). *Abnormal psychology: An integrative approach*. Belmont, CA: Thomson Wadsworth.

developmental change. According to *learning theory*, development occurs as a result of experiencing the positive and negative consequences of behavior, as well as observing and imitating others. Over time, the individual is gradually shaped through interaction with the environment, only passively contributing to his/her own development.

Systematic studies of learning emerged in the late 1800s with Thorndike's (1898, 1911) experiments examining the relationships between learning and intelligence. By 1927, Pavlov had published his famous experiments of *classical conditioning*, that is, learning in which previously existing behaviors come to be elicited by new stimuli. Pavlov taught dogs to salivate when presented with a light by pairing presentations of food and light until the dogs came to associate the light with food (Pavlov, 1927). In the first half of the twentieth century, John B. Watson and then B. F. Skinner extended the classical conditioning paradigm into a more comprehensive theory that explained how learning results from an individual's active, operant responses to the environment (Watson, 1913). *Operant conditioning* occurs when changes in behavior are shaped by the consequences of that behavior, for example, rewards *(reinforcement)* and *punishment*, thereby giving rise to new and more complex behaviors. Beginning in the 1960s and 1970s, our understanding of learning was further expanded by *social learning theorists*. Bandura and his colleagues observed that learning also occurs when we observe and imitate, or model, others (Bandura, Grusec, & Menlove, 1967). Learning theory influenced *information-processing* research in the 1980s. Information-processing theory uses a computer metaphor to examine how humans process, store, and retrieve information (Seifert, Hoffnung, & Hoffnung, 2000). For example, the Wechsler intelligence scales were developed around a concept of intelligence as a single general type (Osterlind, 2006; Valencia & Suzuki, 2000). This general factor assumption has been called into question by numerous researchers including Robert Sternberg (1984, 1985), who used information-processing theory to posit an alternative triarchic model of intelligence. Sternberg views intelligence as consisting of three specific neuroprocessing elements involving the ability to (1) receive and analyze information in an efficient manner (componential elements), (2) easily and efficiently compare new information with stored knowledge and experience (experiential elements), and (3) solve everyday real-life problems (contextual elements). Alternative ways of framing intelligence offer social workers tools for assessing, advocating, and documenting client skills and strengths that often go unnoticed, for example, the intelligence required to survive in a dangerous community is rarely measured, discussed, or labeled.

Research conducted from learning theory and information-processing perspectives has lead to the development of a variety of effective interventions used in social work practice today. *Behavior modification*, that is, the use of learning theory principles to change behavior, continues to be used with clients who are intellectually disabled, harm themselves, harm others, or have autism (Spiegler & Guevremont, 1998; Birk, 1999; Vance & Pumariega, 2001; Courchesne & Pierce, 2005). Research has found therapies based on learning theory, particularly when combined with other approaches, to have some positive effects on clients struggling with mental health, mental retardation, and substance abuse issues (Spiegler & Guevremont, 1998; Vance & Pumariega, 2001; DePaulo, 2002; Taylor, 2002).

Many modern developmental scholars find environmentally based and information-processing theories to be incomplete accounts of psychological and social development. Human beings are not passive "blank slates" at birth waiting to be written upon by the environment, nor are they computers. Human beings are complex biological beings who interpret, find meaning, and respond creatively to the world. To understand the unique ways in which individuals actively contribute to their own development, social workers may turn to *constructivist theories of human development*. From this perspective, individuals are seen as shaping or constructing their own reality. By actively striving to master their environments, individuals construct higher levels of knowledge from elements contributed by both biological maturation and environment. Both biological heritage and environment are viewed as equally important to development. The individual's acquisition of knowledge, however, is not a simple process of copying reality. The knowledge we acquire results from the ways in which we understand, modify, and transform reality (Cole & Cole, 2001).

The constructivist perspective of human development is best illustrated in the theory and research of Jean Piaget, a Swiss scholar often cited as the father of modern developmental psychology. Piaget's work focuses on *cognitive development*, particularly the development of logical scientific reasoning, although the conceptual framework he presents is highly relevant to other areas of development. A number of developmental psychologists have written highly accessible and readable interpretations of Piaget's work (see Hans Furth, 1969) and discussions of implications of Piagetian theory for social and emotional development (see Cowan, 1978).

The constructionist perspective of human development also can be illustrated with an example from early language development. When Sharon was 22 months old, she told a story about the family cat, concluding with the observation: "Midnight ran." A few weeks later, she commented, "Midnight runned." This comment is remarkable for its creative attempt to apply the linguistic rules for past tense markers. Eventually, Sharon returned to the conventional grammatical construction, "Midnight ran," suggesting that she now understood the rule and its exceptions. This order of acquisition in which the child first produces the irregular form correctly, then incorrectly, and then correctly again has been observed in other children for a variety of grammatical forms (see Brown, 1973). How do we account for these patterns? From a constructivist perspective, children's rapid acquisition of a highly complex native language, in part, reflects our human genetic potential. In addition, the environment clearly plays a role: Sharon's family spoke English at home and so she was learning English grammar. Sharon, however, was not passive in this process of language acquisition but actively constructed an understanding of language from innate human ability and input from the environment. When children first use an irregular form correctly, they may be simply imitating others. When they subsequently come to understand the underlying grammatical rule, they may creatively overapply it to the irregular form. From this perspective, Sharon's use of the word "runned" actually reflected a higher level of knowledge than her earlier use of "ran." Finally, children become aware of the exceptions to the rule and once again produce the irregular form correctly. In addition, Sharon's communication occurred within a social and emotional context. She was motivated by her desire to express herself to family members about a beloved pet.

Human development research conducted from a constructivist perspective has many important implications for social work. Most importantly, it draws our attention to the role of meaning in human behavior and development. Social workers intervene with clients with diverse experiences from a wide range of backgrounds. Effective social work interventions go beyond simple biological or environmental manipulations to consider how clients will understand, interpret, and, ultimately, respond to, change.

An example of a constructivist approach to social work is a parenting class for African American grandparents. Many social workers are called upon to conduct parenting classes for parents with children in Head Start, prospective adoptive parents, parents and foster parents involved in the child welfare system, and parents of children with special needs. To be effective, however, parenting classes must go beyond the simple "training" advocated by early learning theorists. From a constructivist perspective, effective classes also consider how parents understand and interpret new skills and techniques. For example, what are generally effective behavioral techniques for managing

> ## BOX 1.4 VIOLENCE ACROSS THE LIFE SPAN
> ### Chronic Aggressive Behavior
>
> A single factor cannot explain chronic aggressive behavior in adolescence and adulthood. Rather, there is growing agreement that violence from repeat offenders results from multiple interacting elements. Researchers hypothesize that combinations of the following environmental and biological factors increase the risk of violent behaviors:
>
> - Abuse during childhood or during adolescent years
> - Poor parenting and inappropriate punishment
> - Observing family violence
> - Living in a culture that promotes aggression and violence
> - Genetic predispositions
> - Central nervous system trauma and neurobiological abnormalities
> - Early temperament and impulse control
> - Early attention problems
> - Abnormal hormonal levels
>
> Growing up in an environment that reinforces violent behaviors significantly increases the risk for chronic aggressive behaviors across the life span. Children living in a violent household or community learn to respond aggressively to cues from the environment perceived to be dangerous. Risk for violent behavior also increases greatly when a person has a genetic predisposition for aggression, or neurobiological abnormalities.
>
> ――――――
> Source: Huesmann, L. R. (1998). Aggression and the self: High self-esteem, low self-control, and ego threat. In R. G. Geen & E. Donnerstein (Eds.), *Human aggression: Theories, research, and implications for social policy* (pp. 73–109). San Diego, CA: Academic Press.

children's difficult behaviors that are consistent with views of appropriate discipline commonly held within these particular parents' community? In a parenting class for African American grandparents fostering their grandchildren, several grandmothers expressed serious reservations about the use of time-out. From their perspective, placing a child in social isolation, even for a short time, was unkind, had the potential to be abusive, and was ineffective. One grandmother expressed the opinion that when a small child misbehaves, the appropriate and effective action is to draw that child closer to you. She advocated a brief spanking immediately following serious misbehavior, accompanied by an explanation and expression of love and concern. The social worker presenting this class had effectively taught the skill of time-out in the sense that the grandmothers responded to questions on a postgroup

BOX 1.5 VIOLENCE ACROSS THE LIFE SPAN

Neighborhood and Crime

Violence is particularly pronounced in certain neighborhoods, but typically violence and related crimes are committed by a small number of people. A study of a high-crime neighborhood in Washington, D.C., found the following:

- Age is a factor in crime. Younger children are less delinquent than older adolescents who are nearing young adulthood.
- Only 7% of the adolescent boys in the studied neighborhoods committed robbery, but these same teenagers were responsible for 36.2% of reported delinquent acts.
- The 7% of youths involved in robberies also committed 20.5% of all juvenile assaults.
- Each of the adolescents involved in robbery physically assaulted an average of approximately twelve people each year.
- Forty-four percent of all drug deals in the neighborhood were committed by the same 7% who participated in robbery.
- Most adolescents involved in selling drugs, but not robbery or other major criminal activities, were less violent.
- Having a job does not appear to prevent delinquency. The most seriously delinquent boys were the most likely to have a paying job.
- Social isolation appears to be a major factor for adolescent boys who get in trouble with the legal system. Seventy-seven percent of the adolescent boys who were involved in robbery identified that they most often keep to themselves, and that they are different from their peers.
- Only 15% of the adolescent boys in the most violent neighborhoods reported having gang connections.

Source: U.S. Department of Justice, Office of Justice Programs, Office of Juvenile Justice and Delinquency Prevention. (2000, March). Violent neighborhoods, violent kids. *Juvenile Justice Bulletin* (NCJ Publication No. 178248, pp. 1–15).

assessment in a manner desired by the social worker. The meaning attached to this behavior by class members, however, made it highly unlikely that they would ever use it. Because this social worker went beyond "training" to consider "meaning," she opened up the opportunity to actively explore the appropriate and inappropriate use of spanking, the actual disciplinary technique traditionally used in these grandmothers' cultural community.

In general, attention to psychological and social factors in human development is important to social work, in part, because it draws our attention to the various ways in which individuals understand and respond to life's challenges. For example, United States society is among the most violent of the industrialized world. Understanding why particular individuals behave aggressively requires an understanding not only of possible biological vulnerabilities, but also individual psychological characteristics (e.g., poor impulse control) and social context (e.g., family or neighborhood violence) (see boxes 1.4 and 1.5).

Cultural and Historical Theories

Culture and history critically affect human development. *Cultural-historical theories of human development* are very compatible with constructivist theories but elaborate upon them in two important ways (Cole & Cole, 2001). First, a cultural-historical perspective views cultural and historical context as a critical third factor in development through which biology and experience interact. *Culture* involves the physical objects, activities, and patterns of living and meaning that are shaped by the experiences of earlier generations and elaborated by later generations. All human beings are born into a community with a variety of rich cultural resources; and these resources, including medicine, language, music, and mathematical systems, profoundly shape development. Each generation does not remake itself from scratch. From the moment we are conceived, our development is profoundly shaped by our cultural and historical context, for example, whether or not our mothers receive adequate prenatal care. As we develop, we act on our world using a particular set of cultural tools, and we view our world through a particular cultural lens. Language is a critical tool for negotiating our social world, but language also shapes the very way we view that social world—even such basic concepts as the way in which we understand ourselves and others.

The second way in which the cultural-historical perspective elaborates upon the constructivist perspective is that it assumes that both less experienced individuals (e.g., children, students, and new social workers) and more experienced individuals (e.g., parents, teachers, and supervisors) are active collaborators in the process of development. The individual is not the "lone scientist" out to discover the world on his/her own. Parents, teachers, and even peers are active in shaping the individual's development; that is, development is "co-constructed" (Rogoff, 1988). For example, parents directly support children's development, for example, by helping them with homework. They also shape the environments in which their children develop, for example, arranging for a child to attend a church-sponsored day care, join scouts, play on a little league team, or enroll in the public high school. Children, of course, are not passive but may take any variety of stances toward the particular socialization messages they encounter. A little girl may embrace, reject, challenge, or ignore her mother's efforts to encourage her active and assertive interactions with boys. Furthermore, the process of negotiating issues such as gender roles may affect the development of both the mother and her little girl.

As this example suggests, the processes through which culture is acquired and elaborated by new generations are complex. From a cultural-historical perspective, development may be seen as occurring throughout the life span through the complex dialectical (interactive) processes of *socialization* and *acquisition*. Socialization is the process by which experts structure the social environment and display patterned meanings for the novice (see Haight, 2002; Wentworth, 1980). Socialization may be direct and intentional, as when a professor assigns students to read the National Association of Social Workers (NASW) Code of Ethics, or indirect and unintentional, as when a student observes a field supervisor grappling with a complex real-life ethical dilemma. Acquisition is the process through which novices interpret, respond to, and ultimately embrace, reject, or elaborate upon the social patterns to which they are exposed (see Haight, 2002; Wentworth, 1980).

These processes of socialization and acquisition are mutually influential. Excellent field supervisors alter the content and structure of their socialization practices in relation to social work interns' various backgrounds, and students adjust their understanding and behavior in relation to their field supervisors' guidance. A school social work supervisor might provide extra support to a student with relatively little background working with young adolescents before allowing her responsibility for a *social developmental study* involving a middle school student. For her part, the student may spend extra time reading about development in early adolescence and interacting with middle school students, their teachers, and families in preparation for participating in a social developmental study. From this dialectical perspective, professional development occurs as students actively read, reflect, observe, discuss, and participate with teachers, field supervisors, and peers in the everyday practices through which the culture of social work is maintained and elaborated.

Lev Vygotsky, a Russian psychologist (1896–1934), had a profound impact on cultural-historical theories of human development (Wertsch, 1985; Vygotsky, 1962). He viewed the mind as developing "in" society. For Vygotsky, all development proceeds from interpersonal processes to intrapersonal processes. Children develop more complex and adequate forms of thought first while interacting with those with more experience and competence. During interpersonal interactions, the experts scaffold, or support, children in developing new and more complex ways of thinking. Eventually, these new forms of thought are internalized by children and they use them independently of the expert.

Modern scholars of human development have elaborated upon Vygotsky's work. The developmental psychologist Barbara Rogoff has spent over twenty years studying children's learning in several countries, including Guatemala and the United States (1990, 2001, 2003). In the Mayan community she studied, children's learning occurred primarily during informal appren-

> ## BOX 1.6 POVERTY ACROSS THE LIFE SPAN
> ### United States Official Poverty Rate
>
> Poverty is increasing significantly in the United States, especially for children. In 2003, 35.9 million people (12.5% of the population) were considered poor by the U.S. government, an increase of 1.3 million people from 2002. Children experienced the highest poverty rates and increase during 2003. The percentage of American children living in poverty (17.6%) was higher than any other age group. In 2003, the poverty rate for adults ages 18 to 64 was approximately 10.8%, and for seniors 65 and older was 10.2%. Furthermore, the number of children in poverty rose from 12.1 million in 2002 to 12.9 million in 2003.
>
> Source: DeNavas-Walt, C., Proctor, B. D., and Mills, R. J. (2004). *Income, poverty, and health insurance coverage in the United States.* U.S. Census Bureau, Current Population Reports (Publication No. P60-226, p. 10). Washington, DC: U.S. Government Printing Office.

ticeship-like everyday interactions. Children learned to interact with others, care for themselves, complete chores, weave, farm, and care for younger children from observing and joining into everyday activities, and from the non-verbal guidance of those with more experience. In the United States white middle-class community Rogoff studied, an important context for children's

> ## Box 1.7 POVERTY ACROSS THE LIFE SPAN
> ### Three-Year Poverty Rates by Race (2001–2003)*
>
> | Racial or minority identity | Percentage living at or below the U.S. poverty line |
> |---|---|
> | Whites | 10.2 |
> | Asians | 10.7 |
> | Native Hawaiians & other Pacific Islanders | 10.8 |
> | Hispanics | 21.9 |
> | Blacks | 23.1 |
> | American Indians & Alaska Natives | 23.2 |
> | All races & minorities combined | 12.1 |
>
> *Rates reflect those who reported themselves as representing only one racial or minority group. Therefore, the rates do not include people who claimed membership in two or more racial or minority groups
>
> Source: DeNavas-Walt, C, Proctor, B. D., & Mills, R. J. (2004). *Income, poverty, and health insurance coverage in the United States.* U.S. Census Bureau, Current Population Reports, (Publication No. P60-226, p. 12). Washington, DC: U.S. Government Printing Office.

> ## BOX 1.8 POVERTY ACROSS THE LIFE SPAN
> ### Worldwide Poverty
>
> According to the World Bank, approximately 1.1 billion people live in extreme poverty. In the poorest areas, individuals may live on less than one dollar per day. Regions with the highest rates of people living in extreme poverty include the Middle East, North Africa, Eastern Europe, Central Asia, Latin America, the Caribbean, East Asia, sub-Saharan Africa, and South Asia. The time has come for social work advocacy to focus beyond the borders of this country and insist on a global perspective of human development and welfare. We can no longer stand by and allow over a billion people across the globe to lose their potential for personal growth and their very lives because of poverty.
>
> Source: Sachs, J. D. (2005). *The end of poverty: Economic possibilities for our time.* New York: Penguin.

learning was formal classroom settings where instruction occurred primarily through verbal instruction. Children learned to interact with others, care for themselves, complete chores, read, write, and do arithmetic often during deliberate, verbal, face-to-face interactions. The content and contexts of learning in Mayan and United States middle-class communities varied, but most children grew to be successful members of their diverse communities.

Cultural-historical theories of human development are highly relevant to social work because they underscore human diversity, especially the rich variety of developmental pathways that lead to healthy adaptation in various contexts. Cultural-historical perspectives do not assume that development is stage-like but consider that it may vary in relation to context. Just as there is not one universal "best" way to develop, there cannot be one "best practice" for social work intervention that applies across cultural and historical contexts.

Figure 1.2.
In the United States, children, especially children of color, are at increased risk of living in poverty. These young children live in a migrant labor camp.

Knowledge of cultural and historical diversity is essential to appropriate and effective social work intervention. It allows social workers to understand the challenges clients may face in particular settings, as well as how they might interpret these challenges and the resources they may bring to bear in meeting them. For example, Mayan immigrant kindergarteners entering the Los Angeles public school system for the first time have been socialized into a very different social role than that of most middle-class European American children. The Mayan immigrant child may be used to interacting in mixed-age settings and taking significant responsibility for her own care as well as that of younger siblings. How will this particular child understand and respond to the new context of school in the United States? What individual psychological resources, as well as external social resources, can be rallied to meet the new challenge of starting school in the United States? Establishing ongoing communication with the child's family or other community members can help the school social worker to identify issues that may facilitate or hinder the child's success in school, including her responses to interaction in a large group of same-age peers.

Although the cultural-historical context, to some extent, shapes the challenges and resources encountered at various ages, a narrow focus on variation across cultural groups can lead to the development of stereotypes. Cultural-historical perspectives also draw our attention to variation within human communities. For example, communities across the United States comprised of individuals from the same ethnic group can reflect diversity because of differing historical conditions and current challenges and resources. The evolution and adaptation of African American communities in Salt Lake City and New York City may be both similar and different because of the various challenges and resources present in the broader cultural-historical contexts of Utah and New York. Furthermore, the individuals within these communities display a wide range of variation in personality, intelligence, and sociability. As social workers, we need to be sensitive to diversity that occurs within as well as across cultural communities to avoid stereotyping.

One area of intracultural diversity in the United States and around the world is poverty. From its inception, social work has been concerned with the devastating effects of poverty on human development. Boxes 1.6 through 1.8 summarize poverty in the United States by age and race, and worldwide.

INTEGRATING ECOLOGICAL-SYSTEMS PERSPECTIVES WITH DEVELOPMENTAL PERSPECTIVES

Cultural-historical theories of human development consider development to be intimately intertwined with the contexts in which it emerges. In order to use this insight fully in social work practice, it is useful to add specificity to the concept of context in relation to human development. What are the critical characteristics of contexts that we expect to affect and be affected by human development? How do the multiple contexts (e.g., family, school, work) that we all occupy interact? To address these and other issues, we consider ecological-systems perspectives.

Physical Ecology

Characteristics of the *physical ecology* relevant to human development include the climate, plant and animal life, and human artifacts. Much of this physical ecology clearly has been shaped by human culture, including the nature and quantity of our food and shelter. Artifacts—man-made products such as tools, toys, books, and musical instruments—emerging over generations reflect our complex human history. They shape and are shaped by current generations.

The physical ecology is an important consideration for social work policy and practice. The forbearers of modern social workers, the "friendly visitors" from charity organization societies and settlement houses, provided assistance to those who were impoverished (Brieland, 1995). Inadequate physical resources is a central issue for social workers today. Debates in child welfare have centered on criteria for identifying and intervening in cases of child neglect. What constitutes adequate food, shelter, and sanitation? Are homeless and destitute parents unable to provide adequate food and shelter for themselves or their children guilty of "child neglect," and should these families be separated?

Social Ecology

Characteristics of the *social ecology* relevant to human development include the people with whom we interact, what we do together, how we interact, and the dynamics of the social groups in which we live. Like the physical ecology, the social ecology has been shaped by generations and both shapes and will be shaped by current and future generations. For example, all human infants require protection and care, but how, what, and by whom such care is provided ranges widely from stay-at-home mothers in middle-class suburban United States, to sibling care in Mayan communities in Mexico, to group care in Israeli kibbutzim.

Social Composition. Social composition refers to the people who are available to interact with us. For a young child, the composition of the social ecology may include parents, siblings, extended family, and neighbors. Awareness of the composition of the social ecology can be extremely important to social work practice. To support the child's developing ability to form close relationships with others, child welfare workers are careful that infants and toddlers in foster care are moved around as little as possible to ensure their opportunity to interact over time with a consistent primary caregiver.

Social Activities. The activities in which we routinely engage with others is another dimension of the social ecology relevant to development. The routine everyday, social activities the young child engages in with parents or older siblings may include chores, book reading, storytelling, bath and meal-times, and play. These activities may support intellectual and social development, language learning, and literacy. Analysis of social activities is also relevant to social work policy and practice. A school social worker contributing to the assessment of a young child with a suspected learning disability affecting reading will consider whether or not the child has had the opportunity to participate with more experienced others at home in everyday routines such as book reading and storytelling that help to support developing literacy skills.

Social Interactions. The ways in which we interact with others is another characteristic of our social ecology critical for understanding development. To return to our example of the infant in foster care: the child's developing ability to form close relationships with other people depends not only on having a relatively constant caregiver, but a caregiver who interacts with the baby in a consistent, supportive, and responsive manner.

Social System Dynamics. The dynamics of the social ecology is also important to understanding development. The social ecology can be thought of as a system. A system is a regularly interacting or interdependent group of parts forming a unified and bounded whole. Depending on the purposes of our social work assessment or intervention, a system may be defined as a family, classroom, mental health facility, school, community, or nation. Social systems have a number of related characteristics that are important to highlight when thinking about social work assessment and intervention.

First, social systems are composed of parts, or subsystems, which interact and can influence one another. Consider the family as a system consisting of several members, including a child suspected of having depression. Social work assessment of the child requires not only knowledge of the child's functioning, but knowledge of the family system in which that child is embedded. Pertinent information includes marital, sibling, and parent-child relationships because these relationships can powerfully affect and be affected by the child's depression (Taylor, in press). An ill child can place enormous strain on parents that can erode the quality of the marital relationship and the quality of parenting and may lead to resentment among the siblings.

Second, social systems tend toward "self-preservation" and not all subsystems have equal power to affect other parts of the system. Lasting meaningful system change often requires multiple interacting factors. Consider the system of slavery in the United States. Despite their centrality to the system, African Americans were virtually powerless to effect lasting and meaningful change in their social, health, or economic situations. Regardless of their intelligence, talent, hard work, artistry, obedience, defiance, or intimacy with whites, African Americans were virtually powerless to effect meaningful change in the slave system. Minor improvements in living conditions were given and taken away, but dismantling the slave system required not only changes in regional and national economics, manufacturing methods, transportation, federal policy, and time, but also a long, bloody civil war.

Third, systems vary in their stability. Family therapists have noticed that in some families change in one subsystem can cause a ripple effect of change throughout the family or system. For example, medical intervention and therapy may result in the lessening of a child's depression, which, in turn, may result in improved marital, parent-child, and sibling relationships. In other families, however, patterns of behavior and interaction are less responsive to change. Treatment of a child's depression may have little or no impact on how his family members respond to him or to one another. Stability may or may not be a good thing depending on whether or not the existing patterns of interaction are satisfactory.

Finally, at any given point in time, we all participate within multiple social systems, for example, home, school, work, neighborhood, community, and nation. These various systems can influence one another; for example, family systems can affect and be affected by school systems. Morning and afternoon routines of families may be structured around school beginning and dismissal times. On the other hand, families may influence schools through social and political pressure. Systems vary in how open they are to influence from other systems. Some public school administrators welcome and act upon input from families, while others are highly resistant.

Urie Bronfenbrenner, a modern American psychologist, describes four interacting levels of social context critical to human development: the microsystem, mesosystem, exosystem, and macrosystem (1979, 1995, 1998). To this framework, D. Norton adds the focal system. The first level of context, the focal system, is our analytic vantage point. It is the perspective from which we view related systems. Depending on the nature and purpose of our social work assessment and intervention, the focal system might be an individual person, family, or community. For the purposes of the following discussion, however, we will consider that the focal system is the individual person. Relevant characteristics of the individual as a focal system include biological, psychological, and social factors. These characteristics are embedded within the cultural-historical context of micro-, meso-, exo-, and macrosystems.

The second level of context is the *microsystem*. The microsystem encompasses the immediate social environment, the day-to-day reality of the focal system (in this case, a person). It usually includes those settings in which we have face-to-face, sustained, and significant relationships with others, for example, our families, peer groups, schools, workplaces, and churches. Microsystems change with the individual's development, and they change across cultural-historical contexts. A young girl's microsystems may include relationships with family, friends, and teachers. As she grows, they may include relationships with a husband and professional colleagues. In 2005, middle-class North American women's microsystems commonly include professional colleagues, but such microsystems were rare at earlier points in history and remain rare in some cultural communities. If major microsystems are missing or are in conflict, the social worker may anticipate that developmental problems could result; for example, a foster child who does not have a permanent family may experience emotional, social, and learning difficulties.

The third level of context is the *mesosystem*. Mesosystems encompass the set of interrelationships between two or more of the person's microsystems; for example, a child's parent takes her to kindergarten on the first day of school and meets the teacher, thereby forming a new home-school mesosystem. A more complex mesosystem can involve a variety of distinct microsystems, for example, from the home, school, church, and neighborhood. The composition and complexity of mesosystems also vary with development and cultural-historical context.

Analysis of the similarities and differences across the microsystems comprising an individual's mesosystems can help the social worker to anticipate challenges and resources for development. Children whose mesosystems are comprised of microsystems homogeneous with respect to beliefs and practices experience a world very different from those experienced by children whose mesosystems are comprised of more diverse or conflicting microsystems. If family, neighborhood, and school are all dominated by a particular religion, then the child's values, beliefs, and identity may be reinforced within multiple homogeneous mesosystems and there may be little stress during childhood. On the other hand, there may be considerable stress in adolescence if the focal system is in conflict with homogeneous mesosystems; for example, the young Mormon teenager living in Utah who discovers he is gay may be condemned by multiple homogeneous mesosystems comprised of his family, neighborhood, school, and church. He may have nowhere to turn for support.

Individuals whose mesosystems are comprised of diverse, even conflicting, microsystems may experience more stress during childhood and less in adulthood. An interracial child, where one parent is Jewish and the other is African American, who lives in a midwestern working-class suburb may experience more conflict and stress within her various heterogeneous mesosystems than the typical Mormon child growing up in Utah. Conflict and stress are not necessarily detrimental and can even facilitate development. If the African American Jewish child receives the support she needs to develop effective coping strategies, then as an adult she may be able to establish ties to diverse groups, thereby enhancing her social resources.

The fourth level of context is the *exosystem*. The exosystem encompasses one or more settings that do not involve the person as an active participant, but in which events occur that do affect the person. A husband may have no contact with his wife's workplace, but the chronic and consistent stress she experiences there may affect her ability to relate to him within their marriage. Other examples of exosystems include the local school board of a child who is attending public school, and the local zoning board of a family whose house is in the path of urban renewal. Exosystems also vary across individual development and cultural-historical contexts. Analysis of a client's exosystems can help social workers to identify sources of stress and support that exist outside of the client's immediate relationships, but that do affect those relationships.

The fifth level of context is the *macrosystem*. It includes the cultural patterns of the larger society that pervade all of the other systems. Macrosystems include widespread societal values such as individual freedom, major institutions such as government and education, and economic structure. They also include the diverse belief systems and practices of subcultures, which vary in terms of ethnicity, income, education, age, ability/disability, urban/rural locale, and sexual orientation.

Analysis of macrosystems can help the social worker identify potential sources of support and stress. In a homogenous world, the macrosystem values and culture closely mirror those of the micro-, meso-, and exosystems, creating little stress on the focal system. In a pluralistic society, the individual's subcultural values, beliefs, and practices may differ from those of the general society and may even be incongruent with that of the societal macrosystem. Jill McLean Taylor (1996) studied the relationships of adolescent Latina and Portuguese girls with their mothers. Some of these dyads described considerable tension resulting, essentially, from the conflicting values and behaviors of the United States mainstream and Hispanic or Portuguese families. Within the school, Hispanic and Portuguese girls were socialized toward independence and self-assertion. In contrast, socialization in the family focused on showing respect to elders and remaining interdependent with the family.

Social climate

In considering physical and social ecologies, it is important to remember that they are not separate but interacting parts of our environment, and that we imbue both our physical and social surroundings with meaning. For example, Rudolf Moos (1990) applied the term "social climate" to refer to a setting's "personality," separate from the characteristics of each individual participating in the setting. Social climate can influence individuals and groups, and people's actions can alter a setting's social climate. Concrete elements of the social climate include a setting's physical characteristics such as size or space, lighting, colors, temperature, objects, decorations, tools, state of repair, neatness or clutter within the space, etc. More abstract elements are the explicit and implicit rules, boundaries, roles, goals, and other expectations placed on individuals participating within the setting. Together a setting's concrete and abstract elements create a social climate. For example, fast-food restaurants use clowns and identifiable play areas to concretely communicate that children are welcomed, and that the abstract rules tolerate a wide range of behaviors. On the other hand, a library uses physical characteristics to announce that individuals of all ages are expected not only to modulate their voices, movement, and activities, but also acknowledge the importance of written and recorded information. Understanding the concept of social climate helps social workers assess a client's goodness-of-fit within and across environmental settings. For example, a home visit from a child welfare caseworker might be a better fit for a quiet child who prefers order and routine than a trip to the fast-food restaurant.

In summary, the developmental-ecological framework in social work reflects an interdisciplinary integration of theory and empirical research in the social and biological sciences. Conceptual frameworks clearly are necessarily given the volume of complex information to which social workers must respond on a daily basis. Systematic consideration of biological, psychological, and social factors as they change over time within particular cultural-historical contexts is critical to adequate assessment and effective intervention. There are, however, a variety of conceptual frameworks or theories available to guide social work practice and policy, and these frameworks will likely evolve considerably over time. You may wonder, then, how professional social workers evaluate conceptual frameworks, and the extent to which any given theory will guide their practices. Such decisions are complex and include many pragmatic considerations, for example, how well a particular framework addresses the challenges facing social workers in various contexts. In addition, evaluation of any conceptual framework requires assessment of the empirical research on which it is based. Thus, some familiarity with social science research is important for modern social workers.

BUILDING THE KNOWLEDGE BASE THROUGH APPLIED SOCIAL SCIENCE RESEARCH

An important characteristic of modern professional social work emphasized throughout this book is the use of empirical social science research to assess theory and to inform practice and policy. Knowledge of empirical research is essential for the modern social worker. The alternatives, including appealing to religious (or other) authority, personal experience, or popular opinion, are simply unacceptable to professional practice in our complex, pluralistic society. Ethical practice necessitates a rigorous assessment of social work practice and policy. Critical questions are: Did the intervention produce the desired results? Did a well-intentioned intervention cause unintended harm? Could scarce resources be spent better elsewhere? Such questions are scrutinized through applied social science research combined with practice experience with particular individuals and communities.

Professional social workers obtain and present information on current applied social science research through a variety of sources including professional journals. *Social Work, Research on Social Work Practice, Social*

Service Review, Social Work Education, Child Welfare, Children and Youth Services Review, and *Affilia—Journal of Women and Social Work* are a few of the journals that report social work research. Such reports typically contain valuable recommendations that have the potential to strengthen practice and policy. Recommendations in some reports, however, may contradict recommendations in other reports or are simply ill-informed. It is essential for social workers to develop the critical thinking skills necessary to evaluate such recommendations (Gambrill, 2000). One way in which the professional social worker can separate the empirical wheat from the chaff is to consider the quality of the research on which the recommendations are based, including: Is the research question or hypothesis relevant or important? Who was sampled to participate in the research? Were the analyses appropriate to address the research question or hypothesis? What is the quality of the argument on which the conclusions and recommendations are based? In addition, consideration of the strengths and limitations of the methods employed to collect the information used to address the research questions posed is a good place to begin a critical analysis of a social work study.

There are a variety of methods used in social work research, each with inherent strengths and limitations. An informal perusal of social work journals suggests that *self-report* is perhaps the most common method in social work research. Self-reports involve the systematic collection of individuals' own reports of their behavior or psychological processes; for example, a group of battered mothers involved in the public child welfare system provide information about how they protected their children from harm during domestic violence. The information may be provided through face-to-face individual or group interviews, mailed questionnaires, or standardized assessments. The questions may range from highly unstructured (e.g., Tell me about your relationship with your partner [husband or boyfriend]) to highly structured (e.g., How many times has your partner struck you?). All these characteristics of self-reports affect the quality of data collected. One consideration for professional social workers deciding whether or not to adopt the recommendations of the research is the inherent strengths and limitations of self-report methods. Strengths include detailed accounts of people's lives that might not otherwise be available (e.g., domestic violence), and a glimpse into the beliefs that motivate behavior (e.g., belief that viewing domestic violence is not itself harmful to children and the failure to shield the child from domestic violence). Limitations include inaccurate or biased reporting resulting, for example, from selective recall (e.g., a woman is motivated to maintain a positive view of her partner and therefore denies or represses memories of abuse).

Systematic observations of behavior is another method of social work research. This method involves the direct observation of the behavior of interest, for example, parenting practices. Data may be collected through videotaping, audiotaping, and paper-and-pencil notes. Data may be collected by the researcher or other person (e.g., a teacher). Direct observations may be highly structured observations that occur within a laboratory setting, or less intrusive, unstructured observations of everyday life. All these characteristics have implications for the type of information that is collected. Strengths of observations include the ability to observe the behavior of interest directly, sometimes as it occurs within real-world settings in participants' everyday lives. Limitations include any effects caused by the presence of an observer, and the cost, including extensive amounts of time.

Some of the strongest social science research combines multiple methods to obtain the most comprehensive understanding. The *ethnographic method* is increasingly popular in social work research. This research method attempts to understand the unique beliefs, values, and practices of a particular social or cultural group. It is characterized by extended contact within a community and the use of multiple methods such as interviews and direct observations in an attempt to provide a "thick description" of social practices and what those practices mean to the participants. Important strengths of the ethnographic method include its rich description and lack of superficiality, and cultural relevance. It is, however, expensive and time consuming. In addition, the goal is to understand a particular community, and so its applicability to other settings is an empirical question.

Recent trends in research go beyond multimethod approaches to create *transdisciplinary research teams* in which scholars from the biological to the social sciences work together to solve complex problems. These scientists create teams with high levels of communication to develop a shared language; pooled bodies of knowledge; and jointly developed research questions, methods, analyses, and interpretations (Gehlert, 2005). For example, a transdisciplinary research team comprised of biologists, psychologists, social workers, and others addressed the problem of racial disparities in breast cancer. Although white women are more likely to get breast cancer, black women are more likely to die of the disease. Working with a complex multilevel model encompassing "genes to geography and back again," these researchers discovered that African American women living in neighborhoods with high crime and poverty rates display high levels of stress, which inhibit DNA repair of cell mutations (see McClintock, Conzen, Gehlert, Masi, & Olopade, 2005). Social work researchers, expert in dealing with communities, familiar with holistic approaches, and accustomed to working on teams, are well suited to participate in such transdisciplinary efforts to creatively tackle some of our most perplexing and persistent social problems.

SUMMARY

American social work has evolved within the complex social and historical forces of the nineteenth and twentieth centuries. With roots in nineteenth-century charity organization societies and philanthropy, social work emerged largely in response to problems associated with industrialization and urbanization. Historically, social workers have been committed to enhancing the welfare of people who encounter problems related to poverty, mental health, health care, employment, shelter and housing, and abuse (Hopps & Collins, 1995). As it evolved, social work developed a dual focus on the needs of individual clients and the ways in which the community and society respond to those needs. Social workers are concerned both with individual well-being and the environmental factors that affect it (Reamer, 1995). Social workers support those in acute need and encourage those in positions of power to use their resources to help meet those needs (Hopps & Collins, 1995).

Understanding human development is central to social work, or any profession whose goal is to enhance the welfare of vulnerable individuals. As illustrated by the life of Clara Brown, human development results from biological, psychological, and social characteristics of the focal system in complex interaction within a particular cultural and historical context. This context includes micro-, meso-, exo-, and macrosystems. By merging insights from human development research with ecological concepts, social workers can better understand and support their clients. A developmental-ecological approach suggests four specific issues to which social workers must attend when assessing problems and planning interventions:

1. *Focal System Characteristics.* What are the characteristics of the focal system? In the case of the individual, what are his/her individual characteristics (physical and mental health, and psychology) at this point in development? How does the client understand and respond to the issue at hand? How might the client's interpretations and reactions, strengths, and vulnerabilities relate to problems (e.g., domestic violence) and possible solutions at this point in time and later in development?

2. *Physical Ecology.* What are the characteristics of the physical ecology in which the client is embedded? What are the client's available physical resources (food, shelter, human artifacts)? Are they adequate for continued development?

3. *Social Ecology.* What are the characteristics of the social ecology in which the client is embedded?

    a. Social composition: Who is present and available for interaction with the client? What is the nature of these relationships? How might these relationships contribute to problems and possible solutions?

    b. Social activities: What is the client doing with others? Are these activities supportive of continued development?

c. Social interaction: How are the client and others interacting together? Are these interactions supportive of continued development? For example, are they mutually respectful?

d. Social system structure: How are various levels (micro-, meso-, exo-, and macrosystems) of the client's social ecology related? How does this social structure relate to problems (e.g., lack of communication between a child's home and school microsystems) and possible solutions (e.g., outreach by school social workers)?

e. Social system dynamics: What are the characteristics of the social system? For example, who has the power to change the system; how does this system interact with other systems; how do system characteristics impact the issue at hand?

4. *Social climate.* What is the goodness of fit between the client and the environment?

The dynamic, developmental-ecological framework underscores the fact that all of us are positioned in complex and changing ways within multiple social systems, for example, of family, school, work, and community. This is true for the white middle-class adult male, as well as the Latina inner-city high school student. We all develop multiple perspectives and frameworks for understanding and operating within diverse systems. For example, our language changes in predictable and systematic ways when we move from speaking to clients, to speaking with supervisors, to speaking with family members. Furthermore, our positions within these diverse interacting systems can vary tremendously over time and place. For example, culturally based differences in adult expectations of child behavior between home and school may be particularly stressful to the beginning kindergartener, but less so as the child becomes familiar with the demands of school and moves on to elementary school. On the other hand, racial differences between home and school may be relatively benign in kindergarten peer groups but become a source of stress in elementary school.

Study and Discussion Questions

1. From the perspective of social work, what are the contributions and limitations of theories or conceptual frameworks of human development that focus on biological, psychological, social, or ecological factors?

2. Describe Bronfenbrenner's descriptions of the micro-, meso-, exo-, and macrosystems. Write down an example of a social work issue. How might Bronfenbrenner's characterization of social context be used to facilitate analysis of this issue?

3. What is a developmental-ecological perspective? To what extent is this conceptual framework relevant to social work? Why?

4. Write down one example of how social work intervention or policy might be approached or affected from a developmental-ecological perspective.

5. We all have folk theories of human behavior and development: values, beliefs, and explanations for how the world works acquired within our families and communities. What are the limitations of folk theories? How do theories within social science (e.g., the developmental-ecological perspective) differ from folk theories?

6. Empirical research is central to the development of theories or conceptual frameworks that guide social work. How is this information obtained? How do we assess the quality of the information that we receive as practicing social workers? How do we apply this information to social work practice and policy? What are the challenges to applying research to practice?

Resources

There are a number of classic scholars to whom students may turn to enhance their understanding of a developmental-ecological framework. They include Lev Vygotsky (1962, 1978; also see Wertsch, 1985) as well as modern scholars such as Bruner (1990), Rogoff (1990, 2003), Bronfenbrenner (1979, 1995), Gibson (1979), Wertsch (1991), Germain (1991), Moen, Elder, and Luscher (1995), and Bronfenbrenner and Morris (1998).

Students also may wish to supplement their understanding of the research methods that generate the knowledge base on which social work is grounded. Students interested in an overview of social work research are directed to Rubin and Babbie (2001). Those interested in more in-depth treatment of various research methods are directed to Denzin and Lincoln (2005) for a discussion of qualitative methods, Tashakkori and Teddle (2003) for an overview of mixed methods, or Shadish, Cook, and Campbell (2002) for a discussion of quantitative research designs. Those interested in the challenges of applying research to practice are directed to Sigel (1998).

Interested students also can supplement this chapter through a number of excellent Web-based resources:

Cornell University's College of Human Ecology is a leader in studies focused on improving the human condition through national policy changes, improved nutrition, innovative housing, and clothing, health care, and legal resources. Available at: http://www.human.cornell.edu

Explore current research focused on ecological development at Cornell University's Bronfenbrenner Life Course Center. Available at: http://www.lifecourse.cornell.edu/default.html

In a radio interview, Jerome Kagan, internationally recognized psychologist and researcher specializing in cognition, social learning, and genetics, outlines many of his more controversial ideas. The interview was conducted by Norman Swan (2000) on Australia's Radio National. Available at: http://www.abc.net.au/rn/talks/lm/stories/s29331.htm

For a brief overview of Lev Vygotsky's social development theory, go to http://chd.gse.gmu.edu/immersion/knowledgebase/theorists/constructivism/vygotsky.htm

For information about genetic conditions and the genes or chromosomes responsible for those conditions, go to Genetics Home Reference, the United States National Library of Medicine's Web site: http://ghr.nlm.nih.gov

For links to research findings and an extensive catalog covering genetics in the biosciences, go to the Genetics Virtual Library: http://www.ornl.gov/sci/techresources/Human_Genome/genetics.shtml

References

Baker, R. (2003). *Clara: An ex-slave in gold rush Colorado*. Central City, CO: Black Hawk Publishing.

Bandura, A., Grusec, J. E., & Menlove, F. L. (1967). Vicarious extinction of avoidance behavior. *Journal of Personality and Social Psychology, 5*, 16–23.

Black, J. E., Jones, T. A., Nelson, C. A., & Greenough, W. T. (1998). Neural plasticity. In N. Alessi (Ed.) & J. T. Coyle (Section Ed.), *Handbook of child and adolescent psychiatry: Vol. IV. Varieties of development, Section I. Developmental neuroscience*. New York: Wiley.

Brieland, D. (1995). Social work practice: History and evolution. In *Encyclopedia of social work* (Vol. 3, pp. 2247–2254). Washington, DC: NASW Press.

Bronfenbrenner, U. (1979). *The ecology of human development*. Cambridge, MA: Harvard University Press.

Bronfenbrenner, U. (1995). Developmental ecology through space and time. In P. Moen, G. H. Elder, Jr., & K. Luscher (Eds.), *Examining lives in context: Perspectives on the ecology of human development* (pp. 619–648). Washington, DC: American Psychological Association.

Bronfenbrenner, U., & Morris, P. A. (1998). The ecology of developmental processes. In R. M. Lerner (Ed.), *Handbook of child psychology: Vol. 1. Theoretical models of human development* (5th ed., pp. 993–1028). New York: Wiley.

Brown, R. (1973). *A first language: The early stages*. Cambridge, MA: Harvard University Press.

Bruner, J. (1990). *Acts of meaning*. Cambridge, MA: Harvard University Press.

Cole, M., & Cole, S. (2001). *The development of children* (4th ed.). New York: Worth.

Courchesne, E., & Pierce, K. (2005). Brain overgrowth in autism during a critical time in development: Implications for frontal pyramidal neuron and interneuron development and connectivity. *International Journal of Developmental Neuroscience, 23* (2-3), 153–170.

Cowan, P. A. (1978). *Piaget, with feeling: Cognitive, social, and emotional dimensions*. New York: Holt, Rinehart and Winston.

Denzin, N., & Lincoln, Y. (Eds.). (2005). *Handbook of qualitative research* (2nd ed.). London: Sage.

DePaulo, J. R., Jr. (2002). *Understanding depression: What we know and what you can do about it*. New York: Wiley.

Furth, H. (1969). *Piaget and knowledge: Theoretical foundations.* Englewood Cliffs, NJ: Prentice Hall.

Gambrill, E. (2000). The role of critical thinking in evidence-based social work. In C. Garvin (Ed.), *Handbook of social work direct practice.* Thousand Oaks, CA: Sage.

Gehlert, S. (2005). *Health disparities and doctoral education in social work.* Keynote address at the annual meeting of the Group for Advancement of Doctoral Education, University of Alabama.

Germain, C. B. (1991). *Human behavior in the social environment: An ecological view.* New York: Columbia University Press.

Germain, C. B., & Gitterman, A. (1996). *The life model of social work practice* (2nd ed.). New York: Columbia University Press.

Gesell, A. (1940). *The first five years of life* (9th ed.). New York: Harper & Row.

Gibson, J. J. (1979). *The ecological approach to visual perception.* Boston: Houghton Mifflin.

Goodwin, F. K., & Jamison, K. R. (1990). *Manic-depressive illness.* New York: Oxford University Press.

Gottesman, I. I. (1991). *Schizophrenia genetics: The origins of madness.* New York: W. H. Freeman.

Greenough, W. T., Black, J. E., & Wallace, C. S. (1987). Experience and brain development. *Child Development, 58* (3), 539-559.

Haight, W. L. (2002). *African-American children at church.* New York: Cambridge University Press.

Hopps, J. G., & Collins, P. M. (1995). Social work profession overview. In *Encyclopedia of social work* (Vol. 3, pp. 2266-2282). Washington, DC: NASW Press.

Irvine, E. E. (1956). Transference and reality in the casework relationship. *British Journal of Psychiatric Social Work, 3* (4), 1-10.

McClintock, M., Consen, S., Gehlert, S., Masi, C., & Olopade, F. (In press). Mammary cancer and social interactions: Identifying multiple environments that regulate gene expression throughout the lifespan. *Journal of Gerontology: Social Sciences.*

McNeil, T. F., Cantor-Graae, E., Torrey, E. F., Sjostrom, K., Bowler, A. E., Taylor, E. H., et al. (1994). Obstetric complications in histories of monozygotic twins discordant and concordant for schizophrenia. *Acta Psychiatrica Scandinavica, 89,* 196-204.

Moen, P., Elder, G. H., & Luscher, K. (Eds.). (1995). *Examining lives in context: Perspectives on the ecology of human development.* Washington, DC: American Psychological Association.

Moos, R. H. (1990). Conceptual and empirical approaches to developing family-based assessment procedures: Resolving the case of the Family Environment Scale. *Family Process, 29,* 199-211.

Moos, R., Finney, J., & Cronkite. R. (1990). *Alcoholism treatment: Context, process, and outcome.* New York: Oxford University Press.

Norton, D. *Ecology and plurality: An ecological systems framework for a pluralistic curriculum: Beyond the dual perspective.* Unpublished manuscript.

Osterlind, S. J. (2006). *Modern measurement: Theory, principles and applications of mental appraisal.* Upper Saddle River, NJ: Prentice Hall.

Pavlov, I. P. (1927). *Conditional reflexes.* Oxford: Oxford University Press.

Payne, M. (2005). *Modern social work theory* (3rd ed.). Chicago: Lyceum Books.

Popper, K. (1999). *All life is problem solving.* New York: Routledge.

Reamer, R. G. (1995). Ethics and values. In *Encyclopedia of social work* (19th ed., Vol. 3, pp. 893-902). Washington, DC: NASW Press.

Rogoff, B. (1990). *Apprenticeship in thinking: Cognitive development in social context.* New York: Oxford University Press.

Rogoff, B. (1998). Cognition as a collaborative process. In D. Kuhn & R. S. Siegler (Eds.), *Handbook of child psychology: Vol 2. Cognition, perception, and language* (5th ed., pp.679–744). New York: Wiley.

Rogoff, B. (2003). *The cultural nature of human development.* New York: Oxford University Press.

Rogoff, B., Turkanis, C., & Bartlett, L. (Eds.). (2001). *Learning together: Children and adults in a school community.* New York: Oxford University Press.

Rubin, A., & Babbie, E. (2001). *Research methods for social work* (4th ed.). Belmont, CA: Wadsworth/Thomson Learning.

Schreibman, L., & Koegel, R. L. (1996). Fostering self-management: Parent-delivered pivotal response training for children with autistic disorder. In E. D. Hibbs & P. S. Jensen (Eds.), *Psychosocial treatment for child and adolescent disorders: Empirically based strategies for clinical practice* (pp.525–553). Washington, DC: American Psychological Association.

Seifert, K. L., Hoffnung, R. J., Hoffnung, M. (2000). *Life span development* (2nd ed.). Boston: Houghton Mifflin.

Shadish, W., Cook, T., & Campbell, D. (2002). *Experimental and quasi-experimental design for generalized causal inference.* New York: Houghton Mifflin.

Sigel, I. (1998). Practice and research: A problem in developing communication and cooperation. In W. Damon, I. Sigel, & A. Renninger (Eds.), *Handbook of child psychology: Vol. 5. Child psychology in practice* (5th ed., pp. 1113–1132). New York: Wiley.

Skinner, B. F. (1975). The steep and thorny road to a science of behavior. *American Psychologist, 30,* 42–49.

Spiegler, M. D., & Guevremont, D. C. (1998). *Contemporary behavior therapy* (3rd ed.). Pacific Grove, CA: Brooks/Cole.

Sternberg, R. J. (1984). Toward a triarchic theory of human intelligence. *Behavioral & Brain Sciences, 7,* 269–315.

Sternberg, R. J. (1985). *Beyond IQ: A triarchic theory of human intelligence.* New York: Cambridge University Press.

Tashakkori, A., & Teddle, C. (Eds.). (2003). *Handbook of mixed methods in social and behavioral research.* Thousand Oaks, CA: Sage.

Taylor E. H. (1987). The biological basis of schizophrenia. *Social Work, 32,* 115–121.

Taylor, E. H. (1997). Serious mental illness: A biopsychosocial perspective. In *Encyclopedia of social work* (Supplement). Washington, DC: NASW Press.

Taylor, E. H. (2005). *An atlas of bipolar disorders.* London: Taylor & Francis.

Taylor, E. H. (In press). Manic depression. In V. S. Ramachandran (Ed.), *Encyclopedia of the human brain.* San Diego, CA: Academic Press.

Taylor, J. M. (1996). Cultural stories: Latina and Portuguese daughters and mothers. In B. J. R. Leadbeater & N. Way, (Eds.), *Urban girls: Resisting stereotypes, creating identities.* New York: New York University Press.

Thorndike, E. L. (1898). Animal intelligence: An experimental study of the associative processes in animals. *Psychological Review Monograph Supplement, 2*(8).

Thorndike, E. L. (1911). *Individuality.* Riverside Educational Monographs. Boston: Houghton Mifflin.

Torrey, E. F., Bowler, A. E., Taylor, E. H., & Gottesman, I. I. (1994). *Schizophrenia and manic depressive disorder: The biological roots of mental illness as revealed by the landmark study of identical twins*. New York: Basic Books.

Vance, H. B., & Pumariega, A. (Eds). (2001). *Clinical assessment of child and adolescent behavior*. New York: Wiley.

Vygotsky, L. (1962). *Thought and language*. Cambridge, MA: MIT Press.

Vygotsky, L. S. (1978). *Mind in society: The development of higher mental processes*. Cambridge, MA: Harvard University Press.

Wallace, C. S., Kilman, V. L., Withers, G. S., & Greenough, W. T. (1992). Increases in dendritic length in occipital cortex after 4 days of differential housing in weanling rats. *Behavioral and Neural Biology, 58* (1), 64–68.

Wallen, J. (1982). Listening to the unconscious in case material: Robert Langs' theory applied. *Smith College Studies in Social Work, 52* (3), 203–233.

Watson, J. B. (1913). Psychology as the behaviorist views it. *Psychological Review, 20*, 158–177.

Watson, J. B. (1930). *Behaviorism*. Chicago: University of Chicago Press.

Wentworth, W. M. (1980). *Context and understanding: An inquiry into socialization theory*. New York: Elsevier.

Wertsch, J. (1985). *Vygotsky and the social formation on mind*. Cambridge, MA: Harvard University Press.

Wertsch, J. V. (1991). *Voices of the mind: A sociocultural approach to mediated action*. Cambridge: Harvard University Press.

Wood, K. M. (1971). The contribution of psychoanalysis and ego psychology to social work. In H. S. Strean (Ed.), *Social casework: Theories in action*. (pp. 45–122). Metuchen, NJ: Scarecrow Press.

Yelloly, M. A. (1980). *Social work theory and psychoanalysis*. New York: Van Nostrand Reinhold.

Figure 2.1. Play is central to development in early childhood. This young mother is taking her young children to visit and play with friends.

2

Social Work with Infants and Young Children: Attachment Relationships in the Family

Wendy L. Haight, Susan A. Cole, and Edward H. Taylor

This chapter considers the infant and young child as the focal system. As you read, consider the child's developing biological, psychological, and social competencies and the physical and social ecologies in which these achievements emerge. This chapter highlights microsystems. Infants and young children participate in many microsystems, for example, with parents, siblings, and extended family members. During this period of life, relationships with caregivers are crucial, especially attachment relationships. As you read, consider the characteristics of caregiver-child attachment relationships, how these relationships emerge, and their implications for the child's future development.

Although caregiver-child microsystems are crucial, they do not exist in isolation but are embedded within a complex social and cultural context. Caregiver-child microsystems may affect and be affected by the macrosystem, for example, the availability of affordable child care. As you read, also consider how mesosystems, for example, the parents' relationships with one another and with the child, affect the attachment relationship. How do ecosystems such as the parents' employment affect the attachment relationship?

If problems emerge in the caregiver-child relationship, social workers in the field of child welfare may intervene. These professionals are called upon to make complex decisions about the safety of the child and interventions to support the caregiver's ability to provide for the child's basic physical and psychological needs. As you read, consider how interventions that may be necessary for the infant's or young child's safety, for example, temporary placement in foster care, can affect the parent-child attachment relationship. What are the side effects of child welfare interventions?

Portions of this chapter draw upon, expand, and update Haight, W., Kagel, J., & Black, J. (2003). Understanding and supporting parent-child relationships during foster care visits: Attachment theory and research. *Social Work, 48(2)*, 195–208.

....

: **BOX 2.1 VIOLENCE ACROSS THE LIFE SPAN**

: **The Impact of Domestic Violence on Infants
and Young Children**

Domestic violence, that is, abuse within close, loving, romantic relationships, is witnessed by an estimated 3.3 to 10 million children annually in the United States (see Stephans, 1999). Witnessing domestic violence is a form of traumatic stress that can threaten children's well-being and development. Traumatic stress involves experiencing or witnessing actual or threatened physical injury to the self or other person, especially a family member, accompanied by fear, helplessness, and horror and, in children, disorganized or agitated behavior (American Psychiatric Association, 1994). Traumatic stress that results from intentional human design, particularly that caused by parents or other attachment figures, is especially challenging for children. There is extensive empirical evidence that witnessing angry and violent exchanges between adults has detrimental effects on children, even if they themselves are not the targets of abuse. Decades of research testify to the relationship between family discord and children's maladjustment. Clear associations have been found between exposure to violence and posttraumatic symptoms and disorders even in infants and toddlers (see Osofsky, 1995a, 1995b). Infants in violent homes may have difficulty eating and sleeping and may cry excessively or very little. Toddlers and preschoolers may show language delays, regress to infant-like behavior, or act out aggressively (see Stephans, 1999). In addition, traumatic stress may disturb children's emerging concepts of self and other, safety, and protection (Osofsky, 1995a, and Pynoos et al., 1996), and interfere with the development of affect regulation (Parens, 1991).

<hr>

Sources: American Psychiatric Association. (1994). *Diagnostic and statistical manual of mental disorders* (4th ed.). Washington, DC: Author; Osofsky, J. (1995a) Children who witness domestic violence: The invisible victims. Social policy report. *The Society for Research in Child Development 9*(3), 1–16; Osofsky, J. (1995b). The effects of violence exposure on young children. *American Psychologist. 50*, 782–788; Parens, H. (1991). A view of the development of hostility in early life. *Journal of the American Psychoanalytic Association, 39*(Supplement), 75–108. Stephans, D. (1999). Battered women's views of their children. *Journal of Interpersonal Violence 14*(7), 731–746; Pynoos, R., Steinberg, A., & Goenjian, A. (1996). Traumatic stress in childhood and adolescence: Recent developments and current controversies. In B. Van der Kolk, A. McFarlane, & L. Weisaeth (Eds.), *Traumatic stress: The effects of overwhelming experience on mind, body and society* (pp. 331–358). New York: Guilford Press.

....

Social work with infants (birth–2 years) and young children (2–5 years) is exciting and vital. In a few short years, typically developing infants transform in size and shape, master their native languages, develop play and humor, and form complex relationships with parents, siblings, extended family members, and peers. Despite the remarkable strengths reflected by these accomplishments, infants and young children remain vulnerable for several years. Dependent on others for their survival, they are more likely to suffer long-term or permanent disabilities because of abuse and neglect than are older children. As described in box 2.1, the development and well-being of infants and young children are also affected by the family context, including the experience of *domestic violence*. Unlike older children, infants and young children cannot care for their own basic physical needs, escape abusive relationships, or seek out supportive adults and peers outside of their families. Furthermore, the rapid physical, psychological, and social growth of infants and young children makes them especially vulnerable to disruptions in development as a result of illness, maltreatment, poverty, or extended separations from their primary caregivers.

CHILD WELFARE WITH INFANTS AND YOUNG CHILDREN

Given their relatively greater vulnerability, infants and young children are a special concern of social workers in *child welfare* practice. Child welfare is the government-organized, formal service delivery system designed to assist children from birth through adolescence who have been abused or neglected, or whose well-being is at risk. In the United States, child welfare services are the responsibility of each state and vary in organization from statewide systems to loosely networked county-by-county systems (Downs, Costin, & McFadden, 1996). Within these systems, government and private agencies provide a range of services supported by federal government policy (Adoption and Safe Families Act, 1997) and intended to support the well-being of vulnerable children and families. Services include in-home support for children and their struggling families, treatment for parents, and out-of-home foster care for children. Agencies also address, with varying success, the social conditions that affect children and families negatively, such as inadequate housing, poverty, substance abuse, domestic violence, and lack of access to adequate health and mental health-care services (Liederman, 1995).

Child welfare services around the world reflect larger social and cultural beliefs regarding the causes and effects of maltreatment and the appropriate responses. The United States child welfare system is but one possible variant. Why do parents abuse their children, and how do we respond to them—with punishment, support? How does maltreatment affect children, and what are the best strategies for dealing with the difficult attitudes and behaviors many children exhibit as a result of their maltreatment? What are our moral and pragmatic obligations as a society to provide resources to support vulnerable families? Examination of child welfare in other societies can provide an important vantage point from which to examine our own assumptions about maltreatment, and the quality of our own practices. Box 2.2 describes aspects of child welfare in Japan.

This chapter focuses on the development of adequate attachment relationships, a central issue in child welfare practice. Attachment refers to close, enduring, affective bonds that develop throughout life (Ainsworth, 1973). More than three decades of empirical research have confirmed what diverse theoretical perspectives have predicted—adequate attachment relationships are necessary for children's healthy development (Zeanah, Boris, & Larrieu, 1997; Shonkoff & Phillips, 2001). Attachment relationships can influence children's expectations for, and responses to, subsequent interpersonal relationships (Carlson, 1998; Crittenden & Ainsworth, 1989). Early attachment relationships can influence a child's basic sense of him/herself as lovable and worthy of attention, of others as trustworthy and reliable, and of the

---

BOX 2.2 INTERNATIONAL PERSPECTIVES
Child Welfare in Japan

One of the problems facing Japanese society is a declining birth rate. In 1970, 24% of the population was younger than 15 years, whereas in 2005 it was projected to be 14.3%. As a consequence, Japanese society has chosen to invest heavily in preventative programs to ensure that its children are healthy and safe and develop to their fullest. These programs include universal child and maternal health care through the preschool years, and antipoverty programs for women who may be plunged with their children into poverty when they lose their spouses.

In Japan, parent social isolation is viewed as a primary risk factor in maltreatment and is addressed more often than poverty. In an urbanized society where interpersonal relationships are highly valued, an individual who lacks a sense of community and informal mutual support systems can feel "socially dead." In their stress and frustration, parents may maltreat their children. At the Hyogo Prefecture Child Maltreatment Prevention Professionals' Meeting (Bamba, 2005), it was argued that child maltreatment is likely to occur when parents live within a "stifling" situation, isolated from the community and relatives. The goal, then, is to create a support system where each parent and child can find their own Ibasho, that is, "place" where they can feel peace, stability, belonging, and security to express themselves fully. Developing accepting and supportive interpersonal relationships where one feels valued typically is central to finding one's Ibasho (Bamba, 2005).

Sources: Segel, U. (2004). Child welfare programs and services: A comparison of the USA and Japan. *International Social Work, 47*(3), 370–390; Bamba, S. (2005). The concept of "Ibasho" and child maltreatment in Japan. Paper presented at the 53rd conference of the Japanese Society for Studying Social Welfare in Japan.

world as a basically safe and interesting place. Children who have experienced poor support from their caregivers, or are uncertain of their caregivers' responses, are less apt to engage in the active exploration of the physical and social environments supportive of optimal development (Cicchetti, 2002).

Unfortunately, an increasing number of infants and young children are entering foster care. Children younger than 1 year of age have the highest placement incidence (Wulcyzn & Brunner, 2000), and infants 3 months and younger are most at risk for foster care placement (Wulczyn, Hislop & Harden, 2002). The rate of placement for children younger than 1 year is more than twice the rate of children entering care ages 1 through 3 years, and more than four times that of children entering care ages 4 through 17 years. Infants in urban areas (primarily African Americans) are at the highest risk with 1.5 percent of all urban children younger than 1 year of age entering foster care (Wulcyzn & Brunner, 2000). Although foster care may protect children's physical safety, it does put their emerging attachment relationships with family members at risk. In addition, when infants and young children experience multiple foster care placements, their subsequent abilities to form attachment relationships can be impaired.

Establishing attachment relationships with foster infants is a central part of foster parenting. Infants and young children in foster care, however, are at special risk and many have multiple, complex needs (Berrick, Needell, & Barth, 1998). They may enter foster care substance exposed, neglected, and with developmental delays and medical problems (Leslie, Gordon, Meneken, Premiji, Michelmore, & Granger, 2005). Infants and young children in foster care have three to seven times more chronic emotional disorders and chronic medical conditions than children of similar socioeconomic backgrounds who remain at home (Blatt & Simms, 1997) and also experience disproportionate rates of developmental delays (Cicchetti & Toth, 1995). This chapter elaborates on how a developmental-ecological analysis of attachment relationships can inform one important issue in child welfare practice: supporting the attachment relationships of infants and young children who are in foster care. The following case illustrates the complexity of this task.

In the following excerpt, 2-year-old Sharon and Priscilla, her mother, are briefly reunited for a visit following a month-long separation. Priscilla, a heroin addict, was charged with child neglect several months earlier when Sharon and her 3-year-old sister were found wandering unsupervised near a busy intersection. Following an investigation by social workers specializing in child welfare, they were placed in foster care with their elderly great-grandmother.

> Sharon [with hair carefully braided and dressed in a beautiful, immaculate Sunday dress] arrived at the playroom before her mother and stood, quietly examining the xylophone mallet. When Priscilla arrived, she and Sharon did not immediately greet one another. Priscilla stood near the door, holding her coat,

and Sharon stood across the room looking down at the mallet in her hands. Priscilla did not bend down or move towards Sharon. She looked over Sharon's head and appeared tense. Sharon initiated the first interaction by holding the mallet out to Priscilla. Priscilla asked if Sharon wanted her to sing, but Sharon made no response. Priscilla then greeted her, "Hi, Sharon," and "Hi, how you doing?" but Sharon did not respond or acknowledge these initiations. Then Priscilla, still standing upright, reached out for the mallet and Sharon handed it to her. They both stood still for a moment, and then Sharon turned away, pulled out a chair and sat, quietly, facing away from Priscilla. . . . Thirteen minutes into the visit, Priscilla drew Sharon to her for a hug. Sharon initially was stiff and unresponsive, but then relaxed, laid her head on her mother's shoulder and cried softly. Priscilla kissed her and asked, "What's wrong? . . . Your mommy love you." (Haight, Black, Workman, & Tata, 2001, p. 330)

Social workers practicing in child welfare settings routinely make complex and difficult decisions regarding the best interests of vulnerable children like Sharon. What are the risks to Sharon of placing her in foster care, particularly to her developing attachment relationships with her birth family? How does one determine when the home environment is safe and, if necessary, with whom an infant or young child should be placed: an elderly relative whom, like Sharon's great-grandmother, the child knows but who may develop health problems necessitating another move, or a foster family, perhaps one pursuing adoption? A brief overview of the rapid developmental changes during infancy and early childhood will provide perspective before discussion of the development of attachment relationships and an examination of child welfare practices to support attachment relationships in infancy and early childhood.

HIGHLIGHTS OF DEVELOPMENT DURING INFANCY AND EARLY CHILDHOOD

Child welfare with infants and young children is challenging both because infants and young children are so vulnerable, and because they experience rapid and complex developmental changes. Illness, neglect, and abuse experienced even for relatively short periods of time can derail these developmental processes and result in significant delays. However, addressing medical needs or changing the caregiving environment can support rapid recovery or developmental catch-up.

Before birth, tremendous biological and psychological development occurs. The fetus's senses develop relatively early in prenatal development. The fetus responds to sounds about five to six months after conception and to light at about six months. Furthermore, the uterine environment provides rich sensory experiences. Sounds from outside the mother's body such as loud noises and voices can be heard by the fetus, as can sounds from within the mother's body such as her heartbeat and digestion. Given this sensory-rich prenatal environment and the relatively early development of the

> ## BOX 2.3 SUBSTANCE ABUSE ACROSS THE LIFE SPAN
> ## Prenatal Exposure to Alcohol
>
> Prenatal exposure to alcohol is teratogenic. Children of heavy drinkers (more than five drinks per day) or alcoholics may develop fetal alcohol effects (FAE) or fetal alcohol syndromw (FAS).
>
> - A child is considered to have FAE if at least one of the following three factors is observed, and FAS if all three factors are observed:
>   1. Growth retardation—low birth weight, microcephaly, decreased fatty tissue, and failure to thrive
>   2. A pattern of craniofacial anomalies including a small, nonsymmetrical head, short nose, slanted eyes, flattened area between the eyes, and a thin upper lip.
>   3. Neurological effects such as fine and gross motor delays; poor muscle tone and tremors; impaired IQ (mean IQ for FAS is 68) or learning disabilities; deficits in verbal learning and memory; problems dealing with multiple sensory inputs; delayed language development and communication deficits.
> - Neurological effects can result in behavioral problems such as impulsivity; decreased attention span; hyperactivity; difficulty developing and maintaining peer relationships; lack of empathy and remorse; poor social judgment; aggressiveness.
> - Adults who were born with FAS often have lifelong cognitive, socialization, and communication deficits.
>
> Source: Malanga, C. J., & Kosofsky, B. E. (2004). Effects of drugs of abuse on brain development. In D. S. Charney & E. J. Nestler (Eds.), *Neurobiology of mental illness* (2nd ed.). New York: Oxford University Press.

senses, it is not surprising that some rudimentary learning occurs in utero. Neonates show a preference for their mother's voice over the voices of other women (Fifer & Moon, 1994), for the native language over other languages (Moon, Panneton-Cooper, & Fifer, 1993), and for the sounds of normal over accelerated heartbeats (Salk, 1993). In contrast to William James's (1890) description of the newborn as occupying a world of impenetrable confusion, we now know that newborns arrive with relatively developed sensory, behavioral, and reflex systems. Full-term, healthy newborns are ready to interact, learn, and form attachment relationships.

During the prenatal period, the developing child is vulnerable to teratogens, which are environmental agents that cause deviations from normal development and lead to abnormalities or death. They include certain viruses, drugs, and pollutants. The use of substances including alcohol, cocaine, and

BOX 2.4 SUBSTANCE ABUSE ACROSS THE LIFE SPAN
Alcohol Abuse during Pregnancy

In the United States, a child born to a mother who has a middle or higher income is at significantly less risk for FAS then children born to low-income mothers. Lower socioeconomic status is associated with ten times more risk for FAS. As a social worker, consider how clustering low-income housing together, limiting prenatal care and addiction rehabilitation centers, and living in a culture that encourages the use of substances for escaping stress may play a major role in pregnant women's abuse of drugs and alcohol.

What other macro- and microsystems issues might increase the probability that low-income pregnant women will abuse a substance? What policy issues could discourage pregnant women from using addictive substances?

Source: Malanga, C. J., & Kosofsky, B. E. (2004). Effects of drugs of abuse on brain development. In D. S. Charney & E. J. Nestler (Eds.), *Neurobiology of mental illness* (2nd ed.). New York: Oxford University Press.

tobacco during pregnancy can have teratogenic effects on the fetus, resulting, for example, in an infant with reduced brain size (Malanga, Kosofsky, & Barry, 2004) or other abnormalities. Boxes 2.3 and 2.4 describe the effects of alcohol abuse during pregnancy.

Another serious risk to development during the prenatal period, infancy, and early childhood is poverty. Boxes 2.5 through 2.8 discuss infant and maternal mortality rates in the United States and internationally, as well as the relatively low rate of immunization in the United States.

Despite the complexity of newborns, they are still entirely dependent on others for their survival and will remain so for several years. This period of dependency results not only in vulnerability to maltreatment; it also provides rich and extensive opportunities for learning. During the first two years of life, infants' abilities to communicate, understand the world, and interact socially in culturally appropriate ways undergo dramatic transformations. By early childhood (approximately 3–6 years of age), children can communicate through language, understand their everyday physical and social worlds, and participate in their own basic care. Their increasing abilities to communicate, think, and play provide them with opportunities for interacting with a range of adults and children in a variety of contexts. Well-developing healthy young children ride tricycles with siblings, join in the pretend play of neighborhood friends, express their opinions forcefully to caregivers, and interact with nonkin adults in the community when out with caregivers.

```
........................................................
:                                                        :
:          BOX 2.5 POVERTY ACROSS THE LIFE SPAN          :
:        The Developmental Link between Focal System     :
:                    and Macrosystems                    :
:                                                        :
```

Healthy development is enhanced when a pregnant woman:
• is physically and mentally healthy before becoming pregnant;
• receives quality prenatal care throughout the pregnancy;
• avoids alcohol, street drugs, and tobacco during the pregnancy;
• avoids certain prescription drugs that can be toxic to the fetus;
• follows health care directives;
• regularly eats well-balanced meals;
• routinely gets a complete night's rest;
• reduces emotional and physical stress;
• is emotionally supported by family, employer, community, and friends.

This list illustrates the partnership that must exist between the pregnant woman and the macrosystem. Unless the government provides health care, education, and nutritional help, many women living in poverty are unable to properly care for their bodies and the developing fetus. On the other hand, women must be willing to use available facilities and educational opportunities. In some cases, women have to overcome personal and community beliefs to trust helping professionals.

An important way in which young children interact with and make sense of their social and physical world is through play. Play, in its many forms, is a universal activity of early childhood. Young children rough and tumble; sing and tease; build creations with mud, sticks, clay, and blocks; and pretend. Such play is important for healthy development. Virtually all major developmental theorists from Freud to Piaget to Vygotsky stress the importance of play. These theorists address fascinating questions such as: Why do children play? What function does play have in development?

Pretending is one form of play in early childhood that has received a great deal of attention. During pretend play, actions, objects, and persons are transformed or treated nonliterally. A child may use a stick as a magic wand, gesture as if sleeping, or take on the role of parent while coordinating a complex plot with several friends. Pretend play has long been recognized as pivotal in facilitating early social and emotional development. Through pretend play, young children can express and communicate with others their emerging concerns and interpretations of the social and cultural world. As in interpretive activity, pretend play allows children to explore, practice, and cri-

BOX 2.6 POVERTY ACROSS THE LIFE SPAN

Infant Mortality Rate in the United States Compared Nationally and Internationally

Infant mortality rates are declining in the United States. However, the death rate for African American infants is 2.5 times higher than for European American infants. The neonatal mortality rate for African Americans in 2000 was 923.5 per 100,000 live births compared to 461.6 per 100,000 live births for European American infants. During the postneonatal period (28 days–1 year), African American infants died at a rate of 468.2 per 100,000 live births compared to 383.9 for European American infants.

The United States ranks twenty-eighth among industrialized countries in prevention of infant deaths. This is a strong indication that the United States does not provide the quality, availability, and accessibility of primary care women need during pregnancy and the medical attention both the child and mother require during the infant's first year of life.

Source: Health Resources and Services Administration, Maternal and Child Health Bureau. (2002). *Child health USA 2002.* Washington, DC: U.S. Department of Health and Human Services.

tique emotions they have observed or experienced (Haight & Sachs, 1995; Haight, in press). Pretend play offers children an important outlet to express negative emotions that result from increasing demands to follow social rules, everyday stresses, and more serious trauma in a context in which there are no real-world consequences. In a study of children experiencing illness (diabetes and asthma), Cindy Dell Clark (2003) described the pervasive and spontaneous use of pretend play by chronically ill children as a means of

BOX 2.7 POVERTY ACROSS THE LIFE SPAN

Maternal Mortality Rates

Racial differences in poverty rates affect maternal as well as infant mortality. Not only do African American infants die at a greater rate than white infants, but black American women die giving birth 3.5 times more often than white women. The maternal mortality rate for African American mothers is 25.4 per 100,000 live births compared to 6.8 maternal deaths per 100,000 for European American women.

Source: Health Resources and Services Administration, Maternal and Child Health Bureau. (2002). *Child health USA 2002.* Washington, DC: U.S. Department of Health and Human Services.

```
..........................................................
:                                                        :
:          BOX 2.8 POVERTY ACROSS THE LIFE SPAN          :
:                   Immunization                         :
:                                                        :
```

In 2001, only 74% of U.S. children received all the recommended preventive immunizations.

Poverty can play a role in a child not getting immunizations because:

- parents may work at low-paying jobs that are at a distance from the clinic;
- taking off from work for well baby care may reduce the parent's pay check;
- parents have difficulty receiving health information and determining the truth of rumors and immunization myths;
- parents have no regular medical care provider and primarily use hospital emergency rooms for medical attention.

Source: Health Resources and Services Administration, Maternal and Child Health Bureau. (2002). *Child health USA 2002.* Washington, DC: U.S. Department of Health and Human Services.

coping with the difficulties of illness and treatment. These children engaged in pretend play to reassure themselves about painful treatments and worrisome symptoms and to compensate for vulnerable feelings related to their illness and treatment. Through pretend play they transformed threatening, painful, or frightening events into occasions for mastery or even celebration.

In addition to facilitating children's learning about emotions, pretend play facilitates adults' learning about children, and children's and adult's learning together. In the words of a young mother of a 2½-year-old:

I have a tendency of watching how she's pretending ... to see if she is having any anxieties or worries or, you know, happiness that she wants to share with me that maybe she, at her age, isn't able to come right out and say, "I'm scared about this." ... It's important for me to see what's on her mind (Haight, Parke, & Black, 1997).

When children and adults pretend together they may spontaneously co-construct an interpretation of the social and cultural world as issues naturally emerge in the contexts of their everyday lives. Such communications may be particularly important when young children experience highly stressful or traumatic events. Indeed, pretend play has been used extensively by play therapists to facilitate children's recovery from trauma (see Webb, 1999).

Despite the centrality of play to development in early childhood, busy adults may devalue this activity. Parents, eager to support their children's success in life, may fill children's days with structured activities such as group music classes for tots, gymnastics classes for preschoolers, and school learning activities at home. In day-care centers, preschools, and kindergartens, academic content is introduced to children at younger and younger ages. In contrast to traditional play-based curriculums, many preschools focus on teaching letters and numbers and other academic skills that are traditionally taught in kindergarten or first grade. These trends have been the subject of much criticism from experts in early childhood development (Zigler, Singer, & Bishop-Josef, 2004; Hirsh-Pasek & Golinkoff, 2003). Social workers, particularly those who are consultants to preschool programs, can have an important role in advocating for the importance of young children's play.

When considering the individual as the focal system, it is important to remember that although we may consider biological, psychological, and social factors separately for the purposes of analysis, in fact, they are interrelated. Children's increasing competence during infancy and early childhood is made possible by a complex ensemble of interrelated biological, psychological, and social developments supported within particular cultural-historical contexts. Children's increasing ability to move around during infancy and early childhood provides one example. During the first few months of life, motor areas of the cortex develop rapidly. In the second half of the first year, physical changes in strength and coordination allow mobility. Different cultural and historical contexts, however, allow different opportunities for the development of mobility. During the nineteenth century, many European American babies spent the first years of life restrained within wagons as their families moved west. Today, the descendents of these babies may career around in walkers in their baby-proofed playrooms. The experience of mobility, in turn, allows for the development of children's understanding of spatial relationships, for example, how objects are positioned relative to one another and various routes through the familiar environment. Mobility also leads to changes in social relationships as caregivers become concerned with the newly mobile infant's safety. During the second and third years of life, children's rapid acquisition of fluency in their native languages allows verbal communication and negotiation with the caregiver regarding safety and separations.

The rapid, complex developmental changes that occur during infancy and early childhood are mediated through relationships with other people, especially primary caregivers (Van Ijzendoorn & Sagi, 1999). Other people provide food, shelter, and a safe and adequate physical environment for the infant and young child. Other people also provide emotional comfort, access to language, and intellectual stimulation. Again, different cultural and historical contexts allow for different opportunities for social interaction. In some families and communities, infants and young children are rarely separated from their mothers even when they sleep; in others, infants are put into their own rooms to sleep at night; in others, they are cared for by a variety of individuals, including older siblings, grandparents, and neighbors, and are rarely separated from human contact. Because of the complex developmental changes in social relationships during the first several years of life, infants and young children are vulnerable to disturbances in their relationships, for example, during foster care placement. Thus, the maintenance and development of adequate attachment relationships is an overarching issue in child welfare with infants and young children.

DEVELOPMENT AND ORGANIZATION
OF ATTACHMENT RELATIONSHIPS

Understanding how attachment relationships are developed is critical to providing child welfare services appropriate to infants and young children. When infants and young children enter foster care, they lose the opportunity to interact extensively with their parents on a daily basis. If they move from foster home to foster home, they lose the ability to interact with those caregivers as well. Frequent and consistent contact with a primary caregiver is necessary for the development of adequate attachment relationships in infancy and early childhood because their organization changes dramatically during the first few years of life (Bowlby, 1969; Ainsworth, 1973; Thompson, 1998).

There are several important developmental changes in infants' early attachment behavior. Infants display innate attachment behaviors such as crying at birth that draw caregivers near, but they do not have a specific relationship with a parent. In this "preattachment" phase, lasting from birth to approximately 6 weeks of age, infants do not become upset when left with an unfamiliar caregiver. In the "attachment-in-the-making" phase, lasting from 6 weeks to approximately 6 to 8 months of age, infants begin to show signs of wariness when confronted with unfamiliar people. For infants placed in foster care early in infancy, their birth mothers are unfamiliar. In reunions with their mothers, infants may display behavior that reflects their perceptions that their mothers are unfamiliar. When reunited with the birth mother after several months in foster care, an infant may stiffen and turn away when his mother picks him up. The reaction of the infant may make it difficult for the mother to continue to engage the infant in order to establish a more secure relationship.

At approximately 7 months of age, infants will display "clear-cut attachment" behaviors. Infants from all over the world become overtly distressed when their primary caregiver is not available, in unfamiliar situations, or with strangers. As children become more mobile (12–18 months), they may use their caregivers as "secure bases" from which to freely explore, checking in with the caregiver if they feel frightened or anxious. By 24 months of age, as the child becomes more mobile and communicatively competent and spends increasing time away from the caregiver, the dyad enters a phase of "reciprocal relationships" in which they share responsibility for maintaining closeness when needed. By 3 years of age, the child enters a more sophisticated phase of attachment, which Bowlby (1969) termed "goal-corrected

BOX 2.9 CRISIS NURSERIES HELP FAMILIES STAY TOGETHER

Crisis nursery services, sometimes called "respite" services, provide temporary emergency care for children. The "emergency" or "crisis" for which the family requests services can range from the need for child care due to a medical emergency (e.g., an automobile accident or surgery) to an unexpected stressful home situation (e.g., domestic violence and homelessness) to a risk of abuse and neglect (e.g., a stressed single parent with no support). Crisis nurseries provide specialized crisis interventions to infants and young children and their families. When families experience crisis situations, the primary caregivers are often unavailable physically or psychologically to meet the needs of their children. The caregivers may be unable to perceive what their young children need or how to best address their needs in the family crisis. When this occurs, both the young children and their caregivers need timely interventions in a safe place where the workers are trained to understand how crisis affects each member of the family (Webb, 1999).

When the environment of infants and young children is chaotic, dangerous, and uncertain, children need the support of people who understand their developmental needs and can provide appropriate interventions until their primary caregivers can again be attentive to their needs (Webb, 1999). Social workers who work in crisis nurseries understand the importance of intervention at the time of the crisis and provide services to infants and young children and their families. These social workers are experts in ameliorating the effects of trauma on young children. The crisis nursery workers have the knowledge and the skills to provide developmentally appropriate interventions for children. Young children in family crises may not have the cognitive sophistication to understand what is happening to them or their families, but they sense the emotionality of the situation and respond to it. Children and their families need assistance in negotiating the immediate crisis and the aftereffects of the event to ensure positive posttrauma child development.

Although crisis nurseries vary in the services they offer to families, many provide an array of services that include initial crisis assessment and intervention services, after-crisis interventions, follow-up care, and/or referral to other community services (e.g., domestic violence shelters). Crisis nurseries prevent families from being separated or the need to place children in foster care when families experience a crisis.

Historically, crisis nurseries in the United States developed from a grassroots movement in the 1960s to provide respite to parents experiencing stress and to prevent child abuse and neglect. A study of 36 parents by Subramanian (1985) found a decrease in parenting stress after accessing services in all areas assessed (e.g., problems with child care, financial problems, and current living situation) except fatigue. Some research suggests that those who use crisis nursery services perceive them as safe places for children (Dougherty et al., 2002). Postcrisis services support development of positive family relationships that enhance the development of secure attachment relationships.

Sources: Cole, S.A., Wehrmann, K. C., Dewar, G., & Swinford, L. (2005). Crises nurseries: Important services in a system of care for families and children. *Children and Youth Services Reviews, 27,* 995–1010; Webb, N. B. (1999). *Play therapy with children in crisis.* New York: Guilford. Subramanian, K. (1985). Reducing child abuse through respite center intervention. *Child Welfare,* 64, 501–509; Dougherty, S., Yu, E., Edgar, M., Day, P., & Wade, C. (2002). *Planned and crisis respite for families with children: Results of a collaborative study.* Chapel Hill, NC: ARCH National Respite Network and Resource Center.

partnership." During this period, caregivers and children communicate and negotiate differences in plans and reach mutual agreement. The child's sense of security no longer depends so much on the actual presence of the caregiver as on mutual trust and understanding. These developmental changes are supported by children's emerging abilities to communicate and understand others' perspectives, motivations, and feelings.

Given the significance and complexity of rapidly changing caregiver-child relationships in infancy and early childhood, child welfare workers must be particularly sensitive to their disruption. Child welfare workers must weigh the potential of harm caused by an inadequate home environment against the potential of harm caused by the disruption of caregiver-child relationships during foster care placement or reunion with the birth parent. Whenever possible, child welfare workers attempt to provide services and support to children and families at home so that out-of-home placement, with the inherent disruption of emerging attachment relationships, can be avoided. When foster placement is necessary, placing an infant or young child with a relative may facilitate the development of existing attachment relationships that may continue even after the child returns home. When an infant is placed at birth with a foster caregiver, the disruption may be experienced at the reunion with the birth parent, or in placement within an unfamiliar adoptive home (Cole, 2005).

One of the ways in which social workers and others work to minimize or avoid early disruptions in care is through crisis nurseries. As described in box 2.9, crisis nursery services provide temporary emergency care for infants and young children whose families are experiencing crisis situations. Such support can alleviate the need for longer-term foster care placement or other separations of the primary caregiver and young child.

A developmental-ecological analysis of attachment relationships provides a framework to assess and support developing attachment relationships when infants and young children must enter foster care. The framework draws attention to the development of attachment relationships as they emerge within particular physical and social ecologies. We consider the interaction of biological, psychological, and social factors as they shape and are shaped within particular cultural contexts over time.

Biological Factors

When thinking about attachment relationships in child welfare, it is important to remember that the formation of attachment relationships appears to be part of our primate heritage. In all human social groups, children and their primary caregivers develop affective bonds and organized behaviors in order to relate in times of stress. These relationships emerge over time and in conjunction with children's and caregivers' experiences. Bowlby (1969, 1973, 1980) argues that such attachment relationships evolved because they enhance our potential for survival. Infants and young children are not able to care for themselves, and the world can be a dangerous place. The attachment relationship between infants and their caregivers provides the basis for a balance of exploration necessary for learning, and proximity-seeking behavior necessary for safety. Infants explore until they begin to feel mild discomfort and then seek the security of their caregivers by going to them or by visually checking in with them over a distance. When the perceived danger diminishes, infants again begin to explore. If an infant experiences the caregiver's response as consistently available for protection in times of perceived danger, the infant is free to explore the physical and social environments, knowing that the caregiver will sensitively respond and provide any needed protection. This confident exploration forms the basis for social and emotional development, as well as for physical and cognitive development.

Recent neuroscience research supports Bowlby's argument that attachment relationships have universal biologically based origins. Like many mammals, human infants appear to have some biologically based behaviors that assist caretaking (e.g., clinging and nursing), as well as other behaviors that make them more attractive (e.g., smiling and cooing) (Stevenson-Hinde, 1994; Shonkoff & Phillips, 2001). Neural processes in neonates and mothers establish behaviors that promote survival and serve as the foundation for later emotional and social development. Human neonates and mothers recognize and prefer one another's unique smell. In mammals, specific brain regions and *neurotransmitters* (chemicals that communicate between brain cells) have been identified that mediate perinatal olfactory learning (Leon, 1992).

Neuroscience research extends Bowlby's theoretical arguments regarding the importance of experience in the development of universal biologically based processes. Biologically based attachment and other processes require enriched and structured experience for their development (Black, Jones, Nelson, & Greenough, 1998). There are extended periods of neural plasticity in childhood during which experiences affect brain structure. Black and Greenough (1986) categorized these processes as either developmentally scheduled for all species members (termed "experience-expectant") or idiosyncratic learning and memory, which is unique in timing and content (termed "experience-dependent").

Experience-expectant developmental processes appear to have evolved to make adaptive use of experience that could be "expected" at a particular time and of adequate quality for nearly all juveniles of a species (e.g., close and sustained early contact with older caregivers). For experience-expectant neural plasticity, experience that is impoverished or distorted can have lasting effects on brain development. It appears that humans and other mammals have developmentally scheduled neural developmental processes for incorporating and using early emotional and social experience relevant to attachment relationships (see Black et al., 1998; Francis & Meaney, 1999). The disruption of these processes by inadequate or grossly distorted experience can have lasting adverse consequences. Indeed child abuse and severe neglect can affect both brain anatomy and physiology (see Kaufman & Charney, 1999; Cicchetti, 2002), which may account for findings that child abuse can result in lifelong vulnerability to depression and personality disorders (Johnson, Miller, & Kirkwood, 1999; Weiss, Lonhurst, & Mazure, 1999). Severe neglect, as in the case of institutionalized Romanian orphans, can substantially impair emotional and cognitive development (Zeanah, Smyke, Koga, Carlson, & the Bucharest Early Intervention Core Group, 2005).

Experience-dependent developmental processes, on the other hand, encompass several forms of lifelong neural plasticity that allow for some modification of earlier brain development. Experience-dependent processes are flexible in their developmental timing and nature of information storage. These processes appear to make new synaptic connections between neurons on demand (e.g., learning of particular vocabulary, spatial information, and social relationships). The presence of experience-dependent processes suggests that positive experiences such as the development of a positive attachment relationship with a foster parent, or therapy, may partially correct the effects of early neglect or trauma. Attachment theory and research indicate that expectations and patterns of attachment behaviors in children with histories of problematic attachment relationships may gradually change if subsequent relationships develop along different lines (Ainsworth, 1989; Ainsworth & Marvin, 1995; Main, Kaplan, & Cassidy, 1985; Sroufe, Carlson, Levy, & Egeland, 2003).

Social-Psychological Factors

Mary Ainsworth conducted the first empirical research on attachment relationships. She conducted extensive naturalistic observations of polygamous families in Uganda and middle-class European American families in Baltimore, Maryland (Ainsworth, 1967; Ainsworth, Blehar, Waters, & Wall, 1978). In both groups, Ainsworth observed consistent differences in the ways in which caregivers and children organized their attachment relationships. To facilitate study of the causes and consequences of this variation in apparently adequately functioning families, she developed a laboratory procedure referred to as the "strange situation" (Ainsworth, Blehar, Walters, & Wall, 1978). The strange situation allows observation of parent-child interaction during gradually escalating, low-level, relatively common, and nontraumatic stressors. During this procedure, the 12- to 36-month-old child and the caregiver enter a playroom. Then a female stranger enters the room. Next, the child remains in the playroom while the primary caregiver and the stranger alternately leave and return.

Several broad categories of attachment relationships have been identified through the strange situation and naturalistic observations (see Thompson, 1998, for review). Across cultures, the majority of attachment relationships are classified as *securely attached* (Van Ijzendoorn, Goldberg, Kroonenberg, & Frenkel, 1992), and parents generally express a preference for secure attachment (Van Ijzendoorn & Sagi, 1999). During the strange situation, children in securely attached relationships use their caregivers as a safe base from which to explore their physical and social worlds. They move away from their caregivers easily but also monitor their physical locations and periodically reestablish contact with them, especially if they become stressed. The child is upset when the caregiver leaves and is unlikely to be comforted by the stranger. When the caregiver reappears, the child establishes physical contact, quickly calms down, and resumes playing.

However, a substantial proportion (approximately 35% in the United States) of parent-child relationships in middle-class intact families fall into one of two subcategories of insecure attachment. During the strange situation, children in *insecure/avoidant* relationships are relatively indifferent to their caregivers' physical locations and may or may not cry if their caregivers leave the room. If they do cry, they are as likely to be comforted by the stranger as by their caregivers. When their caregivers return after brief separations, children may look away instead of approaching their caregivers. These children display fewer attachment behaviors and remain more distant from their caregivers during periods of stress than do securely attached children. Rather than going to the caregiver, they may self-comfort, for example, by playing with a toy (Carlson, Cicchetti, Barnett, & Braunwald, 1989).

During the strange situation, children in *insecure/resistant* relationships generally cling to their caregivers and appear upset even when the caregiver is near. They are distressed when their caregivers leave but are not comforted when they return. Instead, they simultaneously seek contact with their caregivers and protest their efforts to comfort them. They may cry angrily to be picked up but after being picked up immediately struggle to climb down. Children in insecure/resistant relationships do not readily resume play after their caregivers return. In contrast to children in secure attachment relationships, they expend relatively more time and energy monitoring the whereabouts of their caregivers and seeking comfort from them, and less time in independent play and exploration (Carlson, Cicchetti, Barnett, & Braunwald, 1989).

In many family and cultural contexts, secure attachment emerges from sensitive parenting (Van Ijzendoorn & Sagi, 1999). Sensitivity refers to the caregiver's ability to perceive the child's verbal and nonverbal communications accurately, and respond to these signals promptly and appropriately (Ainsworth & Bell, 1969; De Wolff & Van Ijzendoorn, 1997). Caregivers in insecurely attached relationships tend to be less accessible and responsive to their children than those in securely attached relationships. These caregivers are more likely than those in securely attached relationships to have difficulty interpreting children's communications and may respond inappropriately to children's behavioral cues by overstimulating, intruding, or otherwise ignoring children's desires. Caregivers in insecure/avoidant relationships tend to express more anger and rejection and to withhold physical contact more often than caregivers in securely attached relationships.

Caregivers' sensitivity to the children in their care is related to their early attachment experiences with their own caregivers. Human (Main & Hesse, 1990) and primate (Suomi, 1999) studies indicate that parenting behavior is strongly associated with the caregiver's own experience of being parented. Humans' experiences of being parented result in working models, or mental representations, of attachment experiences: their characteristics, values, and meanings. These mental models influence parenting behavior and hence the quality of parents' relationships with their own children. This process is referred to as the "intergenerational transmission" of attachment (Bowlby, 1969/1982). Indeed, the security of parents' mental representations of attachment is associated with the security of their attachment relationships with their own children (Main & Hesse, 1990). Parents who represent their relationships with their own parents as secure tend to have securely attached children, and those who represent their relationships with their own parents as insecure tend to have insecurely attached children (see Van Ijzendoorn, 1995.

Although moderately stable over infancy and early childhood, the organization of attachment behavior can vary with parents' fluctuating levels of stress. Parents who are preoccupied with job or marital problems, family illness, or other common stressors within micro-, meso-, and ecosystems may be less sensitive in their responses to their infants and young children (Belsky, 2005). Infants from intact families show some instability in attachment behaviors when their parents are experiencing stress (Cole, 2005; Thompson, 1998). A previously secure infant may display insecure patterns of attachment behaviors when her parents are experiencing financial or marital difficulties.

Cross-cultural data, although not extensive, indicate that secure attachment typically increases the likelihood of better social competence in the future (van Ijzendoorn & Sagi, 1999). Stable, secure caregiver-child attachment in infancy is associated with positive relationships with parents, peers, and teachers, and enhanced development and self-confidence in childhood (Belsky, Pasco, & Fearon, 2002). Children with insecure caregiver-child relationships in infancy are more likely to experience subsequent behavioral problems, conflicts with caregivers, low self-esteem, and impaired peer relationships (see Cole & Cole, 2001, for review).

Researchers studying children with developmental and social risk factors have identified another problematic pattern of attachment relationship: *disorganized/disoriented* (Type D). Children in Type D attachment relationships do not use their caregivers as a secure base or employ any other coherent behavioral strategy to cope with stress. Rather, they show a range of complex responses to the strange situation atypical of children in secure or insecure attachment relationships (see Barnett & Vondra, 1999). Children with Type D attachment relationships may display disorganized strategies involving interrupted, confused, or undirected behaviors that are unsuccessful in gaining comfort from their caregivers. They may respond to their caregivers with rapidly cycling, contradictory behaviors, such as inappropriate laughter when the caregiver departs, followed by an emotional collapse. Upon reunion, their behavior may alternate between seeking proximity and fleeing, simultaneously avoiding the caregiver and crying. They may attempt to escape the situation even when the caregiver is present. Some children also show disorientation through glazed expressions, mistimed movements, freezing, and anomalous postures. Some children also show severe apprehension in the presence of the caregiver by head banging, wetting, or huddling on the floor; through asymmetrical or mistimed approaches to the caregiver; or by freezing when the caregiver enters the room (Crittenden & Ainsworth, 1989; Main & Solomon, 1990). Such Type D attachment relationships are relatively rare in presumably well-functioning families (Carlson, Cicchetti, Barnett, & Braunwald, 1989).

The pathways to Type D attachment responses are multiple. Certain behaviors associated with Type D attachment relationships (e.g., incomplete strategies for obtaining proximity or anomalous posturing) may reflect symptoms of neurological impairments. A significantly higher percentage of Type D behaviors appears in children with diagnoses of autism and Down syndrome (35%), premature children (25%), and children whose mothers abused alcohol and drugs (43%), but not in children who have severe physical problems that do not involve neurological functioning (see Pipp-Siegel, Seigel, & Dean, 1999). Children who have experienced abuse or neglect are much more likely than those who have not to demonstrate Type D attachment behaviors (Lyons-Ruth, Bronfman, & Parsons, 1999; Barnett, Ganiban, & Cicchetti, 1999; Vondra, Hommerding, & Shaw, 1999). Carlson, Cicchetti, Barnett, and Braunwald (1989) analyzed data from 43 mother-infant pairs: 22 from families receiving protective services for child abuse or neglect, and 21 from demographically matched comparison families who had no history of abuse or neglect. Eighty-two percent of the children who were maltreated met the criteria for Type D attachment relationships. In contrast, only 19 percent of the children in the comparison group exhibited disorganized/disoriented attachment behaviors.

Disorganized/disoriented patterns of attachment behavior are also associated with a history of parental psychopathology (Greenberg, Speltz, & DeKlyen, 1993) such as maternal depression (Van Ijzendoorn, Goldberg, & Kroonenberg, 1992), and parents' own traumatic and unresolved loss of an attachment figure (Main, 1996). The characteristic that these parents may share with maltreating parents is behavior that may alarm a young child. Disorganized/disoriented attachment behavior in neurologically normal children is a response to frightened or frightening caregiver behavior, such as helplessness, distress, or abusiveness (Main & Hesse, 1990).

Disorganized/disoriented attachment relationships in early childhood have been associated with persistent atypical attachment behavior as children develop. During the preschool years, when the strange situation is no longer stressful for most children, some children who were in Type D attachment relationships with caregivers in infancy continue to display signs of distress (Crittenden & Ainsworth, 1989). Other children who showed a Type D attachment strategy in infancy rely on controlling behavior toward the parent (Main & Cassidy, 1988). These children no longer organize their attachment behaviors around their own need for comfort and protection. Instead, they maintain engagement with the parent on the parent's terms, becoming either punitive or caregiving in response to the hostile or helpless parent (Zeanah, Mammen, & Lieberman, 1993). The development of adaptive responses to alarming parental behavior may predispose children to difficulties in other relationships (Schneider-Rosen, Braunwald, Carlson, & Cicchetti, 1985; Crittenden, 1995). For example, a child who is preoccupied with caring for a parent may seek proximity to the parent to avoid punishment but may have relatively little energy to devote to developing relationships with peers.

It is not surprising that Type D attachment relationships in infancy place children at risk for developing psychosocial disorders (Greenberg, Speltz, & DeKlyen, 1993; Main, 1996) and psychopathology (Carlson, 1998). Type D attachment relationships in infancy are linked to such problems as aggressive and hostile behavior toward peers (Lyons-Ruth, Alpern, & Repacholi, 1993), poor overall school adjustment, behavior problems in preschool and elementary school (Lyons-Ruth, Easterbrooks, & Cibelli, 1997), and dissociative disorders and psychopathology in adolescence (Carlson, 1998).

Cultural-Historical Context

Despite the importance of caregiver-child attachment relationships in infancy and early childhood, these relationships do not exist in isolation.

They are embedded within particular families, communities, and cultures at particular points in history. Bowlby's evolutionary perspective on attachment relationships allows for universally adaptive behavior propensities to be realized in specific ways, depending on the niche in which the child must survive. If across cultures all infants used the same fixed strategies to deal with attachment challenges, there would be no room for adaptation to changes in the environment, and to various constraints imposed by particular social and physical contexts. For example, the exploration of Hausa infants in Nigeria is restricted because of environmental hazards. Hausa infants, like their United States counterparts, use their caregivers as secure bases from which to explore the environment, but Hausa infants' exploration is more visual, and done only in close proximity with a caregiver (Marvin, VanDevender, Iwanaga, LeVine, & LeVine, 1977).

Critiques of attachment theory from the perspective of family systems theory (Cowan, 1997) and cultural psychology (Harwood, Miller, & Irizarry, 1995; Shweder et al., 1998) emphasize the relative neglect of cultural-historical context in attachment research. The current cross-cultural database is relatively small and includes only a few studies of non-Western cultures, or families of low socioeconomic status (Tomlinson, Cooper, & Murray, 2005; Van Ijzendoorn & Sagi, 1999). Cross-cultural studies on attachment relationships in Israel (Sagi et al., 1985), Japan (Miyake, Chen, & Campos, 1985), and Germany (Grossmann & Grossmann, 1991, 1981; Grossmann, Grossmann, Spangler, Suess, & Unzer, 1985) suggest how sociocultural context can shape attachment behaviors.

Cultural-historical context can shape attachment behaviors through specific beliefs and related child-rearing practices. The Grossmanns, who studied a nonclinical group of families in northern Germany, found that 49 percent of 12-month-olds were classified as insecure/avoidant during the

Figure 2.2.
This migrant worker is providing her infant son with the kind of positive, responsive parenting that facilitates secure attachment relationships.

strange situation, almost double the percentage usually found in European American samples. Observations of parent-child interactions in German homes, however, did not indicate that German mothers generally were insensitive to their children. Rather, German mothers endorsed a broader cultural belief system emphasizing independence. They believed that babies should be weaned from body contact with their mothers as soon as they became mobile. These cultural beliefs were translated into socialization practices that affected the organization of mother-infant attachment relationships. These mothers maintained a relatively large interpersonal distance from their young children, sometimes pushed their babies away, and left them alone more often than do most middle-class mothers in the United States.

Cultural-historical context also can shape attachment behaviors through the social ecologies in which children are reared. In some Israeli kibbutzim, infants' collective rearing includes sleeping away from their parents in a children's house. During the night, and for significant portions of the day, infants are cared for in groups by child-care workers *(metapelet)*. Infants form attachment relationship with child-care workers as well as family members (Sagi et al., 1985). Furthermore, consideration of the quality of attachment relationships across this extended attachment network predicts a child's social competence at 5 years of age more strongly than any single attachment relationship even to the mother (see Van Ijzendoorn & Sagi, 1999). Attachment research in the United States has focused on the dyadic primary caregiver-child relationship. This cross-cultural research illustrates the importance of examining the wider social networks in which children develop (Harkness & Super, 1996; Thompson, 1998), including those in the United States.

Attachment behaviors also can be influenced by physical ecology. Comparative studies of attachment relationships across diverse groups within the United States suggest that some attachment behaviors are influenced by factors associated with families' socioeconomic status. For example, a meta-analysis of eighteen studies using middle-income samples and eight studies using lower-income samples revealed that maternal sensitivity was more strongly associated with parent-child attachment in middle-income than in lower-income groups (De Wolff & Van Ijzendoorn, 1997). Sensitive middle-income mothers were more likely to have a securely attached child than sensitive lower-income mothers. In some families, environmental factors associated with lower socioeconomic status, such as inadequate food and shelter, and dangerous neighborhoods, may override maternal sensitivity. Despite maternal sensitivity, a child from a lower-income family may adopt an insecure pattern of attachment behaviors. Furthermore, these behaviors may actually be adaptive in the sense of maximizing the child's vigilance and safety in environments beyond the parent-child relationship.

Cultural-historical and socioeconomic factors also interact in complex ways to influence attachment behaviors. Mothers of toddlers were asked to comment on scenarios of toddlers' behaviors in the waiting room of a doctor's office (Harwood, Miller, & Irizarry, 1995). Mothers were middle- and lower-income European Americans, and middle- and lower-income Puerto Ricans. Each scenario was a strange situation analogue and portrayed a child demonstrating behaviors associated with a different attachment classification (e.g., secure, insecure/resistant, insecure/avoidant). In general, mothers' responses varied both with their socioeconomic status and their culture. In discussing what they did or did not like about the toddlers' behaviors, European American mothers were more likely to discuss "self-maximization" (i.e., self-confidence, independence, and development as an individual) and Puerto Rican mothers were more likely to discuss "proper demeanor" (i.e., the child's manners, behavior, cooperativeness, and acceptance by the larger community).

IMPLICATIONS FOR CHILD WELFARE

A developmental-ecological analysis of attachment relationships has important implications for social workers in child welfare working with infants and young children:

1. *Removal of an infant or young child from his/her birth home or foster home must be done with full awareness of the emotional distress and possible harm to the development of adequate attachment relationships that may result from such an intervention.* In our opening example two-year-old Sharon's mother was addicted to heroin and unable to care for her adequately. Placement in foster care clearly was necessary for Sharon's physical survival. Sharon was, however, in her mother's care for her first 18 months of life. During this time they did develop an attachment relationship, however troubled. When separated, both experienced considerable emotional pain and distress. In contrast, 1-year-old George was placed with his foster mother 1 week after his birth when his birth mother left him at the hospital where he was born. George and his foster mother have developed a close and caring relationship. The foster mother is hoping to adopt George, but in attempting to release George for adoption, the child welfare agency has found a cousin who is willing to adopt George.

Child welfare professionals face difficult decisions related to attachment: when should children be placed in foster care, when to recommend the termination of parental rights, and with whom a child should be placed permanently. Some parents are able to recover from substance abuse or domestic violence and go on to successfully care for their children. Others develop strategies for parenting despite developmental disabilities or while suffering from chronic physical or mental illnesses. Given the shortage of adoptive homes for children of color, older children, and children with special needs, the recovery or development of their parents may be the best chance for children like Sharon to have a stable attachment relationship and permanent home.

How child welfare professionals make decisions regarding safety and permanency is a complex topic. In Illinois, a parenting assessment team comprised of social workers, psychologists, and psychiatrists worked together to develop and apply criteria for assessing the ability of parents with severe mental illnesses involved with the public child welfare system to safely care for their children (Jacobsen, Miller, & Kirkwood, 1997). Although severe mental illness disrupts parenting, given appropriate support, some parents are able to parent adequately. Rather than remove infants and young children from their mentally ill parents' care, thus disrupting the attachment relationships developed, the parenting assessment team developed comprehensive evaluative techniques to determine when it was safe for an infant or young child to remain in the care of, or return to the care of, a parent with a major mental illness. These assessments included a complete psychiatric evaluation of the parent and developmental screening of the child, videotaped observations of parent-child interaction to assess attachment and parental behaviors that are associated with maltreatment, parents' responses to a variety of questionnaires, parents' understanding of the child and the parent-child relationship, interviews with parents, appraisal of the home environment, interviews with collateral historians to obtain additional information on families, and a review of pertinent records. These data were then taken into consideration in making well-informed decisions about the safety and placement of children.

2. *Regardless of the safety and permanency plans, a basic issue for child welfare professionals should be how to best support children's early attachment relationships.* Many families, even those who presumably are well functioning, sometimes need support in caring for children. Families with social and financial resources may draw upon family and friends for advice or hire respite child care. Because she was seriously ill and did not have such informal social support or financial resources, Sharon's mother may have benefited from a substance abuse treatment center that could accommodate both her and her daughter, or a foster care provider who would work with her to support her relationship with Sharon in a positive way while she recovered from her addiction. Perhaps George's foster mother and relatives need support in developing a lifelong plan for George that would incorporate all the people who have concern for him, including his foster parents. At the very least, these situations call for a sup-

portive transition to any new environments into which Sharon and George may be placed while in the child welfare system.

3. *If removing the infant or young child from the home is necessary, the development of an adequate relationship between the child and foster parent must be a priority.* Supporting the attachment relationships of infants and young children with their foster families is an important aspect of supporting optimal development for infants and young children entering care. A significant number of infants 3 months and younger are placed with foster caregivers and may be eventually adopted by their foster caregivers. Clearly, for these families to be successful, adequate attachment relationships between children and their foster families must be supported (Dozier & Albus, 2000; Dozier, Higley, Albus, & Nutter, 2002; Stovall & Dozier, 1998, 2000). In supportive families, foster caregivers and their infants can and do develop secure attachment relationships (Cole, 2005).

Even if the foster placement is not permanent, the development of an adequate attachment relationship with a foster care provider will allow the infant or young child the security to continue exploring and learning from the physical and social world, thus minimizing developmental delays. In Sharon's case, she had an existing attachment with her great-grandmother, who was able to provide foster care. The great-grandmother lived close by and had taken care of Sharon when her mother was not home or unable to respond. We know that children like Sharon and George can develop multiple secure relationships with sensitive caregivers whether or not the caregivers are related (Cole, 2002). Sharon's social worker focused on providing her great-grandmother with the resources she needed to care for a young child without exhausting her modest physical and economic resources to the detriment of her relationship with Sharon.

4. *If the goal is to return the child home, as is the case for the majority of children in foster care, then for this goal to succeed, the attachment relationship with the parent must be supported throughout the child's stay in foster care.*

Parent-child visitation, the scheduled face-to-face contact between parents and their children in foster care, is the primary child welfare intervention for supporting the development of adequate attachment relationships while children are in foster care. Ideally, parent-child visits occur in a comfortable homelike setting, and at least weekly (more often for infants and young children). In reality, however, the environment in which children and parents visit may be less than ideal—a sterile office with no toys or other amenities, and under the watchful eyes of foster parents, social workers, or other outsiders. Regular visits are considered so critical to the effort to reunite families that the Adoption

Assistance and Child Welfare Act of 1980 (PL 96-272) requires inclusion of regular visits in family preservation efforts.

Existing research suggests that, too often, visits fall short of meeting their goals. Parents, foster parents, social workers, and adolescents in care report a range of emotional and behavioral responses to visits. Sometimes visits evoke painful feelings about separation and the child's behavior worsens following the visit (see Haight, Kagel, & Black, 2003). Sometimes parent-child interaction clearly is supportive of the development of positive relationships—the parent and child are responsive and positive toward each other—and sometimes more problematic aspects of interaction emerge (see Haight, Black, Workman, & Tata, 2001; Haight et al., 2005). A developmental-ecological perspective on attachment theory and research suggests some strategies for better supporting parent-child attachment relationships during visits.

Research on developmental aspects of attachment relationships points to the need for tailoring visits to children's and parents' changing developmental needs. Regular and frequent visits are especially important during infancy and early childhood. Biological aspects of attachment relationships suggest that when reunification is the permanency goal, regular visits should be encouraged; that families should be supported before, during, and after visits; and that secure attachment relationships should be supported between children and their foster and biological parents.

Social and cultural aspects of attachment relationships highlight the need for understanding and supporting parent-child relationships in the social and cultural contexts in which they are shaped. Visits with infants and young children should occur in homelike settings that allow parents to respond to the children's needs through routine care such as feeding and changing, and to interact comfortably with them.

Social and cultural aspects of attachment relationships suggest that there is limited value to assessment of "secure" versus "insecure" attachment relationships between children and the parents whom they are separated from through foster care. Many otherwise-secure infants and young children respond to their parents in insecure ways after separations much briefer and less traumatic than foster care placement. However, the observation of any problematic aspects of attachment relationships (e.g., disorganized/disoriented relationships) always warrants further investigation, including medical and psychosocial assessments. In cases of problematic attachment relationships, visits typically should be coordinated with other intensive services and may require professional supervision.

5. *When the child welfare intervention is successful and the child returns home, care must be taken with the transition.* If the infant

was removed soon after birth, the only caregiver that infant knows are foster caregivers, who were the surrogate parents. Time with the birth mother is very limited in comparison to the amount of time the infant is with the foster caregiver. The primary relationship becomes the infant-foster caregiver dyad. Through the course of the first year, the birth mother may not notice the development of this relationship until the infant is age 7 to 9 months, when the infant responds fearfully to her during visits and actively protests separation from the foster caregiver. The reunion process with the birth mother after 12 or 15 months can be very traumatic for the child, the foster parent, and the birth mother. The birth mother feels love and has the desire to parent well. The child literally does not know the birth mother and mourns the loss of her known mother—the foster caregiver. The foster mother may mourn the loss of her relationship with the child. It is important in both the transition from the birth parent to the foster parent or from the foster parent to the birth parent that the child's attachment relationships be considered, and time given to establish new attachment relationships.

BOX 2.10 PRACTICE STORIES AND ADVICE

Linda K., rural social worker: "How would you want to be treated if someone came to your home to social work you?"

Linda K. has 25 years' experience working in social work with families and children in rural communities. A masters-level social worker (MSW), she particularly enjoys crisis intervention where she can assist whole families in getting services to meet their needs better. A natural storyteller, Linda describes some of her experiences as a child welfare worker in rural Illinois. She also offers some words of advice to social workers considering child welfare work.

Practice Story

When you are working in child welfare in a rural area, you find yourself in a position where you are out in the middle of nowhere, cell phones don't reach, and you have no protection. I know they train us in child protection very thoroughly about how to protect yourself, the things that you should and should not do when there is, or looks like there is going to be, a physical altercation. A couple Fridays ago I called the deputy, which is protocol. I was going to the middle of nowhere. I didn't know the family. I called the sheriff's office, said, "Tell me how to get to this house." The deputy said, "Oh, go over the hill and turn left on Coon Chase Road. When you get to Coon Chase Road, you are going to go just about a mile along, and you look over there at the right and you'll see this big ole brown house. Just a little heads up," he said. "This guy is a little odd." I said, "Okay. Thanks, Joe, for all your help." And I just go out there, oblivious to what I am walking into. Get out there and this mid 60s grandma greets me. I tell her that I am there because I am investigating her daughter, who has reportedly put bruises on the back of her 13-year-old child when they got into a physical fight. So grandma and I are sitting there visiting, and I am telling her who I am and she has hummingbirds and I commented on the hummingbirds, and she is telling me about her little farm there. And I said, "Would you care if I went ahead and saw your granddaughter?" And she said, "Well, I'd rather you wouldn't 'til my daughter gets here." She said she was at the Wal-Mart, and she'd be back in a little. So, we visit a little bit more. . . . I was 25 minutes from the highway. I really didn't know where I was. I had taken a lot of twists and turns, talked to the deputy, got directions. I really didn't know where I was, and about that time I heard this car screech. This truck screeched into the driveway, gravel flying everywhere, and this older gentleman, probably 60s, got out. "What the hell is going on here!" And he just came right for me. I stood up to shake his hand, and I said, "Hi, I am Linda K. . .", and he wouldn't let me get it out. His face was blood red. "You get off my goddamn property! I don't want any of you sons of bitches around here! You aren't going to come here and tell me how to raise my family!" And I put my hands up like this—one of the things that we are taught in training is very important: You keep a low tone of voice and make direct eye contact. Don't divert your eyes, like you are scared, just make direct eye contact, keep a low voice, and try to de-escalate the situation. So I said, "Now, sir, I am not clear as to why exactly you are upset, but if you can just let me have a minute." Then he started flailling his arms around. "You guys were out here before, you sent out some faggot f—er . . . and you are not going to come out here and treat me that way on my property again." And I said, "Sir, you will have no problem with me." And I said to him, "Sir, this is your property and if you tell me to leave I will be gone, because this is your home, this is your family." And he said, "Yeah, you'll just leave and go get some goddamned cop and bring him out here." And I said, "Well, I do have to ensure the safety of your granddaughter, but I will leave if that's what you want." And then he was just so irate that he slid around the corner of the house, back in this garage-type thing. I had just worked this investigation a week before where there were gunshots involved, so I was very nervous. He slipped around the corner and I said to his wife, I said, "Please have your husband step back around here—that's making me nervous." She goes, "Oh, honey, you don't want him back around here, he is going to hurt you." I said, "No, I'd rather have him back around here where I can see him." So she went and got him, and he came back and they got in an argument, and he pushed her aside and got right up in my space and he was flaying, cussing me, and telling me what he was going to do. I started to back towards my car, but he wasn't having any part of that. He just continued to kind of corner me and then his wife, thank God, stepped in between us and she said, "Now Sam, back off!" And he just pushed her aside and said, "You don't f— with me, woman, when I am getting in a fight." And she said, "Sam, you are not going to fight this woman." And I continued to try to talk to him and he just went off to the camper. By that time, the daughter and the granddaughter were there. I stood there and talked to them. I talked to the 13-year-old and said, "Do you have any bruises now?" And she said, "No." I asked her if she was afraid, kind of quickly assessed the safety, and I said, "I think it would be best if we assessed this in my office." And mom was willing. She was undergoing mental health treatment. She signed a release to talk to her mental health counselor, and when I called her mental health counselor, the mental health counselor assured me that the girls would be safe there. Mom was not violent, and so I left while he was still in the camper. When I left there, I cried half the way into [town], because it was one of the most frightening situations I have ever been in. All I could think of was that my cell phone was dead. I mean it was gone. There was no reception. I was out in the middle of nowhere. Had he walked out of there with a gun, there was absolutely no way I'd be protecting myself. I found out later that he was a chronic alcoholic, and he was just out of it. His grandkids asked me when I interviewed them later, "Were you scared when Grandpa was so mad at you?" "Well," I said, "Actually, I was." And they said, "That's the maddest he's been—reddest we've seen his face—since he pulled the shotgun on the neighbor."

But, most of the time people are very friendly, very hospitable. Seems to be the rural culture. . . . . Almost all people say, "You need something to drink?" I have had so many people say, "Can I get you a glass of water or glass of tea?" I've had experiences with people I was investigating—they have gone above and beyond to make sure that I found their place. I've had people I was leaving say, "Where you going? Because it might be easier if you go this way."

Advice for Beginning Social Workers

The most important thing, I think, is to remember that there are no such things as problem people. There are only people with problems. And every person that you work with is just like you, except that we all get different cards dealt to us. I think it's so easy when you first start into social work—my thinking was to help people be better. Now after over 20 years in the field, my goal is to help Joe [client] with whatever Joe wants help with. In social work we get this mentality that we want everybody to be like us, or at least like what our definition of a successful life is, and, the truth is, Joe's life isn't what I would want for my life, but it's what Joe has chosen for his life and I have to respect that. I just think the most important thing is to recognize that clients are people just like you are—a person. How would you want to be treated if someone came to your home to social work you? Would you want somebody to see your life, figure out what it is that you need to change? I wouldn't. If I said that this is a need that I have, then I would be very grateful for help. But, I wouldn't want you to tell me what my needs are. I remember in all the years in my own life that I have been in therapy, had counseling for the traumatic childhood I went through, the most important thing that all those people did in my life was help me on my journey, to get where I wanted to go. And I think that's what I can do for Joe. Ultimately it is his life.

The other thing you have to recognize is that when you first start, really, you don't know much. You know something. You have some skills. You have some natural and some learned skills, but most importantly you are beginning as a new social worker on a path that the most important teachers are the clients you serve. Every single person that I have come in contact with in doing social work has taught me something. And so, never put yourself on that level that "I am the social worker and because I have a blahblah degree and I know these things, I will come into your home and I will share all my wonderful insights with you and then you—ta-da!—can become as I would want you to be!" Really we should be learning the things that we learn about culture from people—not only different ethnicities, but the culture of poverty or rural culture. We learn that as we serve in these communities.

Also, relationships are the most important thing in social work: relationships with your colleagues, relationships with community members, relationships with, most importantly, the clients. But if you are not a people person, if you can't build relationships, I don't see how you can function in this field. Especially in rural areas where there really is—I hate to call it—but that neighborly good-old-boy network. And if you are not part of that, it's hard to get in. I've been working G. county for over a year. Just last week, I felt that the G. county police department really stepped over into accepting me as part of them. We were doing a court case together and it actually came down that the defendant was accusing them of conducting an interview in a less than professional manner. And since I was present for the interview, I had to testify as to their integrity. They weren't in there to hear me testify, but they knew why I was there. And I am telling you once I did that, when I walked out, in fact, Chief J. gave me a high five. Part of that was because the attorney had said to me when I was on the stand, "So when you went in this interview with the police, you knew that the goal was to get my client to admit to [sexual abuse]." I said," No." I said, "To be honest with you, no, I didn't have that in mind." He smiled at me, the attorney smiled at me, and he said, "So you went into that interview with the police not knowing what the police were looking for?" I said, "I went into the interview with the assumption that the police were looking for the same thing I was, and that was an accurate account of what had happened from the perpetrator's viewpoint." Then the attorney started laughing and said, "Mrs. K., do you really expect this court to believe that you go into an interview with an alleged perpetrator such as my client and you have his best interests in mind?" And, because it is the foundation of my practice, and because it's the heartbeat of what I do, I was able to respond, "Absolutely, sir. I am a child protection services worker. My responsibility is first to ensure the safety of children, but also to offer assistance to any family member who should need help. And, absolutely, I have your client's best interests in mind as well as the child's." And the smile went from his face, and he went right on. When we got outside, the state's attorney's assistant, Tammy, was telling the cops about it. That's when J. gave me a high five and he was just praising me, and he doesn't generally do that. I have often thought about the importance of your integrity, your honesty, and being who you say you are. Nothing will hurt you more in a courtroom than for you to be a different person on that witness stand than you are when you work with your clients, because not only does the client see it, the attorneys see it, and no one respects that. I mean, they expect if you say you advocate for your clients, then you should behave that way, no matter where you are at, because if you don't then it just shows poorly. And I know that we have these humorous conversations and we make light of certain situations just to survive, but the thrust of your practice always has to be the ever-genuine concern for the client, because if you don't have that then you shouldn't be doing this.

SUMMARY

Child welfare is an exciting field to which social workers have made important contributions. Box 2.10 contains practice stories and advice from Linda K., an experienced child welfare worker.

A developmental-ecological analysis of the infant's and young child's attachment relationships provides a framework for child welfare workers to analyze issues in practice and policy. Attachment relationships, part of our biological heritage, are necessary to adequate development. Consideration of biological, psychological, social, and cultural-historical dimensions of attachment relationships allows social workers of infants and young children to flexibly and creatively support the emergence and elaboration of attachment relationships during foster care.

The developmental-ecological analysis illustrated in this chapter also is useful for analyzing social work issues that occur at other points in the life cycle, and in other social contexts. In chapter 3, social work with children in middle childhood in community contexts is explored.

Study and Discussion Questions

1. What is gained and lost through the substitution of a focus on academic skills rather than on play in early childhood programs?

2. What is attachment?

3. How do caregivers and children vary in the quality or organization of their attachment relationships?

4. What experiences are associated with various types of attachment relationships?

5. What are the consequences of various types of attachment relationships to the child's development?

6. How do we interpret variation in attachment behavior within and across cultural communities?

7. Describe problematic aspects of attachment relationships, the experiences associated with them, and impact on children's development.

8. What is the child welfare system?

9. What are parent-child visits, and why are they important?

10. What are the implications of attachment theory and research for parent-child visitation?

11. What are some of the moral and ethical dilemmas faced by child welfare professionals in considering the placement of infants and young children in foster care? How can these be resolved?

12. To return to our opening example: Sharon's great-grandmother suffered a debilitating stroke shortly after her placement in her care. If you were Sharon's caseworker, what would you recommend and why? What information would you want to have before making this recommendation?

13. Why is the infant mortality rate so high in the United States? What can we do about this?

Resources

For students interested in deepening their understanding of attachment relationships and child welfare with infants and very young children, we recommend the following sources: Berrick, Needell, Barth, and Jonson-Reid (1998); Ainsworth, Blehar, Waters, & Wall (1978); Carlson, Cicchetti, Barnett, and Braunwald (1989); Cole (2005); Crittenden & Ainsworth (1989); Main, Kaplan, and Cassidy (1985); Sroufe, Carlson, Levy, and Egeland (2003); Van Ijzendoorn and Sagi (1999); Zeanah, Mammen, and Lieberman (1993); and Haight et al., (2001, 2003, 2005). For those interested in learning more about play, see Zigler et al. (2004); and Hirsh-Pasek and Golinkoff (2003).

Interested students can supplement this chapter through a number of excellent Web-based resources.

The American Academy of Family Physicians provides an excellent article, "Primary Care of Infants and Young Children with Down Syndrome." Available at: http://www.aafp.org/afp/990115ap/381.html

The Center for Disease Control provides safety tips for protecting infants and young children around domestic pets. Available at: http://www.cdc.gov/healthypets/child.htm

The United Nations'World Health Organization provides an online booklet on issues of feeding and nutrition of infants and young children. Emphasis is placed on specific problems and solutions faced by families in countries that were formally part of the Soviet Union and are currently struggling economically. Available at: http://www.euro.who.int/InformationSources/Publications/Catalogue/20010914_21

Infants & Young Children is an interdisciplinary journal of special care aimed primarily at medical health care professionals. The journal's core focus is the clinical management of infants and young children with, or at risk for, developmental disabilities. The articles provide research, educational methods, diagnostic and treatment techniques, and therapeutic steps for supporting families. Available at: http://www.iycjournal.com/pt/re/iyc/ home.htm

The President's Advisory Commission on Educational Excellence for Hispanic Americans is charged with strengthening the nation's capacity to provide high-quality education while increasing opportunities for Hispanic American participation in federal education programs. The Web site provides information for enhancing development and learning from infancy through adolescents. Available at: http://www.yic.gov/wwa/index.html

The United Nations' World Health Organization provides an excellent international overview of the importance and methods for preventing HIV transmission to infants. Available at: http://www.ahfgi.org/global_pdf/infant_hiv_prevention.pdf

The Audiology Department of Boys Town National Research Hospital offers details on hearing problems faced by infants and young children. The Web site provides information on how hearing aids work and why certain types of hearing instruments are preferred for younger children. Available at:

http://regensburg.de/Fakultaeten/Medizin/HNO/audio/childhg.htm

Autism and other pervasive developmental disorders strike the very young and last a life time. The Autism Society of America (ASA) is the leading voice and provides resources and support for the entire autism community. Available at: http://www.autism-society.org

References

Abrams, R. M., Gerhardt, K. J., & Peters, A. J. M. (1995). Transmission of sound and vibration to the fetus. In J. P. Lecanuet, W. P. Fifer, N. A. Krasnegor, & W. P. Smotherman (Eds.), *Fetal development: A psychobiological perspective* (pp. 315–330). Hillsdale, NJ: Erlbaum.

Adoption and Safe Families Act of 1997, PL 105-89, 111 Stat. 2115.

Adoption Assistance and Child Welfare Act of 1980, PL 96-272, 94 Stat. 500.

Ainsworth, M. (1967). *Infancy in Uganda: Infant care and the growth of love.* Baltimore: Johns Hopkins University Press.

Ainsworth, M. (1973). The development of infant-mother attachment. In J. L. Gewirtz (Ed.), *Attachment and dependency.* Washington, DC: Winston.

Ainsworth, M. (1989). Attachments beyond infancy. *American Psychologist, 44,* 709–716.

Ainsworth, M., & Bell, S. (1969). Some contemporary patterns of mother-infant interaction in the feeding situation. In A. Ambrose (Ed.), *Stimulation in early infancy* (pp.133–163). New York: Academic Press.

Ainsworth, M., Blehar, M., Waters, E., & Wall, S. (1978). *Patterns of attachment.* Hillsdale, NJ: Erlbaum.

Ainsworth, M., & Marvin, R. (1995). On the shaping of attachment theory and research: An interview with Mary D. S. Ainsworth, fall 1994. *Monographs of the Society for Research in Child Development, 60*(2–3, Serial No. 245), 3–21.

Barnett, D., Ganiban, J., & Cicchetti, D. (1999). Maltreatment, negative expressivity, and the development of Type D attachments from 12 to 24 months. In J. Vondra, & D. Barnett (Eds.), *Atypical attachment in infancy and early childhood among children at developmental risk* (Monographs of the Society for Research in Child Development, Vol. 64, No. 3, pp. 97–118). Chicago: University of Chicago Press.

Barnett, D., & Vondra, J. (1999). A typical patterns of early attachment: Theory, research and current directions. In J. Vondra & D. Barnett (Eds.), *Atypical attachment in infancy and early childhood among children at developmental risk* (Monographs of the Society for Research in Child Development, Vol. 64, No. 3, pp.1–24).

Belsky, J. (2005). Attachment theory and research in ecological perspective: Insights from the Pennsylvania Infant and Family Development Project and the NICHD Study of Early Child Care. In K. E. Grossman, K. Grossman, & E. Waters (Eds.), *Attachment from infancy to adulthood: The major longitudinal studies* (pp. 71–97). New York: Guilford.

Belsky, J., & Pasco Fearon, R. M. (2002). Early attachment security, subsequent maternal sensitivity, and later child development: Does continuity in development depend upon continuity of caregiving? *Attachment and Human Development, 4,* 361–387.

Berk, L. E. (2000). *Child development* (5th ed.). Needham Heights, MA: Pearson.

Berrick, J. D., Needell, B., Barth, R. P., & Jonson-Reid, M. (1998). *The tender years*. New York: Oxford University Press.

Black, J., & Greenough, W. (1986). Induction of pattern in neural structure by experience: Implications for cognitive development. In M. E. Lamb, A. L. Brown, & B. Rogoff (Eds.), *Advances in developmental psychology: Vol. 4. Varieties of development—developmental neuroscience* (pp. 1-50). Hillsdale, NJ: Erlbaum.

Black, J., Jones, T., Nelson, C., & Greenough, W. (1998). Neural plasticity. In A. Alessi (Ed.), *The handbook of child and adolescent psychiatry: Vol. 4* (pp. 31-51). New York: Wiley.

Blatt, S, Simms, M. (1997, April). Foster care: Special children, special needs. *Contemporary Pediatrics, 113.*

Bowlby, J. (1969/1982). *Attachment and loss: Vol. 1. Attachment.* New York: Basic Books.

Bowlby, J. (1973). *Attachment and loss: Separation: Vol. 2. Anxiety and anger.* New York: Basic Books.

Bowlby, J. (1980). *Attachment and loss: Vol. 3. Sadness and depression.* New York: Basic Books.

Carlson, E. (1998). A prospective longitudinal study of attachment disorganization/disorientation. *Child Development, 69,* 1107-1128.

Carlson, V., Cicchetti, D., Barnett, D., & Braunwald, K. (1989). Finding order in disorganization: Lessons from research on maltreated infants' attachments to their caregivers. In D. Cicchetti & V. Carlson (Eds.), *Child maltreatment: Theory and research on the causes and consequences of child abuse and neglect* (pp. 494-528). New York: Cambridge University Press.

Cicchetti, D. (2002). How a child builds a brain: Insights from normality and psychopathology. In W. Hartup & R. Weinberg (Eds.), *Minnesota symposia on child psychology: Vol. 35. Child psychology in retrospect* (pp. 23-71). Mahwah, NJ: Erlbaum

Cicchetti, D. & Rogosh, F. A. (2001). The impact of child maltreatment and psychopathology on neuroendocrine functioning. *Development and Psychopathology, 13,* 783-804.

Cicchetti, D., & Toth, S. L. (1995). Developmental psychopathology perspective on child-abuse and neglect. *Journal of the American Academy of Child and Adolescent Psychiatry, 34*(5), 541-565.

Clark, C. (2003). *In sickness and in play: Children coping with chronic illness.* New Brunswick, NJ: Rutgers University Press.

Cole, M., & Cole, S. (2001). *The development of children* (4th ed.). New York: Scientific American Books.

Cole, S. A. (2005). Infants in foster care: Relational and environmental factors affecting attachment. *Journal of Reproductive and Infant Psychology, 23,* 43-61.

Cowan, P. (1997). Beyond meta-analysis: A plea for a family systems view of attachment. *Child Development, 68,* 601-603.

Crittenden, P. (1995). Attachment and risk for psychopathology: The early years. *Developmental and Behavioral Pediatrics, 16,* 12-16.

Crittenden, P., & Ainsworth, M. (1989). Child maltreatment and attachment theory. In D. Cicchetti & V. Carlson (Eds.), *Child maltreatment: Theory and research on the causes and consequences of child abuse and neglect* (pp. 432-463). New York: Cambridge University Press.

De Wolff, M., & Van Ijzendoorn, M. (1997). Sensitivity and attachment: A meta-analysis on parental antecedents of infant attachment. *Child Development*, *68*, 571-591.

Downs, S., Costin, L., & McFadden, E. (1996). *Child welfare and family services: Policies and practice* (5th ed.). White Plains, NY: Longman.

Dozier, M., & Albus, K. E. (2000). Attachment issues for infants in foster care. In R. Barth, M. Freundlich, & D. Brodzinsky (Eds.), *Adoption and prenatal drug exposure: The research, policy, and practice challenges.* Washington, DC: Child Welfare League of America Press.

Dozier, M., Higley, E., Albus, K. E., Nutter, A. (2002). Intervening with foster infants' caregivers: Targeting three critical needs. *Infant Mental Health Journal*, *23*, 541-554.

Fifer, W. P., & Moon, C. M. (1994). The role of mother's voice in the organization of brain function in the newborn. *Acta Paediatrica* 397, (Suppl.), 86-93.

Francis, D., & Meaney, M. (1999). Maternal care and the development of stress responses. *Current Opinion in Neurobiology*, *9*, 128-134.

Greenberg, M., Speltz, M., & DeKlyen, M. (1993). The role of attachment in the early development of disruptive behavior problems. *Development and Psychopathology*, *5*, 191-213.

Grossmann, K., & Grossmann, K. E. (1981). Parent-infant attachment relationships in Bielefeld. In K. Immelman, G. Barlow, L. Petrovich, & M. Main (Eds.), *Behavioral development: The Bielefeld interdisciplinary project* (pp. 694-699). New York: Cambridge University Press.

Grossmann, K., & Grossmann, K. E. (1991). Newborn behavior, the quality of early parenting and later toddler-parent relationships in a group of German infants. In J. Nugent, B. Lester, & T. Brazelton (Eds.), *The cultural context of infancy: Vol.2* (pp. 3-39). Norwood, NJ: ABLEX.

Grossmann, K., Grossmann, K. E., Spangler, G., Suess, G., & Unzer, L. (1985). Maternal sensitivity and newborns' orientation responses as related to quality of attachment in northern Germany. In I. Bretherton & E. Waters (Eds.), *Growing points of attachment theory and research* (Monographs of the Society for Research in Child Development, Vol. 50, No. 1-2, pp. 233-256). Chicago: University of Chicago Press.

Haight, W. (In press). A sociocultural perspective of parent-child pretend play. In D. Fromberg & D. Bergen (Eds.), *Play from birth to twelve: Contexts, perspectives, and meaning* (2nd ed.). New York: Garland Press.

Haight, W., Black, J., Workman, C., & Tata, L. (2001). Parent-child interaction during foster care visits. *Social Work, 46*, 325-338.

Haight, W., Kagel, J., & Black, J. (2003). Understanding and supporting parent-child relationships during foster care visits: Attachment theory and research. *Social Work, 48*(2), 195-208.

Haight, W., Mangelsdorf, S., Black, J., Szewczyk, Schoppe, S., Giorgio, G., et al. (2005). Enhancing parent-child interaction during foster care visits: Experimental assessment of an intervention. *Child Welfare, 84*(4), 459-481.

Haight, W., & Miller, P. (1993). *Pretending at home: Early development in a sociocultural context.* Albany: State University of New York Press.

Haight, W., Parke, R., & Black, J. (1997). Mothers' and fathers' beliefs about and spontaneous participation in their toddlers' pretend play. *Merrill-Palmer Quarterly, 42*, 271-290.

Haight, W., & Sachs, K. (1995). The portrayal of emotion during mother-child pretend play. In W. Damon (Series Ed.), L. Sperry, & P. Smiley (Eds.), *Exploring young children's concepts of self and others through conversation. New Directions in Child Development.* San Francisco: Jossey-Bass.

Harkness, S., & Super, C. (1996). Introduction. In S. Harkness & C. Super (Eds.), *Parents' cultural belief systems: Their origins, expressions, and consequences.* New York: Guilford.

Harwood, R., Miller, J., & Irizarry, N. (1995). *Culture and attachment: Perceptions of the child in context.* New York: Guilford.

Hepper, P. G., & Shahidullah, S. (1994). The beginnings of mind: Evidence from the behavior of the fetus. *Journal of Reproductive and Infant Psychology, 12*(3), 143-154.

Hirsh-Pasek, K., & Golinkoff, R. (2003). *Einstein never used flash cards.* New York: Rodale.

Jacobsen, T., Miller, L. J., & Kirkwood, K. P. (1997). Assessing parenting competency in individuals with severe mental illness: A comprehensive service. *Journal of Mental Health Administration, 24,* 189-199.

James, W. T. (1890). *The principles of psychology.* New York: Holt, Rinehart and Winston.

Johnson, J., Cohen, P., Brown, J., Smailews, E., & Bernstein, D. (1999). Childhood maltreatment increases risk for personality disorders in early adulthood. *Archives of General Psychiatry, 55,* 600-606.

Kaufman, J., & Charney, D. S. (1999). Neurobiological correlates of child abuse. *Biological Psychiatry, 45,* 1235-1236.

Krasnegor, N. A., & Lecanuet, J. P. (1995). Behavioral development of the fetus. In J. P. Lecanuet, W. P. Fifer, N. A. Krasnegor, & W. P. Smotherman (Eds.), *Fetal development: A psychobiological perspective* (pp. 3-14). Hillsdale, NJ: Erlbaum.

Lecanuet, J. P., & Schaal, B. (1996). Fetal sensory competencies. *European Journal of Obstetrics, Gynecology, and Reproductive Biology, 68*(1-2), 1-23.

Leon, M. (1992). The neurobiology of filial learning. *Annual Review of Psychology, 43,* 377-398.

Liederman, D. S. (1995). Child welfare overview. In R. L. Edwards & J. Hopps (Eds.), *Encyclopedia of social work* (19th ed.). Washington, DC: NASW Press.

Lyons-Ruth, K., Alpern, L., & Repacholi, B. (1993). Disorganized infant attachment classification and maternal psychosocial problems as predictors of hostile-aggressive behavior in the preschool classroom. *Child Development, 64,* 572-585.

Lyons-Ruth, K., Bronfman, J., & Parsons, E. (1999). Maternal frightened, frightening, or atypical behavior and disorganized infant attachment patterns. In J. Vondra & D. Barnett (Eds.), *Atypical attachment in infancy and early childhood among children at developmental risk* (Monographs of the Society for Research in Child Development, Vol. 64, No. 3, pp. 67-96). Chicago: University of Chicago Press.

Lyons-Ruth, K., Easterbrooks, M., & Cibelli, C. (1997). Infant attachment strategies, infant mental lag, and maternal depressive symptoms: Predictors of internalizing and externalizing problems at age 7. *Developmental Psychology, 33,* 681-692.

Main, M. (1996). Introduction to the special section on attachment and psychopathology: 2. Overview of the field of attachment. *Journal of Consulting and Clinical Psychology, 64,* 237-243.

Main, M., & Cassidy, J. (1988). Categories of response to reunion with the parent at age six: Predicted from infant attachment classifications and stable over a one-month period. *Developmental Psychology, 24,* 415-426.

Main, M., & Hesse, E. (1990). Parents' unresolved traumatic experiences are related to infant disorganized attachment states: Is frightened or frightening parental behavior the linking mechanism? In M. Greenberg, D. Cichetti, & M. Cummings (Eds.), *Attachment in the preschool years* (pp. 161-182). Chicago: University of Chicago Press.

Main, M., Kaplan, N., & Cassidy, J. (1985). Security in infancy, childhood, and adulthood: A move to the level of representation. In I. Bretherton & E. Waters (Eds.), *Growing points of attachment theory and research* (Monographs of the Society for Research in Child Development, Vol. 50, No. 1-2, pp. 66-104). Chicago: University of Chicago Press.

Main, M., & Solomon, J. (1990). Procedures for identifying infants as organized/disoriented during the Ainsworth strange situation. In M. Greenberg, D. Cicchetti, & N. Cummings (Eds.), *Attachment in the preschool years: Theory, research, and intervention* (pp. 676-678). Chicago: University of Chicago Press.

Malanga, C. J., & Kosofsky, B. E. (2004). Effects of drugs of abuse on brain development. In D. S. Charney & E. J. Nestler (Eds.), *Neurobiology of mental illness* (2nd ed.). New York: Oxford University Press.

Marvin, R. S., VanDevender, T., Iwanaga, M., LeVine, S., & LeVine, R. (1977). Infant-caregiver attachment among the Hausa of Nigeria. In H. McGurk (Ed.), *Ecological factors in human development* (pp. 247-259). Amsterdam: North-Holland.

Miyake, K., Chen, S., & Campos, J. (1985). Infant temperament, mother's mode of interaction, and attachment in Japan. An interim report. In I. Bretherton & E. Waters (Eds.), *Growing points of attachment theory and research* (Monographs of the Society for Research in Child Development, Vol. 50, No. 1-2. pp. 276-297). Chicago: University of Chicago Press.

Moon, C., Panneton-Cooper, R. P., & Fifer, W. P. (1993). Two-day-old infants prefer native language. *Infant Behavior and Development,* 16, 495.

Pipp-Siegel, S., Siegel, C., & Dean, J. (1999). Neurological aspects of the disorganized/disoriented attachment classification system: Differentiating quality of the attachment relationship from neurological impairment. In J. Vondra & D. Barnett (Eds.), *Atypical attachment in infancy and early childhood among children at developmental risk* (Monographs of the Society for Research in Child Development, Vol. 64, No. 3, pp. 25-44). Chicago: University of Chicago Press.

Sagi, A., Lamb, M., Lewkowicz, K., Shoham, R., Dvir, R., & Estes, D. (1985). Security of infant-mother-, -father-, and -metapelet attachments among kibbutz reared Israeli children. In I. Bretherton & E. Waters (Eds.), *Growing points of attachment theory and research* (Monographs of the Society for Research in Child Development, Vol. 50, No. 1-2, pp. 257-275). Chicago: University of Chicago Press.

Salk, L. (1973). The role of the heartbeat in the relationship between mother and infant. *Scientific American, 228*(3), 24-29.

Schneider-Rosen, K., Braunwald, K., Carlson, V., & Cicchetti, D. (1985). Current perspectives in attachment theory: Illustration from the study of maltreated infants. In I. Bretherton & E. Waters (Eds.), *Growing points of attachment theory and research* (Monographs of the Society for Research in Child Development, Vol. 50, No. 1-2, pp. 194-210). Chicago: University of Chicago Press.

Shahidullah, S., & Hepper, P. G. (1993). The developmental origins of fetal responsiveness to an acoustic stimulus. *Journal of Reproductive and Infant Psychology, 11*(3), 135-142.

Shweder, R., Goodnow, J., Hatano, G., LeVine, R., Markus, H., & Miller, P. (1998). The cultural psychology of development: One mind, many mentalities. In W. Damon (Ed.), *Handbook of child psychology: Vol. 1. Theoretical models of human development* (5th ed., pp. 865-938). New York: Wiley.

Sroufe, L. A., Carlson, E. A., Levy, A. K., & Egeland, B. (2003). Implications of attachment theory for developmental psychopathology. In M. E. Hertzig & E. A. Farber (Eds.), *Annual progress in child psychiatry and child development: 2000-2001* (pp. 43-61). New York: Brunner-Routledge.

Stevenson-Hinde, J. (1994). An ethological perspective. *Psychological Inquiry, 5,* 62-65.

Stovall, K. C., & Dozier, M. (1998). Infants in foster care: An attachment theory perspective. *Adoption Quarterly, 2,* 55-88.

Stovall, K. C., & Dozier, M. (2000). The development of attachment in new relationships: Single subject analyses for 10 foster infants. *Developmental Psychopathology, 12,* 133-156.

Suomi, S. J. (1999). Attachment in rhesus monkeys. In J. Cassidy & P. R. Shaver (Eds.), *Handbook of attachment: Theory, research, and clinical implications* (pp. 181-197). New York: Guilford.

Thompson, R. (1998). Early sociopersonality development. In W. Damon (Ed.), *Handbook of child psychology: Vol. 3. Social, emotional and personality development* (5th ed., pp. 25-104). New York: Wiley.

Tomlinson, M., Cooper, P., & Murray, L. (2005). The mother-infant relationship and infant attachment in a South African peri-urban settlement. *Child Development, 76,* 1044-1054.

Van Ijzendoorn, M. H. (1995). Adult attachment representations, parental responsiveness, and infant attachment: A meta-analysis on the predictive validity of the adult attachment interview. *Psychological Bulletin, 117,* 387-403.

Van Ijzendoorn, M. H., Goldberg, S., Kroonenberg, P. M., and Frenkel, O. J. (1992). The relative effects of maternal and child problems on the quality of attachment: A meta-analysis of attachment in clinical samples. *Child Development, 63,* 840-858.

Van Ijzendoorn, M. H., & Sagi, A. (1999). Cross-cultural patterns of attachment: Universal and contextual dimensions. In J. Cassidy & P. R. Shaver (Eds.), *Handbook of attachment: Theory, research, and clinical applications* (pp. 713-734). New York: Guilford.

Vondra, J., Hommerding, K., & Shaw, D. (1999). Stability and change in infant attachment in a low-income sample. In J. Vondra & D. Barnett (Eds.), *Atypical attachment in infancy and early childhood among children at developmental risk* (Monographs of the Society for Research in Child Development, Vol. 64, No. 3, pp. 119-144). Chicago: University of Chicago Press.

Weiss, E., Longhurst, J., & Mazure, C. (1999). Childhood sexual abuse as a risk factor for depression in women: Psychosocial and neurobiological correlates. *American Journal of Psychiatry, 156,* 816-828.

Wulczyn, F. H., & Brunner, K. (2000). Infants and toddlers in foster care. *Protecting Children, 16,* 4-12.

Wulczyn, F. H., Hislop, K. B., & Harden, B. J. (2002). The placement of infants in foster care. *Infant Mental Health Journal, 23,* 454-475.

Zeanah, C. H., Boris, N. W., & Larrieu, J. A. (1997). Infant development and developmental risk: A review of the past 10 years. *Journal of the Academy of Child and Adolescent Psychiatry, 36,* 165-178.

Zeanah, C., Mammen, O., & Lieberman, A. (1993). Disorders of attachment. In C. Zeanah (Ed.), *Handbook of infant mental health* (pp. 332-349). New York: Guilford.

Zeanah, C. H., Smyke, A. T., Koga, S. F., Carlson, E., & the Bucharest Early Intervention Core Group. (2005). Attachment in institutionalized and community children in Romania. *Child Development, 76,* 1015-1028.

Zigler, E., Singer, D., & Bishop-Josef, S. (Eds.). (2004). *Children's play: The roots of reading.* Washington, DC: Zero to Three Press.

Figure 3.1. Individuals of mixed racial heritage are among the fastest growing segments of the U.S. population. These twin girls are of African American and Chinese heritage.

3

Social Work with Children in Middle Childhood: Spiritual Development in the Community

This chapter considers the 6- to 11-year-old child as the focal system. As you read, think about the child's developing biological, psychological, and social competencies as they emerge within physical and social ecologies. The focus of this chapter will be on the macrosystem as it affects the focal system, using as an exemplar the cultural beliefs and practices within an African American community as they affect children's spiritual development. The chapter highlights an ethnographic study and an oral history of spiritual development conducted in Salt Lake City, Utah. In this research, children's emerging spiritual development is discussed as a protective factor for their exposure to racism. As you read, consider what is to be learned from these ethnographic and case-based approaches to social work scholarship. Also consider the relationship of cultural beliefs and practices related to spirituality and racism and microsystems, for example, the relationships of adults and children; mesosystems, for example, those formed through connections between the church and home, or the church and university; and ecosystems, for example, the impact of decisions made by church boards on resources available for children's Sunday school.

Middle childhood, broadly the period from 6 through 11 years of age, is an exciting time of change ushering in many new experiences and roles. While family ties remain central, children's increased intellectual and social competences allow their independent participation in widening social contexts of neighborhood peer groups, school, and community organizations. Some of these contexts, for example, scouting or elementary school, may provide new experiences and relationships. Other contexts, such as church

---

This chapter draws upon and elaborates Haight, W. (2002). *African-American children at church: A sociocultural perspective*. New York: Cambridge University Press; Haight, W., & Carter-Black, J. (2004). His eye is on the sparrow: Teaching and learning in an African American church. In E. Gregory, S. Long, & D Volk (Eds.), *Many pathways to literacy: Young children learning with siblings, grandparents, peers and communities*. New York: Routledge Falmer.; Hudley, E., Haight, W., & Miller, P. (2003). *Raise up a child: Human development in an African-American family*. Chicago: Lyceum Books.

and family, may be familiar, but school-age children begin to take on new roles, for example, watching over younger siblings at home in the afternoon or actively participating as ushers in church. Not surprisingly, social workers encounter school-age children in a wide variety of community contexts.

Everyday after school, Mitchell, a bright, outgoing and intelligent 8-year-old, attended an after-school program at his church. Although he was an active and enthusiastic participant in this program, for some perplexing reason, he had developed an active dislike of school. The social worker in charge of Mitchell's after-school program approached his parents. They, too, were concerned about Mitchell. They had read to Mitchell on a regular basis since he was a toddler, an activity he loved and still requested frequently, and could not understand why, by the third grade, Mitchell had failed to learn to read independently. The social worker helped Mitchell's parents request from their local public school an assessment of Mitchell for a possible *learning disorder.* A thorough neuropsychological assessment revealed that Mitchell had a perceptually based learning disorder. He was not "lazy," or "unmotivated," nor did he suffer from "low academic potential," common misattributions made regarding children with learning disorders. As an African American male, racial stereotyping further increased Mitchell's vulnerability to such misattributions. Mitchell , however, had difficulties in discriminating letters, for example, M from W, and seeing, at a neurological level, punctuation. This disorder is not something that Mitchell will outgrow, but, like blindness or other more obvious physical disabilities, he can learn to compensate. With intervention to support his reading, as well as the use of assistive technology including books on tape and voice-activated software, Mitchell was able to achieve in school and attend a distinguished liberal arts college.

Regaining his confidence and love of learning, however, required more than academic intervention. Psychosocial support also was an important part of the intervention for Mitchell. Supported by the social worker in his after-school program, Mitchell used the Internet to research dyslexia. He then provided education for his peers at school through a science presentation on the brain and dyslexia, which included famous scientists with learning disorders. Mitchell's emotional recovery was also supported within his church community. An important belief within this community is in the inherent worth of each individual as a child of God. This resistance to a definition of self-worth based upon external achievements provided to be enormously comforting and, ultimately, quite motivating to Mitchell.

Regardless of the context in which they encounter school-age children like Mitchell, social workers consider biological, psychosocial, and cultural dimensions of experience. In addition, religion and spirituality may play an increasing role in the experiences of children in middle childhood, and many social workers argue for the inclusion of spirituality in social work assessment and intervention. Mitchell has a biologically based disorder that affected his cognitive and psychosocial development in a cultural context (school) in which literacy and achievement are highly prized and expectations of African American males too often are low. Religiously based beliefs within his African Methodist Episcopal church provided a comfort and way of interpreting his learning disorder in a way that helped Mitchell to persist in the face of these difficulties.

HIGHLIGHTS OF DEVELOPMENT DURING MIDDLE CHILDHOOD

In contrast to the rapid and dramatic changes that occur in infancy, early childhood, and adolescence, development in middle childhood is slower and less dramatic. Nevertheless, considerable interrelated changes in physical, cognitive, social, and emotional development do occur in children ages 6 through 11. By the end of middle childhood, most typically developing children have made remarkable progress towards acquiring many of the complex skills and attitudes necessary to participate in a variety of everyday activities within their cultural communities. In the United States, most typically developing children have mastered basic literacy skills and successfully negotiate increasingly complex social relationships with peers. These achievements allow them to participate in physical work and chores around the home and community, to successfully participate in recreational activities such as organized sports, and to develop culturally valued skills such as dance and playing a musical instrument (see Cole and Cole's [2001] excellent overview of development in middle childhood, which we draw upon here).

In a wide variety of cultures, middle childhood is marked by increased independence and responsibilities. Anthropological research indicates that by 5 to 7 years of age, children from around the world are expected by adults to monitor their own behavior and well-being, and to take on increased responsibilities (Sameroff & Haith, 1996). Children are no longer restricted to home settings where they are carefully supervised by adults. Among the Mayan people in highland Guatemala, boys assume responsibility for gathering wood, an important chore that takes them beyond the supervision of adults (Rogoff, 2000). In the United States, children spend hours in school and in the company of peers. The increased responsibility and autonomy of children in middle childhood are made possible by important biological and cognitive developments and are supported by widening social opportunities (Cole & Cole, 2001).

During middle childhood, children's brains continue to develop. Neural maturation makes possible more complex thinking. Myelination, the formation of an insulating sheath of tissue around a nerve fiber, speeds up the transmission of nerve impulses in the *prefrontal cortex*. The prefrontal cortex coordinates the activities of other brain centers in more complex ways, enabling children to control their attention, to form explicit plans, and to engage in self reflection (Cole & Cole, 2001).

BOX 3.1 POVERTY ACROSS THE LIFE SPAN
Poverty and Children's Health

Poverty affects children's health in a variety of ways, including access to routine health care. More than 8 million American children (20.6%) are without health insurance. Despite the recommendation of the American Academy of Pediatrics that children see a doctor at least annually, in 2000 nearly 17% of children ages 10 through 17 years did not see a medical doctor. Hispanic children were nearly twice as likely as white children not to visit a medical doctor.

Source: Health Resources and Services Administration Maternal and Child Health Bureau. (2002). *Child health USA 2002* (p. 54). Washington, DC: U.S. Department of Health and Human Services.

During middle childhood, children become physically stronger and more agile. In the United States and around the world, poverty can threaten children's physical development and well-being. Boxes 3.1 and 3.2 describe the impact of poverty on children's access to medical and dental care in the United States.

Among the cognitive competencies made possible by increased brain development include the ability to reason more logically, follow through on a problem, keep track of more than one aspect of a situation at a time (see classic research by Piaget, 1928), and reflect on thinking (Flavell, Green, & Flavell, 1995). On a given afternoon, many 11-year-old children travel independently home from school, complete homework (e.g., construct a logical argument to explain a multistep word problem in math, employ mnemonic devices to recall the spelling of vocabulary words), supervise a younger sibling, and set the table for dinner.

As suggested by the above list of competencies, planning is a hallmark of cognitive development in middle childhood. "Planning is the deliberate organization of a sequence of actions oriented toward achieving a specific goal" (Gauvain, 1999, p. 176). It is necessary for children to successfully meet increased adult demands for responsible behavior. By the end of middle childhood, the planning abilities of many children in the United States will be sufficient to allow them to keep track of, complete, and hand in class assignments from multiple teachers as they transition into middle school.

The cognitive abilities that underlie planning include the ability to set goals and identify the means and coordinate actions to reach those goals. Children learn about planning through the course of everyday activities, especially as they interact with more experienced planners, for example, parents and older siblings at home. Planning in a social context involves collaboration as participants coordinate and direct their future activities to

```
BOX 3.2 POVERTY ACROSS THE LIFE SPAN
           Access to Dental Care
```

Children living in poverty have limited access to dental care. However, in 1999–2000 only 19% of children from low-income families eligible for dental services under Medicaid Early and Preventive Screening, Diagnosis, and Treatment (EPSDT) program received preventive dental care. In 1999–2000 approximately 30% of low-income children had not had a dental checkup for 12 or more months. This represents a macro- and microsystem problem that needs to be addressed by social workers.

Something is wrong when the macrosystem provides a means for low-income children to receive preventive dental care, but families fail to take advantage of the program. This may represent a lack of understanding by parents that preventive dentistry is important, or a sign that the program's benefits are not understood. It may also occur because parents have difficulty taking off time from work or finding a dentist who accepts Medicaid payments. Dentists and doctors are not required to take Medicaid insurance. As a result, finding an available dentist who does not have an extremely long waiting list can be difficult. It is impossible for parents to accurately predict whether they will be able to take a child to an appointment that is months away. Changes in work requirements, parental or child health, transportation, and other problems may force the most well-meaning and organized parent to cancel an appointment made months in advance.

Source: Health Resources and Services Administration Maternal and Child Health Bureau. (2002). *Child health USA 2002* (p. 52). Washington, DC: U.S. Department of Health and Human Services.

satisfy mutual interests and needs, for example, planning a meal or weekend trip. As children's ability to plan expands, adults gradually transfer to children responsibility for planning their everyday activities. By the end of middle childhood, children show increasing competence in devising a range of elaborate and effective plans (Gauvain, 1999). They independently deliver newspapers and Girl Scout cookies, plan birthday parties, finish chores, and complete homework.

In many parts of the world, the increased biological and cognitive competencies of middle childhood are supported by participation in school. An important challenge to children entering middle childhood is to master learning in school. School is a formal and specialized context for learning that differs in a variety of ways from learning in informal everyday contexts. Unlike the informal learning environment of the home, in the school

Figure 3.2.
After-school tutoring programs can support children's understanding of basic concepts and teach them good study habits.

environment children are expected to learn and demonstrate their learning primarily through symbols: spoken and written language, and mathematical notations. School learning typically is led by one adult supervising a large group of same-age children. It often involves developing skills learned out of context, whose significance are not immediately clear. It may be unclear to a child completing a worksheet of division problems at her school desk why this skill is important. On the way home from school, however, this child may eagerly and actively cooperate with friends to calculate how many packs of gum they can buy with their pooled allowances.

If formal learning in school initially presents challenges unusual to children from majority communities, it can be even more daunting for children unfamiliar with European American culture. In the United States, public schools include children from an increasing variety of cultural communities. Many of these otherwise-competent children struggle to succeed in school. Suina and Smolkin (1994) describe the experience of Pueblo children and their European American teachers. The Pueblos of the southwestern United States have their own languages, governments, social patterns, and other cultural components. Pueblo children experienced uncertainty and confusion in response to common practices of their European American teachers such as asking children to introduce themselves individually to a class visitor, or asking them to vote in the absence of group consensus. Although the European American teachers viewed these practices as innocuous, they were in conflict with traditional Pueblo culture. To engage and teach Pueblo

BOX 3.3 ADULT OUTCOMES FOR CHILDREN WITH LEARNING DISORDERS

Once they learn to compensate for specific deficits, people with learning disorders often can excel academically. Richard Jed Wyatt, MD, an internationally known expert in molecular biology, neuro-psychiatric interventions, psychiatric medications, and advocacy for people suffering with mental illness, was in special education programs throughout his school experience including medical school because of a learning disorder. Even as a senior psychiatrist and researcher, his reading skills remained so poor that important professional articles and chapters had to be read into a tape recorder for him. Yet, before his death in 2002, he was the director of an internationally recognized neuropsychiatry research program. Most people consider Dr. Wyatt a modern pioneer in mental health research who, among other accomplishments, found time to volunteer at homeless shelters where he provided psychiatric care and researched homelessness and mental illness. Although reading and organizing material was always difficult for him, he managed to develop educational materials designed to help people better understand depression, bipolar disorder, and schizophrenia.

It is important to recognize that Dr. Wyatt's accomplishments required the interaction of social systems and personal motivation. Without social support for discovering how to learn and live with a learning disorder, as well as personal motivation, sacrifice, and unwillingness to accept academic defeat, Dr. Wyatt's talent for scientific inquiry would not have blossomed. Unfortunately, far too many children with learning disorders do not receive the level of educational and social support needed to help them realize their potential.

Compensating for a learning disorder, however, is more than discovering alternative ways to achieve academically. The child must be assisted in discovering that she/he can be competent. An older adult interviewed by the authors illustrates the importance of social validation and support in discovering one's talents. Throughout his childhood, adolescence, and early adulthood, this individual secretly feared that he was mildly mentally retarded. He believed that others had simply tried to be kind and not confront him with his retardation. The man was aware that his academic learning in school was hampered by his reading and writing skills, which remained far below the ability of others. He believed he was passed from grade to grade and given a high school diploma as a consolation prize for not dropping out. He was unable to give up the fear of being mentally retarded until he was drafted into the army. To his surprise, the U.S. Army identified him as a potential leader, sent him to Officer Candidate School (OCS), and then commissioned him as a second lieutenant. The self-efficacy gained from completing OCS, becoming a military officer, and successfully leading combat troops in Vietnam convinced him that he was not mentally retarded. Without experiencing successes across major ecological systems, people with learning disorders can have great difficulty freeing themselves of self-destructive beliefs. Once the above individual accepted that he was normal but had to learn differently than others, he completed a college degree. With this further validation, he entered and successfully completed a master's degree and PhD.

Sources: American Psychiatric Association. (2000). *Diagnostic and statistical manual of mental disorders* (text revision, pp. 94–51). Washington, DC: Author; Hale, J. B., & Fiorello, C.A. (2004). *School neuropsychology. A Practitioner's handbook*. New York: Guilford Press. Lavoie, R. (2005). *It's so much work to be your friend*. New York: Simon & Schuster.

children successfully, European American teachers not only had to incorporate appropriate content from the Pueblo community, they also had to learn culturally appropriate ways of teaching that content.

Formal learning in school also presents challenges to approximately 5 percent of children in the United States who, like Mitchell in the opening case study, have learning disorders (also called "learning disabilities" or "learning differences"). Children are diagnosed with cognitive learning disorders when their academic skills in reading, mathematics, or written expression are significantly below what is expected for their intelligence, age, and experience (see Hale & Fiorello, 2004; American Psychiatric Association, 2000; Lavoie, 2005). The challenges experienced by a child with a learning disorder are not the result of mental retardation, cultural differences, deprivation, lack of school attendance, trauma, hearing or visual problems, physical illness, or mental disorders. Learning disorders result from neurologically based differences in information processing, for example, how the child discriminates sounds, comprehends visual information, recalls factual information, and communicates with others. If not addressed, children with learning disorders can experience frustration in school, stigmatization, and other negative feedback from adults and peers. These experiences can lead to social, behavioral, and mental health problems. With adequate support, however, children with learning disorders can achieve in school and beyond. Box 3.3 provides examples of how some children with learning disorders have found their way as adults.

School provides children in middle childhood increasing amounts of time with peers. In the United States, children ages 6 through 12 spend approximately 40 percent of their waking time with peers (Cole & Cole, 2001). Positive relationships with peers are important for children's well-being and development. Children who are popular with their peers generally are good at initiating and maintaining positive social relationships, compromising, and negotiating (e.g., see Rubin, Bukowski, & Parker, 1998). Good relationships with peers can provide a feeling of belonging, provide opportunities for exploring social relationships, and develop moral understanding and personal identity. In the United States, many children in middle childhood also spend increasing amounts of time in the community participating in boys and girls clubs, after-school programs sponsored by churches, scouting, and sports.

Children may experience problems in peer interactions for a variety of reasons, including poor social skills or even physical appearance. Children who are actively rejected by peers are at risk for school failure and mental health problems (e.g., see Rubin, Bukowski, & Parker, 1998). Such experiences can have a profound impact on a child's sense of self, as illustrated in Lucy Grealy's (1994) remarkable, first-person account, *Autobiography of a Face*. After being smacked on the jaw at school during a game of dodge ball, the obviously bright, outgoing, and socially skilled 9-year-old Lucy was diagnosed with Ewing's sarcoma, a virulent form of cancer with a 5 percent survival rate. Her treatment included the removal of part of her jawbone. As a result of the discomfort that others felt with her changed face, as well as the cruel taunting she experienced from other children, Lucy describes feeling set apart as different from her peers, guilty, and ashamed. Although she survived the cancer, she subsequently endured years of painful and unsuccessful plastic surgeries in an attempt to change her appearance to gain, and feel worthy of, others' love and acceptance.

Despite their increased autonomy and time spent with peers, most children in middle childhood remain closely connected with their parents. Their

BOX 3.4 VIOLENCE ACROSS THE LIFE SPAN
Child Abuse and Poverty

National surveys indicate that child abuse increases the farther a family falls below the poverty line. Poverty places parents under enormous stress, and some lash out at their children. Social workers focusing at the level of the macrosystem may help reduce child abuse by:

- working to eliminate poverty through affordable housing and living wages;
- providing supportive case management people under a set income;
- providing systematic high-quality day care, after-school care, and evening child care, because all parents need time for work and rest away from children.

BOX 3.5 SUBSTANCE ABUSE ACROSS THE LIFESPAN

Problems Found in Families with
a Substance-Abusing Parent

Addiction and substance abuse change the family system and can affect each of the members. Children from a family living with addiction have a higher probability for experiencing;

* alcohol and other substance abuse beginning in late childhood or early adolescence;
* severe family problems over extended time periods;
* inconsistent family involvement, and fragmented and unhealthy coalitions between family members;
* reduced or poor school achievement;
* increased social and behavioral problems while attending school;
* increased antisocial behavior and child conduct problems across community and home settings.

Adapted from Mack, A. H., Franklin, J. E., Jr., & Frances, R. J. (2003). Substance use disorders. In R. E. Hales & S. C. Yudofsky (Eds.), *The American psychiatric publishing textbook of clinical psychiatry* (4th ed., p. 365). Washington, DC: American Psychiatric Publishing.

relationships, however, may undergo changes. There may be a decrease in overt affection, an increase in parental expectations for competent and appropriate behavior, and an increased concern with school performance. In addition, there may be changes in control strategies, with parents increasingly relying on reasoning to keep children safe when not under direct adult supervision (Cole & Cole, 2001).

Unfortunately, many children do not experience the benefits of a supportive relationship with a parent. Child abuse remains a significant risk factor for development in middle childhood. Box 3.4 describes poverty as a macrolevel risk factor for child abuse. Most parents struggling with poverty do not abuse their children. Nevertheless, poverty places enormous stress on adults. Effective long-term prevention of child abuse must address macrolevel factors such as poverty.

The intellectual competencies and social and emotional maturity displayed by children in middle childhood are significantly more advanced than that of children in early childhood. It is important to remember, however, that despite the impressive developmental advances of children in middle childhood, they are still children and need considerable adult supervision and support. Although children reason logically about concrete objects and events, their ability to reason abstractly and hypothetically is limited. They have made great strides in their ability to plan daily activities but may need

··
:
: **BOX 3.6 SUBSTANCE ABUSE ACROSS THE LIFE SPAN**
: **The Problem of Parent Methamphetamine Abuse**
:
: The abuse of methamphetamine, a powerful central nervous sys-
: tem stimulant and neurotoxin, is a growing and urgent problem across
: the United States, including the rural Midwest. Rural law enforcement
: officers and health, mental health, and child welfare professionals
: increasingly encounter children living in homes where methampheta-
: mine is produced and abused. In a study of school-age children in the
: rural Midwest, children whose parents abused methamphetamine
: were growing up within a rural drug culture with distinct antisocial
: values, beliefs, and practices. This culture includes environmental dan-
: ger, chaos and neglect, abuse, loss, and exposure to adults' antisocial
: behavior (criminal activities, substance abuse, domestic violence).
: Many children displayed psychological, social, and educational distur-
: bances. There was, however, individual variation across children that
: may be attributed, in part, to individual (e.g., an easy-going, sociable
: temperament; intelligence), familial (e.g., support from extended fami-
: ly), and community (e.g., support from school) protective factors.
: There is a need for effective child mental health services in rural com-
: munities, and for a positive environment for children's future develop-
: ment through education of children, foster parents, and community
: members.
: _____
: Source: Haight, W., Jacobsen, T., Black, J., Kingery, L. Sheridan, K., & Mulder, C. (2005).
: "In these bleak days": Parental methamphetamine abuse in a rural Midwestern commu-
: nity: Implications for child mental health services. *Children and Youth Services Review,*
: *27,* 949-971.
··

considerable support in planning for the more distant future; for example,
they may be quite competent at completing nightly homework assignments
but need considerable adult supervision to complete longer-term projects.
They are increasingly autonomous but still need adult monitoring and supervision because they can be mislead or tricked by potential abusers. They
spend increasing amounts of time in peer groups, but peers can be difficult
and adults may need to intervene to discourage bullying and other aggressive behavior as well as provide emotional support and comfort.

Sadly, there are children who for various reasons do not receive adequate adult support and supervision. Parent substance abuse, for example,
can result in inconsistent parental discipline and inadequate monitoring of
children's activitioes (Dishion & McMahon, 1996). Boxes 3.5 and 3.6
describe challenges to children growing up in homes where parents abuse
alcohol or drugs.

DEVELOPMENTAL-ECOLOGICAL ANALYSIS OF SPIRITUAL DEVELOPMENT IN MIDDLE CHILDHOOD

This section focuses on spiritual development and its implications for social work practice with school-age children. Religion and spirituality play an increasing role in the experiences of some children in middle childhood, and many social workers argue for the inclusion of spirituality in social work assessment and intervention. During the past twenty years, the field of social work has seen a resurgence of interest in religion and spirituality (e.g., see Bullis, 1996; Canda, 1997; Canda & Furman, 1999; Haight, 1998; Pinderhughes, 1989; Sheridan, Bullis, Adcock, Berlin, & Miller, 1992). Spirituality may be defined as "the direct, personal experience of the sacred; the awareness of a higher power, a causal force beyond the material or rational, that operates in all aspects of existence" (Potts, 1996, p. 496). Spirituality has to do with the search for life's ultimate meaning and purpose. Religion, a related concept, is a system of symbols, beliefs, rituals, and texts shared by a community of believers. Although religion provides a collective framework for expressing spirituality, individuals' search for meaning may lead them to embrace spiritual precepts and practices that are not specifically religious.

The concern of contemporary social workers with religion and spirituality is not surprising given social work's origins in nineteenth-century sectarian ideologies regarding charity and community service, and institutions such as the Charity Organization Society, the Settlement House movement for immigrants, and Jewish communal services. During the twentieth century, however, as social work became increasingly professionalized, serious concerns arose with sectarian approaches. Critical questions focused on issues of moralistic judgments about the "deserving" and "undeserving" poor, combining proselytizing with the provision of social services, and the increasing religious diversity of the United States. Social work shifted from a sectarian to an academic approach drawing upon social scientific theories, assessments, and intervention (Canda, 1997).

At first blush, the focus of some contemporary social workers on religion and spirituality may seem regressive. An important distinction, however, should be made between proselytizing, advocating for one's personal spiritual and religious beliefs and practices, and the attempts of contemporary social workers to understand an important component of clients' diverse worldviews and resources. For many individuals, spirituality is the legacy into which they are born, spiritual experiences form the grid on which other life events are located, religious beliefs form the foundation for interpretation and evaluation of one's life, and a church "family" provides critical support in times of need (Haight, 2002; Hudley, Haight, & Miller, 2003). If social workers ignore such fundamental belief systems, they may fail to understand their client's worldview, which is necessary to effective professional intervention.

Consideration of religion and spirituality is not necessarily incompatible with modern scientific approaches to social work—it can provide a more complete understanding of clients' worldviews and can suggest potential sources of stress and support in times of crisis.Attention to religion and spirituality is compatible with *strengths-based practice* (see Saleebey, 2003). For some children, religious teachings and spirituality are a strength and protective factor.They are a source of joy, comfort, meaning, and interpretation of life's trials.There is a growing awareness that spirituality may illuminate the mysterious quality of *resilience* (Garmezy, 1985; Masteen, Best, & Garmezy, 1990). People who are resilient are able to find meaning in their lives even in the face of extraordinary hardship. Robert Coles provides a memorable example, quoting the words of an 8-year-old girl who helped to desegregate a North Carolina school in 1962:

I was all alone, and those people [segregationists] were screaming, and suddenly I saw God smiling, and I smiled....A woman was standing there (near the school door), and she shouted at me, "Hey, you little nigger, what are you smiling at?" I looked right at her face and I said, "At God." Then she looked up at the sky, and then she looked at me, and she didn't call me any more names (Coles, 1990, pp. 19–20).

As this quote suggests, the spiritual and religious experiences of middle childhood often have remarkable emotional depth.Tamminen's (1991, 1994) studies of Finnish children and adolescence found that spiritual experiences are relatively common in middle childhood and adolescence.The percentage of individuals who reported experiencing "God's nearness," however, was greatest during middle childhood prior to a period of questioning and analysis during adolescence. During their discussions of morality and political issues, Robert Coles (1990) was so impressed with children's spontaneous use and elaborations of their religious beliefs that he embarked on an exploration in *The Spiritual Life of Children*. He found that spirituality was central to the lives of children of Jewish, Muslim, and Christian traditions. Sarah Moskovitz (1983) concluded from her study of child survivors of the Nazi Holocaust that a sense of hope for the future rooted in religious faith enabled children to love and behave compassionately toward others in spite of the atrocities they had experienced. Recent collections including the religious and spiritual experiences of children include works by Karl Rosengren and colleagues (Rosengren, Johnson, & Harris, 2000) and Donald Ratcliff (Ratcliff, 2004). In her oral history, *Raise up a Child*, Edith Hudley (Hudley, Haight, & Miller, 2003) describes human development in a rural African American community as rooted in spirituality. Scholarship within African American studies portrays spirituality as a common cultural value (Boykin, 1994; Schiele, 1996) and as an agent of socialization (Brown, 1991).

A developmental-ecological analysis of children's spiritual development considers beliefs and practices as they emerge within complex social and cultural-historical contexts. This chapter elaborates on children's spiritual development within the macrosystem of an African American community. The center of this community for children and families was an African American Baptist church.

Historically, the African American church has been a key context within African American communities. Throughout its history, the African American church has played a significant role in providing social support services. Strong involvement in churches has been one of the means by which African American families have coped with adversity (see Haight, 2002, for a review). Within the African American church, Sunday school has been a particularly significant context for children's socialization (Mitchell, 1986).

The African American church is an important context for the acquisition of a culturally distinct alternative identity and view of reality (see Haight, 2002, for a review). This alternative system of beliefs is not a simple imitation or derivation of European American Christianity (Long, 1997) but evolved in relation to a distinct, African heritage, shaped by experiences in North America (Smitherman, 1977; Hale-Benson, 1987; Long, 1997). General characteristics of this meaning system and related practices seem particularly relevant to children's resilience. First, African American religion has been described as the pragmatic intertwining of the sacred and the material (Smitherman, 1977). Consistent with both a traditional African worldview and with the experience of racism within the United States, a key to the African American notion of spirituality is its importance in facilitating survival (Hale-Benson, 1987). African American religion addresses specific human needs and experiences, and it helps individuals cope with traumatic aspects of human existence (Lincoln, 1999).

A second feature of African American religion is an emphasis on community. Community is central to African American culture (Stack, 1974). This emphasis on community has religious underpinnings. A common theme in spirituals is the threat of loneliness and despair to disrupt the community of faith (Hale-Benson, 1987).

A third feature, viewed by some as a cornerstone of contemporary African American theology, is the belief in the inherent dignity and worth of each individual. Each child, each individual, is special because he or she was created by God (Hale-Benson, 1987). The belief that God recognizes African Americans as equal to European Americans—each personally as one of God's children—has given many the inner resolve to "keep on keeping on" (Hale-Benson, 1987).

One of the contexts in which systems of belief are co-constructed is storytelling. Storytelling appears to be a cultural universal and is particularly prominent in African American culture (Gates, 1989). Stories of personal experience, in which past events personally experienced by the narrator are related, have been observed in the language of children and adults from a wide variety of cultural communities, including African American ones. Several scholars have argued that the study of socialization through stories should be expanded to include more than only past events. Linda and Doug Sperry (1996) found that at home, young children within a rural African American community preferred telling stories about fictional events, rather than past events, as is common in European American families.

Ethnographic Portrait of First Baptist Church

To illustrate the role of the macrosystem in children's spiritual development, we provide an in-depth discussion of First Baptist Church (a pseudonym). The research began with the collection of developmental and ethnographic materials over a four-year period (1991–1995) within an African American Baptist community in Salt Lake City, Utah (Haight, 2002). The goal was to understand, in depth, the coherence and diversity of adults' socialization beliefs and practices, and children's emerging participation within this specific cultural context. In the long run, the complex differentiated portrait emerging from this case-based strategy provided a basis for meaningful comparisons with other communities. In the short run, it highlighted and perhaps challenged culturally based assumptions about educational practices and social service interventions with children and families.

First Baptist Church is an important case for at least two reasons. First, the African American community in Utah shares many similarities with African American communities in other parts of the United States. Many African American Utahns experience racial discrimination in employment, housing, education, and everyday social interactions (Coleman, 1981). The developmental literature, however, is virtually silent with respect to the impact of racism on children's development (Fisher, Jackson, & Villarruel, 1998). Second, the African American Utahn community has characteristics distinct from many other African American communities. The overwhelming majority of African American Utahns find themselves in the religious as well as the racial minority. In contrast to the predominantly Baptist African American community, most of the population of the state of Utah belongs to the Church of the Latter-day Saints (whose members are commonly known as Mormons). Despite the diversity across African American communities, there remains an unfortunate tendency in some of the developmental, educational, and social service literatures to minimize complexities of group variation. This case provides an important illustration of adaptation and development within a particular African American community in relation to a geographically and culturally distinct larger community.

This study focused on socialization practices, including storytelling, verbal conflict, and role-playing, through which adults, particularly Sunday school teachers, and their students, ages 3 to 15 years old, constructed personal meanings from an important cultural resource, the Bible. These observations focused on Sunday school. A total of forty Sunday school classes for children ages 3 to 16 years old were audiotaped and the context was described in field notes. From these materials, detailed verbatim transcripts of Sunday school classes and descriptions of nonverbal contexts were reconstructed. These observations were contextualized by multiple in-depth semi-structured interviews with the pastor, Sunday school superintendent, and Sunday school teachers. These interviews were also audiotaped and transcribed. Practices and beliefs associated with Sunday school were further contextualized through description of yearly events such as vacation Bible school, monthly events such as youth emphasis day, weekly events such as the pastor's sermons for children, a variety of other special occasions focusing on children, adult Sunday school classes, and weekly Sunday school teachers' meetings. Observations and interviews were further contextualized through historical and social background information obtained from a variety of sources including local newspaper articles, historical documents, and church publications.

Mother Edith Hudley's Oral History

A "mother" and deaconess of First Baptist Church and a master storyteller, Edith Hudley deepened our understanding of the cultural-historical context through her in-depth oral history (Hudley, Haight, & Miller, 2003). Mrs. Hudley was born in 1920 on a small family farm in Kennard, Texas. The sixth of eight surviving children, Edith was her mother's helper and apprentice. Before she attended a segregated school, beginning when children were 7 years of age, Edith was taught at home by her mother. Her mother taught her to cook, sew, and care for infants. Edith described feelings of great pride and self-worth at her increasing abilities to help her family in such concrete ways. When she was 10 years of age, and her mother died from complications of childbirth, Edith was able to perform these tasks independently. The family's burdens, however, were lessened through their close community ties, especially to the church. When Edith brought her father questions that he found inappropriate for a father to answer, he sought out his older sister, cousins, and other female community members. He also encouraged Edith to form relationships with the "mothers of the church," the ones with experience who would keep her to the right path. In turn, as an adult, Mrs. Hudley became a mother of First Baptist Church, mentoring and teaching the children.

Mrs. Hudley recounted her life story during several days in the fall of 1998 and the winter of 1999. Although she had never narrated so much of her life story in a single sitting, her stories had a shape that had been honed over multiple tellings. Her collaborators (Wendy Haight and Peggy Miller) respected the integrity of her tellings by not interrupting or redirecting her talk. Twenty-three hours of audio recordings were transcribed verbatim, yielding 346 typed single-spaced pages. The transcripts were edited to retain the essence of Mrs. Hudley and the conviction of her telling (see Hudley, Haight, & Miller, 2003, for a further description of methods).

There is a growing awareness that children cannot be understood apart from the cultural and historical contexts that shape their lives. This is true of all children, but because African American children and other minorities have been underrepresented in studies of child development, the need to imagine the contexts of their lives is especially urgent. Edith Hudley's story stimulates our imaginations and prompts us to question, enlarge, or reaffirm certain assumptions about child rearing. Mrs. Hudley's strong opinions about child rearing are grounded in the messages that she received from the family and community into which she was born—religious faith is the most important force in life, the compass by which all conduct is oriented.

The Macrosystem: Spiritual Development at First Baptist Church

Adults like Mrs. Hudley were central to the spiritual socialization of children at First Baptist Church. Complex cultural beliefs and practices were conveyed to the children during observation of and interaction with adults and other children during informal and formal church activities. Several key cultural concepts and socialization practices emerged from the *ethnography* and *oral history*.

Spirituality Is a Lifeline. At First Baptist Church, religious beliefs— such as the inherent worth of each individual, and the value of freedom, justice, and forgiveness—are viewed as lifelines both to healthy spiritual development and also to effective coping with the challenges of everyday life. The primary goal of Sunday school teachers is to "bring the child to God" for spiritual salvation. In addition, they argued that children must be familiar with religious beliefs so that they may reach for them in times of need. In the words of one Sunday school teacher, children must know how to "put on the armor of God." This protection can be carried inside of each child to school, to work, and in the community (Haight, 2002).

Consistent with this emphasis on spiritual protection, Mrs. Hudley provided numerous illustrations of how her faith provided her with a coherent framework for coping with life's challenges including racism, poverty, violence, and, in the following excerpt, death.

I was a little girl and they was building a chimney....And Mama had this baby. It was a pretty baby, and I was in the house....They let me stay in the kitchen, and Mama was in the room when the baby was born. That was the prettiest baby. It had a full head of hair. And the baby died....And I went and I was lookin at the baby, and Papa had to stop buildin the chimney to build a little box to go bury the baby. And I was just lookin for the baby to say somethin. And I said, "Mama, the baby ain't sayin nothin!" I was listenin for the baby to cry. And Mama said, "Well the baby won't be sayin anything. The baby's goin back to Jesus." That's the way she told me the baby's dead. (Hudley et al., 2003, p. 11)

Meaningful Involvement in Community. Consistent with the literature in African American studies, a key finding from the ethnographic

research and the oral history concerns the emphasis on community. The significance of community as it relates to the African American church is exem-
plified in the common reference to one's "church home," indicating member-
ship in a particular church. At First Baptist Church, children are valued members of a cultural community stretching back in time, and including members of the church highly esteemed for their wisdom and spirituality. Each
child participated in meaningful ways beside these esteemed community
members, for example, ushering worship services, leading devotions, singing
in the choir, or providing service to families in need. In describing her own
participation as a child with adults at church, Sister Irma noted, "I gathered
my spirit from them. I saw what they did. I saw them pray. I saw them read
the Bible. I saw them sing, and they would sing joyously" (Haight, 2002, p.
69).

Adults also described the necessity of knowing the child's family and
community in order to teach effectively. During Sunday school, teachers
often referred to individuals and events class members knew. When Davon
misbehaved, Sister Justine reminded him of their mutual connection to his
grandmother. A sense of community also was fostered during the "children's
story," a part of the regular Sunday morning worship services when the pastor or other church leaders would tell the children stories relating biblical
concepts to the lives of famous African Americans or to African or African
American folktales. These stories encouraged a sense of pride in being
African American and connected the child to a broader African or African
American heritage.

Community ties were seen as central to survival. When Mrs. Hudley told
the story of her rural home burning down when she was a child, it was
neighbors and community members who provided the family with shelter,
food, and clothing necessary for survival (Hudley et al., 2003).

Inherent Worth of Each Individual: Love and Respect. Another
key concept to emerge from this research program is the inherent worth of
each individual. This worth exists independently of material success and
social status. In the words of a popular hymn, each individual is a "child of
the King" with unique God-given gifts. Each child is entitled to love and
respect and, with opportunity and effort, will go far. As elaborated within the
stories told in Sunday school, vacation Bible school, and other church contexts, however, the journey will be difficult. Just as many were blind to
Jesus—a powerful personal role model for many African American children—many will not see the black child's inner resources and strengths. Just
as the Egyptians enslaved and oppressed Moses's people, some will attempt
to oppress the black child. These and other stories told to children, however, also stress that through faith, effort, and community, they too, like the
Hebrew people, can prevail. The challenge is to remain a loving and moral
person throughout the journey and to maintain a deep optimism in the ultimate rewards of a successful journey.

The following excerpt from Mrs. Hudley's narrative of her experiences walking to segregated school as a 7-year-old illustrates how religious beliefs can aid children in that successful journey despite racism.

The whites would be walking one way. And we'd be walking the other. They'd yell at us, "You dirty, black niggers! We hate you! We hate you!" I'd go to Mama and ask her, "Why do they hate us?" She'd always take me to the Bible. She taught me that God loves us all. God is the judge. She taught me not to take hate inside of myself. (Haight, 1998, p.213).

Mrs. Hudley went on to explain that when we hate, we destroy that part of God that he left inside each of us when he created us. From Mrs. Hudley's perspective, the black children were not the victims of this story, rather, their taunters were.

The inherent worth of children also was communicated through the love they were shown by adults. Indeed, a love for children pervaded the narratives collected in this research program as well as the practices observed. For example, when asked what made a good Sunday school teacher, adults at First Baptist Church did not refer to intellectual qualities or professional achievement. A good Sunday school teacher loves children. In describing her life's work, Mrs. Hudley repeatedly emphasized, "I love children, period." This love provides a basis for a relationship that was viewed as prerequisite to effective socialization.

A respect for children also pervaded adults' beliefs and practices. At First Baptist Church, children were seen as the hope of the future but were also respected as models for spiritual salvation. The pastor exhorted the congregation to "learn to be more childlike," that is, to trust and have faith in God. Furthermore, children's spiritual experiences were taken seriously. For example, 10-year-old Edith repeatedly interacted with visions of her dead mother. These visions were interpreted by her father and pastor as legitimate spiritual experiences. Mrs. Hudley's belief that the dead remain connected to the living was introduced and reinforced through relationships in middle childhood with these adults.

Appropriate Adult-Child Relationships. Love and respect for the child and the child's spiritual experiences, however, did not lead to dissolution of generational boundaries. Haight (2002) described the nature of adult-child relationships at First Baptist Church as "child sensitive and growth oriented." Sunday school teachers and Mrs. Hudley clearly were sensitive to children's emotional, social, and cognitive immaturity. On the other hand, they demanded respect and took very seriously their charge to pass down spiritual lifelines to children. In a narrative relating a conversation with her son, Mrs. Hudley emphasized, "Honor your mother and father that your days may be longer....God gave y'all to me to raise, and if I fail to raise you, I have failed God. And I have to suffer the consequences" (Hudley et al, 2003, p. 158).

Adults' leadership roles, however, did not result in children's passivity. Sunday school classes clearly were lead by the teachers who initiated narratives, posed questions, and made demands on children's behavior and performance. Children, however, were not passive. They actively contributed by responding to questions, debating issues, and putting forth their own interpretations, for example, how scriptures related to their own lives.

Storytelling. Another key finding from this research program has been the importance of storytelling to relating new and complex concepts to children's own lives and experiences. Helping children to understand and then to apply biblical concepts in their everyday lives was described by every informant as a central goal of Sunday school. When asked how they accomplished their goals, adults consistently discussed storytelling. Pastor Daniels explained:

We are convinced that it is out of life that the best applications of any kind of principles can be found. And, certainly if you're going to make sense of it, you have to relate it to life. And, when we tell our own personal stories, there's almost an immediate connection with the youngsters. (Haight, 2002, p. 83).

Observations of Sunday school classes revealed that storytelling was a central part of lessons. Children's formal Sunday school lessons included reading extended excerpts form the King James Bible, which the children struggled to understand. It was through the stories that accompanied or followed these texts that the ideas really came to life. These stories had several characteristics. First, stories frequently contained comments that explicitly linked the biblical texts to children's everyday lives. Sunday school teachers routinely concluded a story with challenges such as "And how is this lesson relevant to our lives today?" Stories sometimes contained deeply personal, spiritual meanings. In her oral history, Mrs. Hudley related numerous stories told to her more than seventy-five years ago by her own parents that have provided guidance during difficult times, and remain a touchstone for her life.

Second, narratives related a variety of types of events. Consistent with adults' emphasis on the significance of biblical text, many narratives involved retelling the biblical text. Stories also related personal experiences and elaborated hypothetical events. These stories always followed the biblical text and were used by teachers to illustrate and elaborate key points from the text. Sister Irma ended a particularly dramatic story from her own life with the explicit comments, "Now I share that with you not that you need to be worried about it . . . but that's something that happened to me that's in line with today's lesson" (Haight, 2002, p. 96).

Typically, adults used stories of personal experience to communicate to children how biblical principles are important to their lives. After discussing with her class several examples from the New Testament of storms at sea, Sister Justine challenged the 8- to 12-year-old children to understand the metaphorical meaning of "storm." Embedded within this discussion was Sister Justine's personal story of recovery from alcoholism, the "major storm" in her life "calmed by Jesus."

Although stories of personal experience can be very powerful, they also have limitations. First, teachers are concerned about keeping children focused on the biblical text—and children's own personal experiences can be highly distracting to them. Second, teachers are concerned with respecting the privacy of families, and children are not always discrete in relating their stories. On the other hand, teachers needed to check children's abilities to apply the lesson to their own lives. Hypothetical talk referring to temporally sequenced hypothetical events within narratives was common in Sunday school. Like stories of personal experience, hypothetical stories provided children with concrete instances of how biblical concepts relate to modern everyday experiences and elaborate upon biblical text. Sister Justine routinely asked the 8- to 10- year-olds, "If Jesus was walking with us today, what would he want you to do?" Unlike personal narratives, they frequently cast a child in the role of protagonist. By middle childhood, some children began to initiate hypothetical narratives. The following excerpt is conversation between 9-year-old Latasha and Sister Justine:

Latasha: If, if you were good and—say you were really good.
SJ: Ahha.
Latasha: And an angel when you were a child, but you got up and when you got grown up you were just mean in a gang—but then turned back over to God and then when you die—say you were shot by a gang member. So where would they go then? Because their sins were there?
SJ: All you have to do is ask for forgiveness! You're saying this person went to church, came back hard-headed, then came back to church, and then got accidentally killed in the line of fire of a gang member? All it takes is believing.
Latasha (interrupting): Yeah, but you believe yes and you believe no.
SJ: You can't waiver in your faith. (Haight, 2002, p. 99)

Social Work Intervention

Information and insights gained from Mrs. Hudley and from the ethnography were used to inform the development of an intervention for children. This intervention had two goals. First, community members identified computer literacy as a weak area in the education of many children who had little access to computers either at home or in their relatively poorly funded public schools. As the pastor expressed, adults worried that children would be "behind the eight ball" (be at a disadvantage academically to other children) in their secondary school education and beyond if they did not receive some meaningful computer experience. Second, community members identified multicultural education as a relatively weak area of preparation at the local university. Experience at First Baptist Church could provide a context for white middle-class students, especially those who intended to become teachers, social workers, or other helping professionals, to learn from the local African American community.

In collaboration with community members, we developed a computer club for children ages 3 to 18. Computers were donated from the local university and housed in the church basement. The computer club operated on Thursday evening and Saturdays. It was staffed by university students taking a child development class. These students were made aware of research findings regarding adult-child interaction in church, and supervised in their interactions with the children by university staff and community members (see Haight, 2002, for discussion of the computer club).

IMPLICATIONS FOR SOCIAL WORK WITH SCHOOL-AGE CHILDREN AND THEIR FAMILIES

Within the United States and other industrialized societies, school is a central context of development in middle childhood. Despite the strong value African American communities historically have placed on academic achievement and educational attainment (see Comer, 1988), educational underachievement in public schools remains a sad reality for many African American children and youth. Yet the context of the African American church appears to facilitate competence and motivation in children, even those who experience difficulty in the public school setting. The findings presented below, in conjunction with those of Robin Jarrett (1995), Jan Carter-Black (2001), and others, provide clues for social workers concerned with supporting children's development, especially in school (see Haight & Black, 2004).

Respect the Inherent Worth of Every Individual

The Sunday school teachers at First Baptist Church taught the children to believe in the inherent dignity and worth of each individual. Regardless of racism and other indignities in the world, they are always "children of the King." Crucial to the development of African American children are curriculums, programs, and services that incorporate strategies for dealing with racism in ways that diminish the experience as a risk factor. Adults must display beliefs and practices that promote children's healthy racial identity, and awareness of and constructive responses to racism, without promoting hatred or discrimination toward members of other racial groups (Sanders, 1997).

Gain Familiarity with Culturally Normative Styles of Adult-Child Interactions

Adult-child interactions at First Baptist Church were described as "child-sensitive" and "growth-oriented" (Haight, 2002). Adults prioritized their relationships with children and their families, and they also held very high standards for conduct and achievement. As is not uncommon for Sunday school teachers in African American churches, teachers at First Baptist Church presented in a manner that conveyed strong conviction, absolute authority, and clear generational boundaries. While these teaching techniques may vary from the norm of middle-class white strategies, social workers must realize that the meaning African American children and their families attach to diverse teaching strategies may in fact be quite different from their own. Within the African American community, teachers who love children and feel a personal calling to teach are easily identified. European American social workers may respond negatively to tone of voice, volume, or cadence of speech, and relatively authoritarian demeanor and affect. African American children and their families may be more likely to pay attention to the teacher's motivation and intentions. Does she care about the children? Is she able to convey that caring? Is she willing to be nurturing and encourage children to be strong, competent, and ambitious yet conform to church community and parental values and goals? Does she love the children?

Recognize the Centrality of Spirituality

Spirituality was the central value at First Baptist Church and a lifeline for Mrs. Hudley. Certain values expressed in public schools, however, may be in conflict with the strong spiritual orientation of many African American families (Jarrett, 1995). Awareness by school social workers of a family's spiritual orientation may minimize misunderstanding and facilitate home-school relations. Many adults at First Baptist Church seemed less concerned with concepts such as individuality, competition, or personal achievement—considerations more reflective of the analytical learning environment in schools—and more concerned about instilling in children the importance of placing God first in their lives.

Understand Community

At First Baptist Church children participated as valued members of the community. School social workers need to be cognizant of the meaning of community as programs and services are being developed that will enhance the resilience in African American children. The inclusion of members of a child's extended kinship system, including fictive kin, in planning and decision-making resonates with the construction of "family" within the African American church and larger social community.

Use Storytelling to Engage Children in Learning

Storytelling is a historically and culturally prescribed strategy for passing along lessons for living to children from which social workers may draw. Mrs. Hudley and teachers in Sunday school use stories to bring the biblical meanings to life and relate central concepts to everyday life. Stories provide a venue for engaging children's imaginations. The use of stories including hypothetical talk keep children focused on the lesson and minimize opportunities for childish indiscretions. Furthermore, stories provide powerful and coherent frameworks for interpreting even the most difficult experiences.

BOX 3.7 PRACTICE STORY AND ADVICE FROM THE FIELD

Steve A.: Social work professor and policy expert: "You don't develop coalitions overnight."

After completing his MSW, Steve A. worked for 10 years in the Michigan state legislature. He then completed a PhD in political science and currently is a social work professor. He conducts research on social policy and teaches MSW- and PhD-level social work students. In this excerpt, he discusses the ways in which social workers are involved in policy, relates a practice story, and offers advice for students interested in policy work.

What are some contexts in which social workers interested in social policy could work?

There is a huge need for advocacy, and there are a lot of social advocacy organizations out there. They can play an important role in the political process, and in policy development. And I mean anything from local community organization types of advocacy to the state-level associations and federal types of associations, like Children's Defense and the Center for Budget priorities. There are a lot of social service-oriented think tanks. But there are a lot of possibilities at the local, state, and federal levels for some types of advocacy-oriented type positions.

Another route for those who come out of policy is to go into government; for example, I had a couple of [MSW] policy students who did their placements down there at the Illinois Department of Human Services and then got hired at either the local or state offices to keep working. So they could do a number of things. Some of them go into management, in terms of running a local office; others go into state evaluation units, which would be closer to the work that I did in the House. So there are a lot of different opportunities along government lines.

You know I never went this route [local agency] myself, but I did some research in aging and I got to be friends with a guy who is running an area agency on aging and I saw the types of things that he could do in terms of just developing service networks, and his role was very interesting. It was a role of management, because he had to manage programs, but also he had to be out advocating on behalf of seniors in his region. He became very familiar with government funding sources and what it is that they advocate, so I thought it was a very rich world and I thought of going that way for a while—heading a local agency.

One of our graduates went in at the ground level of the agency and she has moved up to program director. And I have no doubt that someday she will be the director of the agency. You know you can start out in practice and move up, or you start out in policy and move up more as a manager type, and I have seen it happen both ways. Those are interesting jobs, running a local agency or even being a program director in a local agency, where you have a lot of say in what direction the agency might go in terms of initiatives, and how they go about coming up with the money to do that, or convincing the public it's a good thing to do. Those are viable roles I have seen our students take. **What were some people or experiences that helped you to understand policy?**

The guy that I mentioned before who was my subcommittee chair, the thing that I always admired about him was he was just dogged. He had that perspective. He knew that things didn't change very quickly, and I think a lot times the staff would have given up, but every year you know he had his little tick list of things that he was going to bring up again. And, he was the author of the mandatory seat-belt law in Michigan. And when I got there [the state legislature], he had already proposed the seat-belt legislation about ten times. Finally got it passed in its sixteenth year. And I talked to him about that. When I first got there, he was still a lot of votes short. He said, "I'm going to get this sooner or later. I get a few votes every year, and I go back and I work more people every year. And every year it's gone up, but sooner or later I am going to get this passed." You know, when I got there I was a little skeptical, but you know, fifteen or sixteen years out he got it passed, and it was because he did it every year. He worked somebody every year, and he kept making these little gains and he finally got it changed. And it's not the biggest change in the world, but it's a fairly major change in that state. But it couldn't have happened without somebody just pushing and pushing every year and building coalitions and not getting too frustrated by getting beaten every year. You have to be very persistent and recognize the complexity of things, and the resistance to change, and the importance of going at it year in and year out. **What advice do you have for social workers interested in going into policy?**

Respect diverse views. In legislature you have people who are all over the board. We had 110 members, and you had some really right-wing people, and you had some very liberal people. One of the problems I see with some of our students—and I try and work with them on this because I was that way—social workers tend to come in having pretty strong views about things. When you go into a legislature or even a bureaucracy that's focused just on social services, you get a range of views that are quite a bit different from your own—often, quite a bit more conservative than your own. And if you come on too strong and don't learn to respect those views and don't really put quite an effort into understanding them, it compromises your ability to be effective. I mean I have heard members and legislators say the same thing, just what an experience it is of broadening your perspectives on what people think—because you have to. I think in general for our students that's a real important thing if they go into that kind of broader arena where there are a lot of conflicting interest groups wanting things, it's just a way of thinking about things that most people don't have when they start out.

Understand that change is incremental. Unless you are really lucky, changes that are big don't happen very often—it's just the nature of things. Most changes tend to be small and incremental and a lot of times that flusters people because they are in this partially because they think big changes are needed or else [they] would have gone and done something else in the first place. So, then you get into the environment and first of all you find out that its much more complex than you thought and there are a lot of people who don't think like you. So you have to be pretty patient learning who the players are and learning how things actually work. But then you also have to be persistent in terms of long-term perspective on change. You might get lucky and you might see a big change right away. But usually that doesn't happen and most successful change efforts that I have seen really have been the combination of long periods of work by a lot of different people. So there is really the importance of knowing people and forming coalitions with them, which again has something to do with being able to work with people who don't think quite like you. But also realizing that things don't happen very quickly and a lot of times it's a small change. If you keep making small changes every year, they accumulate over time into something that makes a lot of sense.

Make a time commitment. You have to make a little bit of a time commitment, and I mean you have to stay several years so that you learn the actors. You don't develop coalitions overnight. You have to meet people. They have to trust you and you have to develop working relationships. People who end up being most effective, in terms of advocacy change efforts, usually have been around awhile. You know, it's almost like an industry. You have to do the leg work and the development because credentials really become important. I mean we tend to be seen as specialists—you are not asked to talk about every area. You are asked to talk about an area where you are seen as having credibility, and that credibility tends to come with time and being tested.

SUMMARY

Development in middle childhood, although not as dramatic as that in infancy and adolescence, nonetheless reflects significant biological, psychological, and social growth. As with other periods of development, growth is intertwined with the context. Unfortunately, many children in middle childhood continue to experience risk because of poverty, maltreatment, parental substance abuse, and racial discrimination. Social workers address such issues through direct practice and through policy. Box 3.7 contains practice stories and advice from a social worker who has spent a significant part of his career working to change policy.

By middle childhood, spirituality has become, for many individuals, an important part of their experience and a tool for coping with adversity. Social workers and those engaged in community-based youth programs who have some knowledge of the ethos and principles of the African American church will understand how the church, especially Sunday school, functions as a significant context for children's socialization. This increased knowledge can be called upon as a guide in the development of various community-based youth programs that support rather than conflict with the characteristics of the African American alternative system of beliefs. Programs designed to reach children and youth can model effective child development strategies employed by the church as they seek to develop culturally appropriate programs that are tailored to specific communities. Similarly, academic and extramural school-based programs that reflect dimensions of the relationships and interactions between African American children and their Sunday school teachers, pastors, mother's boards, and other significant church leaders may find that children exhibit competencies where previously they were struggling. Such strategies are examples of strengths-based social work practice.

Study and Discussion Questions

1. When and how is it appropriate for social workers to discuss spiritual issues with their clients? How do these discussions differ from proselytizing?

2. How might the relationships that children formed at First Baptist Church serve as protective factors in public school?

3. What might social workers learn from the interactions of teachers at First Baptist Church with school-age children?

4. Considering development in middle childhood, how do you explain Tamminen's finding that children in middle childhood are especially moved or responsive to spiritual experiences?

5. What are some of the risks to development in middle childhood, and how might these risks be addressed by social workers through direct practice and policy?

6. Consider again the case of Mitchell. How might his undiagnosed biologically based learning disorder have affected the ways that adults and peers responded to him, as well as his perceptions of himself? What interventions might be appropriate for Mitchell's family members and peers? How might religiously based beliefs, such as the inherent worth of each individual, serve as protective factors for Mitchell?

Resources

For students interested in an excellent overview of development in middle childhood, see chapters in Cole and Cole (2001). For those interested in learning more about children's spiritual development in various cultural communities, see Coles (1990), Ratcliff (2004), Boyatzis (2004), and Haight (2002). To learn more about spirituality in social work, see Canda (1997), or Sheridan and colleagues (1992). For students seeking more information about strengths-based social work practice, see Saleebey (2003).

Interested students can supplement this chapter through the following excellent Web-based resources.

The MacArthur Network on Successful Pathways through Middle Childhood systematically studies the course of development during middle childhood. Additionally, the program explores how normal developmental experiences are similar and different within and across cultural and racial groups. Available at: http://childhood.isr.umich.edu/mission/index.html# purpose

The Center for Disease Control outlines physical and psychosocial changes parents and professionals can expect as a child moves to middle childhood. Available at: http://www.cdc.gov/ncbddd/child/middlechild hood.htm

The Research Network on Successful Pathways through Middle Childhood, sponsored by the MacArthur Foundation, offers parents and professionals access to comprehensive bibliographies and research reports. Available at: http://www.middlechildhood.org/mission/themes.htm

Lois Melina offers thoughts about the impact of adoption on the child during middle childhood. The Web site also provides links to other adoption sites. Melina is the editor of the *Adopted Child* newsletter and is on the Evan B. Donaldson Adoption Institute's (EBDAI) board. The EBDAI is dedicated to improving information about adoption and advocating for practice and policy change in the field. Available at: http://parenting.ivillage.com/gs/gsfam dynamics/0,,6nwb,00.html

A book chapter by Kerns, Schlegelmich, Morgan, and Abraham (2004) explores how professionals can more correctly assess attachment in middle childhood. Available at: http://www.guilford. com/excerpts/kerns.pdf #search='Middle%20Childhood'

The Children, Youth, and Family Consortium at the University of Minnesota provides information on normal and abnormal development for children and teens. The consortium also provides links and academic information on family development. A brief overview of middle childhood development is available at: http://www.cyfc.umn.edu/publications/connection/pubs/04winter/overview.html

The U.S. Department of Education's National Center for Education Statistics has prepared a sixty-seven-page working paper, *Measures of socioemotional development in middle childhood*. The paper is available in a PDF format at: http://nces.ed.gov/pubs2001/200103.pdf#search='Middle%20Childhood

References

Boyatzis, C. (2004). The co-construction of spiritual meaning in parent-child communication. In D. Ratcliff (Ed.), *Children's spirituality: Christian perspectives, research, and applications*. Eugene, OR: Cascade Books.

Bullis, R. (1996). *Spirituality in social work practice*. Washington, DC: Taylor & Francis.

Canda, E. R. (1997). Spirituality. In R. L. Edwards (Ed.), *Encyclopedia of social work* (Supplement). Washington, DC: NASW Press.

Canda, E. R. (1998). *Spirituality in social work: New directions*. Binghamton, NY: Haworth Pastoral Press.

Canda, E. R., & Furman, L. D. (1999). *Spiritual diversity in social work practice: The heart of helping*. New York: Free Press.

Carter-Black, J. (2001). The myth of "the tangle of pathology": Resilience strategies employed by middle-class African-American families. *Journal of Family Social Work, 6*(4), 75–100.

Cole, M., & Cole, S. (2001). *The development of children* (4th ed.). New York: Worth.

Coleman, R. (1981). Blacks in Utah history: An unknown legacy. In H. Z. Papanikolas (Ed.), *The peoples of Utah*. Salt Lake City: Utah Historical Society.

Coles, R. (1990). *The spiritual life of children*. Boston: Houghton Mifflin.

Dishion, T. J., & McMahon, R. J. (1996). *Parental monitoring and prevention of problem behavior: A conceptual and empirical reformulation* (NIDA Research Monograph No. 177). Rockville, MD. (NTIS No. PB 99-124315/LL).

Fisher, C. B., Jackson, J. F., & Villarruel, F. A. (1998). The study of African American and Latin American youth. In I. Sigel & K. Renninger (Eds.), *Handbook of child psychology: Vol. 4. Socialization, personality, and social development* (5th ed.). New York: Wiley.

Flavell, J. H., Green, F. L., & Flavell, E. R. (1995). Young children's knowledge about thinking. *Monographs of the Society for Research in Child Development, 60* (1, Serial No. 243), 1–95.

Fraser, M. W. (Ed.). (1997). *Risk and resilience in childhood: An ecological perspective*. Washington, DC: NASW Press.

Gates, H. L. (1989). Introduction. In L. Goss and M. E. Barnes (Eds.), *Talk that talk: An anthology of African-American storytelling*. New York: Simon and Schuster.

Gauvain, M. (1999). Everyday opportunities for the development of planning skills: Sociocultural and family influences. In A. Goncu (Ed.), *Children's engagement in the world: Sociocultural perspective*. New York: Cambridge University Press.

Grealy, L. (1994). *Autobiography of a face*. New York: Houghton Mifflin.

Haight, W. (1998). "Gathering the spirit" at First Baptist Church: Spirituality as a protective factor in the lives of African American children. *Social Work, 43,* 213–221.

Haight, W. (2002). *African-American children at church: A sociocultural perspective*. New York: Cambridge University Press.

Haight, W., & Carter-Black, J. (2000). His eye is on the sparrow: Teaching and learning in an African American church. In E. Gregory, S. Long, & D. Volk (Eds.), *Many pathways to literacy: Young children learning with siblings, grandparents, peers and communities*. New York: Routledge Falmer.

Haight, W., Rhodes, J., & Nicholson, M. (2001). Cross-race mentoring: Perspectives of mentors over time and strategies for support. *The Mentor: Journal of Mentoring and Field Experience, 1*(1), 8–17.

Hale-Benson, J. (1987). *The transmission of faith to young black children*. Paper presented at the Conference on Faith Development in Early Childhood, Henderson, NC.

Hudley, E., Haight, W., & Miller, P. (2003). *Raise up a child: Human development in an African-American family*. Chicago: Lyceum Books.

Jarrett, R. L. (1995). Growing up poor: The family experiences of socially mobile youth in low-income African-American neighborhoods. *Journal of Adolescent Research, 1*(1), 111–135.

Jarrett, R. L. (1997). Resilience among low-income African-American youth: An ethnographic perspective. *Ethos, 25*(2), 218–229.

Jessor, R., Colby, A., & Shweder, R. A. (Eds.). (1996). *Ethnography and human development: Context, and meaning in social inquiry*. Chicago: University of Chicago Press.

Lincoln, C. E. (1999). *Race, religion, and the continuing American dilemma*. New York: Hill and Wang.

Long, C. H. (1997). Perspective for the study of African-American religion in the United States. In E. Fulop & A. Raboteau (Eds.), *African-American religion: Interpretive essays in history and culture*. New York: Routledge.

Mitchell, E. P. (1986). Oral tradition: Legacy of faith for the black church. *Religious Education, 81,* 93–112.

Piaget, J. (1928). *Judgment and reasoning in the child*. London: Routledge & Kegan Paul.

Pinderhughes, E. (1989). *Understanding race, ethnicity, and power: The key to efficacy in clinical practice*. New York: Free Press.

Potts, R. (1996). Spirituality and the experience of cancer in an African-American community: Implications for psychosocial oncology. *Journal of Psychosocial Oncology, 14,* 1–19.

Ratcliff, D. (Ed.). (2004). *Children's spirituality: Christian perspectives, research, and applications.* Eugene, OR: Cascade Books.

Rogoff, B. (2000). *Culture and development.* New York: Oxford University Press.

Rosengren, K. S., Johnson, C. N., & Harris, P. L. (2000). *Imagining the impossible: Magical, scientific, and religious thinking in children.* New York: Cambridge University Press.

Rubin, K., Bukowski, W., & Parker, J. (1998). Peer interactions, relationships, and groups. In W. Damon (Series Ed.) & N. Eisenberg (Vol. Ed.), *Handbook of child psychology: Vol. 3. Social, emotional, and personality development* (5th ed.). New York: Wiley.

Saleebey, D. (2003). Strengths-based practice. In R. English (Ed.), *Encyclopedia of social work* (Supplement). Washington, DC: NASW Press.

Sameroff, A. J., & Haith, M. M. (1996). *The five to seven year shift: The age of reason and responsibility.* Chicago: University of Chicago Press.

Sanders, M. G. (1997). Overcoming obstacles: Academic achievement as a response to racism and discrimination. *Journal of Negro Education, 66*(1), 83–93.

Sheridan, M., Bullis, R., Adcock, C., Berlin, S., & Miller, P. C. (1992). Practitioners' personal and professional attitudes and behaviors toward religion and spirituality: Issues for education and practice. *Journal of Social Work in Education, 28,* 190–203.

Smitherman, G. (1977). *Talkin and testifyin: The language of black America.* Boston: Houghton Mifflin.

Sobel, M. (1988). *Travelin' on: A slave journey to an Afro-Baptist faith.* Princeton, NJ: Princeton University Press.

Sperry, L., & Sperry, D. (1996). Early development of narrative skills. *Cognitive Development, 11,* 443–465.

Stack, C. B. (1974). *All our kin: Strategies for survival in a black community.* New York: Harper & Row.

Suina, J., & Smolkin, L. (1994). From natal culture to school culture to dominant society culture: Supporting transitions for Pueblo Indian students. In P. Greenfield & Cocking (Eds.), *Cross-cultural roots of minority child development* (pp. 115–130). Hillsdale, NJ: Erlbaum.

Tamminen, K. (1991). *Religious development in childhood and youth: An empirical study.* Helsinki: Suomalainen Tiedeakatemia.

Tamminen, K. (1994). Religious experiences in childhood and adolescence: A view point of religious development between the ages of 7 and 20. *International Journal for the Psychology of Religion, 4*(2), 61–85.

Figure 4.1. A positive, supportive relationship with an adult such as a mentor is a protective factor for young teens. This 13-year-old girl is enjoying a visit with her grandmother, a retired middle school teacher.

4

Social Work with Adolescents: Mentoring in Schools

Susan A. Cole, Wendy L. Haight, and Edward H. Taylor

This chapter considers the adolescent as the focal system. As you read, consider the emerging biological, psychological, and social characteristics of the 11- to 22-year-old. In the United States and other industrialized societies, school remains an important context for development for many individuals throughout adolescence. The school is also the context in which social workers play important roles delivering services to adolescents. An intervention that has grown tremendously in popularity is mentoring, including school-based programs. As you read, consider the mesosytems created between microsystems formed at school, home, and the community through school-based mentoring programs. How might such mesosytems affect and be affected by the developing adolescent?

Social work with adolescents can be challenging and rewarding. Jean-Jacques Rousseau (1762/1911) likened adolescence to a violent storm, and G. Stanley Hall (1904) called it a period of storm and stress brought about by raging hormones. Researchers no longer view adolescence as necessarily more stressful than childhood or adulthood. Adolescents display a wide range of responses to puberty and other developmental changes, from pride and enjoyment of new roles to more cautious or even negative responses. Nevertheless, the legacy of Rousseau and Hall remains and adolescents have become one of the most stereotyped groups in contemporary society, widely portrayed in the media as delinquent, sex crazed, or tormented (Steinberg, 2002).

Although modern scholars would disagree with such stereotypes, they agree that adolescence is a time of rapid development. From approximately 11 to 22 years of age, adolescents negotiate biological, psychological, social, and economic transitions as they prepare to assume adult roles. The expectations of adults for how and when adolescents make the transition to adulthood, and what roles and responsibilities are appropriate for them, vary by culture. The gradual acquisition of new roles is shaped within an increasing variety of social contexts including family, work, leisure, and community organizations. For many individuals, especially in the United States and other industrialized nations, school remains a central context of development throughout adolescence. The mentoring interventions that are the focus of school social work interventions described in this chapter often support students who feel alienated, unsupported, or confused by traditional school programs.

SCHOOL SOCIAL WORK WITH ADOLESCENTS

School social work emerged at the turn of the twentieth century from a concern for underprivileged children and youth. School social workers, called "visiting teachers," visited the homes of immigrant children to develop links between families and schools. A primary role of modern school social workers remains that of home-school-community liaison. Today, school social work is an active and growing profession with approximately 15,000 members in the United States (Allen-Meares, 1999). It blends the fields of education and social work to support the well-being and academic achievement of children in school. To accomplish these objectives, school social workers provide direct interventions to children and families (e.g., school-based tutoring programs), arrange for services in the community (e.g., ongoing evaluation and counseling for a child identified with possible *attention deficit disorder* or *attention deficit disorder with hyperactivity*), and advocate for children to make schools more responsive to their needs (e.g., advocate for schools to adopt positive approaches to discipline). The school social worker functions in all three roles when serving on the multidisciplinary team with parents, psychologists, and other relevant school staff members who develop *individual education plans* (IEPs), formal plans to address difficulties students may be experiencing in school.

How school social workers support and advocate for children varies by state and by school district. In some areas, school social workers primarily do assessment and referral to community resources for therapeutic interventions. In other areas, the school social worker actually engages the student and family in therapeutic interventions. In rural areas, the school social worker may be an especially important resource to children, adolescents, and their families because resources are limited for psychosocial screening, assessment, intervention, and referral (Cole, 1993).

Typically, the specific tasks of a school social worker are diverse. On any given day in Illinois a social worker may facilitate a group of students experiencing grief from the death of a family member, struggling with their parents' divorces, or experiencing pregnancy and parenting. Box 4.1 describes some of the challenges faced by pregnant and parenting teens. The social worker may then meet with a group of community volunteers to educate them for working as mentors for middle school children. The social worker may then meet with teachers, school administrators, and community leaders to develop school policies for responding to the increasing cultural diversity of our public schools. Later, the social worker may meet with parents in

BOX 4.1 TEEN PREGNANCY

Although adolescent birth rates in the United States have declined, the U.S. teen pregnancy rate exceeds those in most developed countries. In 2002 approximately 860,000 American teens became pregnant and about half this number gave birth. Girls younger than 18 accounted for about 43% of all teen pregnancies.

Teen pregnancy is an important risk factor to development in adolescence. Teen mothers and their babies face increased physical health risks and decreased future opportunities. With proper support, adolescent mothers can finish their educations, sustain lasting romantic and other interpersonal relationships, and successfully parent their children. As a group, however, they face more economic, health, and developmental difficulties than other young women. To adequately support young women, we need to:

- develop programs that help prevent teen pregnancy;
- provide a gateway for physical, emotional, and educational support early in the pregnancy;
- prepare and assist the teen in making an informed choice on whether or not to carry the fetus to term;
- prepare and assist the teen for making an informed choice on whether or not to parent the child upon delivery or place the child in an adoptive home;
- ensure that teen mothers who choose to parent know how to care for a baby, have a safe environment, and have the required financial and emotional support;
- intervene to minimize the risk that the young woman will become pregnant again soon, thereby overwhelming her and her social support system;
- find productive ways to ensure that the father provides financial, physical, and emotional support for the child.

A challenge for social workers is to discover interventions and educational methods that increase sexual responsibility in both adolescent boys and girls. Teenage boys can be left out of the psychosocial education equation once the girl is pregnant. This not only penalizes the girl but may also stand in the way of the teenage male's emotional and social growth. That is, the boy is not challenged to develop sexual responsibility or efficacy before or after the pregnancy. In addition to understanding the dangers of unprotected sex, adolescent boys need help comprehending that once pregnancy occurs, they have moral responsibilities to the mother, developing baby, and society. The goal is not to prevent or delay sexuality by threatening adolescents but rather to improve and increase their abstract thinking skills, empathy, and understanding of moral-social responsibilities.

Source: *Teen pregnancy*. (2005). White Plains, NY: March of Dimes Birth Defects Foundation. Available at: http://www.marchofdimes.com/professionals/681_1159.asp

their home to discuss the development and functioning of a child referred for assessment of a possible learning disorder.

As this overview suggests, school social work relies both on ecological and developmental theories. Ecological perspectives in school social work emphasize the relations of the child, family, school, and community as they affect educational outcomes (Allen-Meares, 1999; Germain, 1999; Monkman, 1999). Understanding children's development alerts the school social worker to potential problems and suggests intervention strategies (Haight, Carpenter, & Tata, 1999). Understanding adolescent development may help a school social worker distinguish depression from normative stress, and whether referral to a therapist, community psychiatrist, or school mentoring program is most appropriate. It also alerts school social workers to potential mismatches between children's developmental needs and the demands of the school system (Allen-Meares, 1999). Puberty is a universal, socially significant developmental transition that occurs at about the same time that many young adolescents move from small, personal elementary school classrooms to large middle schools with multiple teachers and new peers (Germain, 1999). School social workers, anticipating the stress that may emerge as a result of the mismatch between children's developmental needs for support during early adolescence and large school systems, may advocate for change in the school system (e.g., for elementary-style education to extend through eighth grade). In addition, they may develop prevention interventions such as school-based mentoring programs to establish personal, trusting relationships for children with an adult to compensate for the impersonal nature of the existing middle school system.

The following excerpt describes the informal mentoring between a young adolescent in foster care and a retired child protective service worker.

> Jeremy is a 13-year-old child living in the rural Midwest. He is in foster care following his parents' arrest for manufacturing methamphetamine. His parents are now serving long prison sentences and Jeremy is facing adolescence in long-term foster care. Fortunately, Jeremy has been placed with loving foster parents who genuinely care for and support him. He is thriving in a home with structure: regular meals, bedtimes, school attendance, leisure activities, and, most of all, available parents. Nevertheless, Jeremy is aware of the stigma associated with methamphetamine abuse in his small community and feels pressure to be a "perfect child" for his foster parents. In addition, Jeremy feels great ambivalence about distancing himself from the parents he loves. He also feels tremendous rage at being separated from his parents.
>
> Shortly after entering foster care, Jeremy was matched through a mentoring program with Lydia, a retired child protection worker who lives in his community. Lydia picks Jeremy up from school every Thursday and they go to "their restaurant" for a treat and to talk. Because she lives in the same small town as Jeremy, Lydia has had the opportunity to videotape one of Jeremy's baseball games. Jeremy treasures his time with Lydia, in part, because it makes him feel special. As a child who experienced neglect in his birth home and is one of seven foster children, he has received precious little one-on-one time

with adults. As their relationship has deepened, Lydia has proven to be an invaluable sounding board for Jeremy to express his anger and grief. By listening, providing an adult perspective, and communicating her unconditional positive regard, Lydia has become a major source of support for Jeremy.

In this excerpt, the term "mentor" is used to refer to a relationship between an older, more experienced adult and an unrelated younger person in which the adult provides ongoing guidance, instruction, and encouragement. Over time, the mentor and young person may develop a special bond of mutual commitment, respect, identification, and loyalty. This relationship supports the adolescent's well-being and development and facilitates the transition into adulthood (Rhodes, 2002).

Research suggests that informal relationships with caring adults such as Lydia can make an important difference in the lives of vulnerable children and adolescents (Garmezy, 1985; Robins & Rutter, 1990; Werner & Smith, 1982). Adolescents who grew up under extremely difficult circumstances and yet somehow succeeded often credit their success to the influence of an informal role model or mentor (Anderson, 1991; Fisher, 2001; Freedman, 1995; Lefkowitz, 1986; Levine & Nidiffer, 1996). Support from natural mentors—more experienced people with whom the adolescent has established an informal supportive relationship—is associated with improvements in the psychological, social, academic, and career functioning of at-risk adolescents (McLearn, Colasanto, & Schoen, 1998; Rhodes & Davis, 1996). Adolescents with natural mentors are less likely to smoke marijuana or engage in delinquent activities (Zimmerman, Bingenheimer, & Notaro, 2002). Unfortunately, relatively few adolescents spontaneously develop such relationships with natural mentors (Rhodes & Davis, 1996). Even for those adolescents predisposed to do so, families, schools, and communities have changed in ways that have dramatically reduced the availability of caring adults. Families are increasingly mobile, and, because crime rates have risen, parents increasingly sequester their children at home, cutting off opportunities for contact with supportive, caring adult neighbors (Rhodes, Bogat, Roffman, Edelman, & Galasso, 2002).

One approach to intervention with adolescents has been to develop formal mentoring programs, which pair supportive adults with vulnerable adolescents. In recent years, thousands of mentoring programs have emerged. These efforts have included a wide range of youth (pregnant teenagers, African American boys) and volunteers (teachers, community members, executives, and elderly people) (McLearn, Colasanto, & Schoen, 1998). Beyond their intuitive appeal, research suggests that mentors assigned through more formal volunteer programs can positively affect youth outcomes through a combination of emotional support, practical assistance, and role modeling (Rhodes, 2002). Formal mentors promote social and emotional development and school achievement, provide critical support to pregnant and parenting teenagers, and reduce delinquent behavior and substance abuse (Grossman & Tierney, 1998; Morrow & Styles, 1995; Rhodes,

2002; Rhodes, Contreras, & Mangelsdorf, 1994; Sipe, 2002; Tierney, Grossman, & Resch, 1995).

Mentoring programs exist in a wide variety of forms. A promising trend is site-based mentoring (Rhodes, 2002). Currently, approximately 45 percent of mentoring programs are site based, and more than 70 percent of these are located in schools. These programs can capitalize on the knowledge, referrals, supervision, and support of the many adults who are already in the setting. Although existing empirical evidence is still sparse, there is some evidence that school-based mentors can positively affect academic outcomes and relationships with teachers (Herrera, 1999; Curtis & Hansen-Schwoebel, 1999; Rhodes, 2002). High-quality school-based mentoring programs are promising prevention interventions for which school social workers may advocate, support, and provide services.

HIGHLIGHTS OF DEVELOPMENT DURING ADOLESCENCE

Mentoring is an intervention particularly well suited to adolescence, a time of life when young people increasingly explore relationships outside of the family. Roughly speaking, adolescence is the second decade of life. Although at one time adolescence was synonymous with the teenage years (13–19), the adolescent period has lengthened in the past century both because young people mature earlier physically and because so many people remain economically dependent on their parents into their 20s. In the United States and other industrialized countries, adolescence begins around 10 years of age and ends in the early 20s. Because of the vast changes that occur between 10 and 22 years of age, developmental psychologists find it useful to divide adolescence into three periods: early adolescence (10–13 years), middle adolescence (14–18 years), and late adolescence or youth (19–22 years). For those who remain in school, these periods roughly correspond to the middle school, high school, and college years (Steinberg, 2002).

An analysis of 175 societies around the world indicates that adolescence is a widespread, if not universal, social stage (Schlegel & Barry, 1991). Adolescents master the skills necessary for economic survival, learn the appropriate social roles associated with adult status, develop emotional independence from parents and other adults, acquire a deeper understanding of their culture's values and ethical system, and learn to behave in a socially responsible fashion as defined by their culture (Grotevant, 1998). For some adolescents, this developmental period is cut short because of poverty or victimization, and the young person may never acquire the skills and values necessary to participate in mainstream society. Box 4.2 describes research by a Taiwanese social worker involved in an intervention designed to help aboriginal girls in Taiwan victimized by prostitution to develop the values and vocational skills necessary to function in mainstream society.

BOX 4.2 INTERNATIONAL PERSPECTIVES
Juvenile Prostitution in Taiwan

As in other parts of the world, juvenile prostitution is a serious issue in Taiwan. The government has responded by creating and supporting residential vocational centers to protect and counsel adolescent girls arrested for prostitution. Such institutions provide young women with a safe home, opportunities to develop alternative means of self-support, and role models. Sadly, a number of the teenagers return to prostitution after leaving the vocational centers. In an effort to better understand the problem of juvenile prostitution in Taiwan and strengthen intervention programs, Mary Ku, a Taiwanese social worker, researched the risk and protective factors for juvenile prostitution. She found that children's experiences of crushing poverty, domestic violence and maltreatment in their homes, identification as a "bad girl," and sexual abuse were among the risk factors for entry into prostitution. Protective factors that facilitated adolescents' reentry into a conventional lifestyle included cutting ties with previous boyfriends, changes in attitudes toward sexuality, negative experiences in prostitution such as rape and other forms of violence, successful substance abuse rehabilitation, and a positive relationship with a family member.

Source: Ku, M. (2003). *Life stories of aboriginal juvenile prostitutes in Taiwan.* Unpublished doctoral dissertation, University of Illinois, Urbana-Champaign.

The length of adolescence and the degree to which it is associated with social and psychological disruptions vary greatly across societies. In the United States and other industrialized societies, a gap of seven to nine years typically separates biological changes that mark the onset of sexual maturity from the social changes that confer adult status, such as the right to vote or to marry without parental consent. This lengthy adolescent period has developed in mainstream society in the United States because of the time required to acquire the knowledge and skills necessary to be independent and to perpetuate society (Cole & Cole, 2001). It is also linked to a lengthy life expectancy and limited training and economic opportunities for older adolescents outside the educational track (Boonstra, 2002).

By contrast, in some societies there is a relatively brief delay between the beginning of sexual maturity and the beginning of adulthood (Whiting et al., 1986). These are usually societies in which biological maturity occurs late by Western standards and in which the level of technology is relatively low. By the time biological reproduction becomes possible, at about 15 years of age in many nonindustrial societies, young people already know how to perform the basic tasks of their culture such as farming, weaving cloth, preparing food, and caring for children (Cole & Cole, 2001).

Biological Factors

Because of the variation across time and place in the age of onset and length of adolescence, many developmental psychologists prefer to define adolescence as a series of intertwined biological, psychological, social, and economic transitions from immaturity to maturity (Sternberg, 2002). The biological transition, known as puberty, results in dramatic changes in the adolescent's physical appearance and in capability for sexual reproduction. One of the first visible signs of puberty is the adolescent growth spurt. People grow more quickly during the adolescent growth spurt than at any other time of life except infancy. In the span of two to three years, boys may grow as much as 9 inches, and girls as much as 6 or 7 inches. Muscle tissue and fat also increase dramatically (Cole & Cole, 2001). The magnitude and rate of physical changes experienced during puberty may be more significant than those of infancy because of their psychological effects as the adolescent reflects upon and interprets those changes. As described in box 4.3, the physical and mental health of adolescents in the United States may be threatened by inadequate access to health care because of poverty.

There is wide variation in the age at which puberty begins and its duration. The first pubertal changes (growth of breasts for girls, and growth of testes and scrotal sac for boys) typically occur between 7 and 9½ years of age for girls, and 9½ and 13 for boys (Steinberg, 2002). The age at which puberty begins depends on complex interactions of genetic and environmental factors such as caloric intake, health, nutrition, and stress. Perhaps because of changes in living standards, there have been striking historical changes in the onset of puberty. In the 1840s, the average age of menarche among women of European descent was between 14 and 15 years, whereas today it is between 12 and 13 years (Steinberg, 2002).

BOX 4.3 POVERTY ACROSS THE LIFE SPAN
Hospitalization

Many low-income families either have no health insurance or have policies that do not adequately cover pregnancies and mental disorders. Yet the leading cause of hospitalization for children ages 10 through 14 years is mental disorders. For individuals ages 15 through 21 years, pregnancy and childbirth account for the largest number of inpatient admissions, with mental disorders accounting for the second highest cause for hospitalization. With adequate ongoing mental health care, many youth experiencing mental health problems could avoid hospitalization. Likewise, with adequate prenatal care, many problems of pregnancy and childbirth could be reduced.

Source: Health Resources and Services Administration, Maternal and Child Health Bureau. (2002). *Child health USA 2002* (p. 25). Washington, DC: U.S. Department of Health and Human Services.

Mentors can provide support and reassurance to young adolescents experiencing puberty. Many parents and young adolescents find discussing pubertal changes to be awkward and uncomfortable. Mentors can serve as resources, helping young people to interpret and respond to the psychological and social implications of physical maturity by supporting the young person in maintaining a positive body image, examining body image and sexual norms presented in the media, and coaching him/her about developing positive interpersonal relationships.

During puberty, many individuals also experience a consolidation of their sexual orientation as heterosexual, bisexual, or homosexual that will remain largely stable throughout their lives (Zucker & Bradley, 2004). There is growing evidence that sexual orientation is biologically based, a result of interactions of genes and other physiological factors (Gladue, 1994). There also is some evidence that differences in brain structure and hormone production may relate to sexual orientation (LeVay, 1993; Berenbaum & Snyder, 1995). As would be predicted from a biological model, a higher rate of joint homosexuality is found in identical twins than fraternal and nontwin siblings (LeVay, 1993). Environmental factors may delay or suppress the expression of a gay, lesbian, or bisexual identity, but research on sexual orientation has largely discredited theories that posit a causal role to family relationships (Freud, 1922/1959) and social learning (Isay, 1990).

Adolescents who find themselves in the sexual minority face real and significant challenges. Throughout modern history, sexual minorities have been penalized and labeled as deviant. Hitler placed gay men and lesbian women in concentration camps, religions demonized and excommunicated them, previous psychiatric diagnostic manuals called them disordered and in need of treatment, and public laws stripped away their civil rights. While progress has been made, stigma remains. In part this occurs because of the popular belief that one becomes homosexual by choice—a position not supported by modern research.

Mentors can play an important role in the lives of children who are sexual minorities. Often family members respond insensitively to young people because of their personal religious values or their own confusion (Longres & Etnyrem, 2004). Youth who come out during adolescence may be at risk for homelessness, victimization (Rivers & D'Augelli, 2001; Jucovy, 2000; Ryan & Fetterman, 1998), sexual exploitation (Graber & Archibald, 2001), and suicide (Proctor & Groze, 1994; Hershberger & D'Augelli, 2001). Mentors can provide such youth with perspective, psychological support and affirmation, and advocacy.

Psychological Factors

The psychological transitions of adolescence are also dramatic and include changes in thinking (Piaget & Inhelder, 1958). Compared to children, adolescents are better able to think about hypothetical situations and abstract concepts such as friendship, democracy, and morality. These changes have far-reaching effects in the adolescent's ability to plan ahead, reason scientifically, and consider moral dilemmas. Adolescents can begin to think in logical ways about what their lives will be like in the future, about their relationships with friends and family, and about politics, religion, and philosophy (see Steinberg, 2002; Anda, 1995; Cole & Cole, 2001). These changes in thinking are facilitated by school attendance. Unfortunately, poverty forces many adolescents in the United States to drop out of school (see box 4.4).

Mentors can facilitate psychological development, including intellectual changes in their protégés, through social interaction. The twentieth-century Russian psychologist Lev Vygotsky described intellectual development as proceeding from the interpersonal to the intrapersonal (Wertsch, 1985). Through interaction with others (interpersonal processes) who are more

··

Box 4.4 POVERTY ACROSS THE LIFE SPAN

School Drop Out

Between 1999 and 2000 approximately 488,000 youths dropped out of high school. Adolescents living in poverty or near poverty are five times more likely to drop out of school than teens from middle- and high-income families. Youths living in poverty may experience hunger, lack of clothing, the need to work to help support their families, illness, multiple family moves, safety concerns, and lack of academic support.

Since 1970 Hispanic youths have had the highest school drop-out rate:

• School drop-out rate for foreign-born Hispanic youths in 2000 was 44.2%.

• School drop-out rate for first- and second-generation Hispanic youths born in the United States in 2000 was 14.6% and 16%, respectively.

_____

Source: Health Resources and Services Administration, Maternal and Child Health Bureau. (2002). *Child health USA 2002* (p. 6). Washington, DC: U.S. Department of Health and Human Services.

··

experienced and who scaffold and support the developing person's emerging competencies, the developing person functions at a higher level of intellectual competence. As a result of such interpersonal processes, the less experienced individual, over time, acquires the independent cognitive abilities (intrapersonal processes) to function at that higher level. For example, the mentor scaffolds the youth's emerging abilities to think in more abstract ways about the self in relation to others. As a result of this support, the adolescent's competence increases, and she gradually acquires the ability to engage in abstract thought independently of the mentor.

Social Factors

As changes in physical, cognitive, and social abilities emerge throughout adolescence, social relations with adults and peers are reconstructed. Relationships with peers remain central, but now may include a sexual and romantic component. In early adolescence, peers begin to socialize in mixed-gender groups, for example, going to the movies or the mall with a group of boys and girls, and attending parties. Later in adolescence, individuals may pair off and begin dating (see Steinberg, 2002).

Relationships with parents also remain central in adolescence. The changes in responsibilities and social roles that occur during adolescence, however, may cause some friction as adolescents and their parents renegotiate their social relations (Cole & Cole, 2001). This may be especially difficult for young people who mature into adults different from the one imagined or planned for by their parents due to physical or mental disabilities, gender identification, or chosen career pathways. As youth remain dependent on their parents for longer and longer periods of time to obtain increased levels of education or as an economic strategy, such negotiations may occur repeatedly.

BOX 4.5 VIOLENCE ACROSS THE LIFE SPAN
Teens and Guns

Thousands of adolescents are killed annually by firearms. In 2000, 2,524 adolescents ages 15 through 19 years were killed by guns. Fifty-nine percent of these youths were murdered, 35% committed suicide, and 4% of the deaths resulted from an accidental shooting.

Source: Health Resources and Services Administration, Maternal and Child Health Bureau. (2002). *Child health USA 2002* (p. 47). Washington, DC: U.S. Department of Health and Human Services.

Sadly, these important social transitions in relationships may be skewed when adolescents must live and learn in violent peer groups, schools, and communities. Violence not only threatens the physical well-being of adolescents; it also affects the development of their relationships with adults and with peers (see boxes 4.5–4.8).

The transitions of adolescence inevitably result in profound shifts in an adolescent's sense of self and understanding of others: parents, teachers, siblings, and peers. Changes in social status permit young people to try new roles and engage in new activities, such as work and intimate relationships, which dramatically alter how they perceive themselves and their relationships with others. This newfound independence can make discussing these important changes with parents difficult for many adolescents, thus making the role of mentors very important.

BOX 4.6 VIOLENCE ACROSS THE LIFE SPAN

Homicide, Suicide, and Accidental Death of Older Teens

For adolescents ages 15 through 19 years living in the United States, homicide is the second leading cause of death, followed by suicide. Fifteen percent of all deaths in this age group result from murder, and 12% from suicide.

Forty-nine percent of the deaths in this age group result from accidental injuries. Seventy-eight percent of accidental deaths in this age group are the result of automobile crashes. Approximately 14% of youths in this age group report that they rarely or never use seat belts when riding in a car driven by another person.

Source: Health Resources and Services Administration, Maternal and Child Health Bureau. (2002). *Child health USA 2002* (p. 546–47). Washington, DC: U.S. Department of Health and Human Services.

Parents are also experiencing a role transition from decision maker to facilitator, coach, and cheerleader. This transition is often difficult for parents, who naturally continue to feel responsible for their children's struggles, are not quite sure of their children's new competencies, and want to help their adolescent solve problems as quickly as possible. Although relationships with parents continue to be very important for most adolescents, conflicts with parents typically increase, especially during early adolescence. Family members' physical proximity and vested interest in an adolescent can cause them to overreact or become judgmental. Parents who have been the primary relationship in their children's lives also may experience difficulties as adolescents' peer relationships gain in importance.

Informal and formal mentors such as extended family members, teachers, coaches, church elders, and other community members have the advantage of standing outside these family struggles. They can provide a safe haven

BOX 4.7 VIOLENCE ACROSS THE LIFE SPAN

School Violence

School violence continues to be a problem in the United States. Bullying can take many forms including verbal and nonverbal threats, physical attacks, and destruction of property. Although the number of high school adolescents carrying weapons to school decreased 21% between 1993 and 2001, 9% of students reported being threatened with a weapon while attending school.

Source: Health Resources and Services Administration, Maternal and Child Health Bureau. (2002). *Child health USA 2002* (p. 6). Washington, DC: U.S. Department of Health and Human Services.

BOX 4.8 VIOLENCE ACROSS THE LIFE SPAN

Adolescent Risk and Protective Factors for Violent Behavior

Between 1994 and 1995 more than 90,000 adolescents in grades 7 through 12 were surveyed in approximately 80 communities across the United States. The research concluded that several factors place adolescents at a greater risk for violent behaviors. For both boys and girls, the most predictive factors for violent behavior were previous involvement in violence and a history of victimization. For boys, the third-ranked predictors included having repeated a grade in school and having carried a weapon to school. For girls, the third-ranked predictors included having carried a weapon to school, used alcohol, and experienced emotional distress.

A number of factors appear to help adolescents control aggressive impulses and avoid participation in violence. For boys, protective factors include positive parental school expectations, ability to discuss problems with parents, and positive relationships with adults. For girls, protective factors include school achievement, strong relationship or connectedness within their families, religious participation and beliefs, and feeling connected to their school.

Another survey of 250 rural students found that many high school students have difficulty applying these protective factors. Sixty percent of the students reported a belief that no adult really understands teenagers, 42% believed that not being part of the right peer group prevented personal acceptance at school, and 34% reported knowing someone in school who was often lonely. More worrisome is that 29% of the students admitted that they often feel depressed, and 15% stated that they have thought about committing suicide. These responses demonstrate that many adolescents feel alone, cut off from meaningful dialogue with adults, and disconnected from peers and school.

Resnick, M., Ireland, M., Borowsky, I. (2004). Youth violence perpetration: What protects? What predicts? Findings from the National Longitudinal Study of Adolescent Health. *Adolescent Health, 35,* 424–434; Taylor, E. H. (2005). *A survey of violent perceptions and self-destructive thoughts in rural students.* Unpublished manuscript.

for teens to air sensitive issues, while still transmitting adult values, advice, and perspectives. Unlike parental advice, which adolescents are often quick to dismiss, guidance and encouragement from a concerned adult noncaregiver is sometimes considered more seriously, particularly if the mentor has experience that the primary caregiver lacks. Peers, who also stand outside the family, are often struggling with similar transitions and lack the experience, knowledge, and intellectual sophistication to assist with complex issues. Mentors can fill a unique niche for adolescents, somewhere between their parents and peers (Rhodes, 2002).

The economic transitions of adolescence include the initiation of paid work. Work often provides affirmation that the educational system is not providing. Some adolescents contribute to the economic well-being of their families. They are drawn into the work of the family, for example, migrant workers and small business owners. Such activities may have psychological as well as financial payoffs through increased self-esteem for their necessary contribution to their family. Too many hours of work, however, can interfere with school achievement.

Many adolescents also choose to engage in some form of part-time paid work, which has the potential to increase responsibility, teach skills, and provide adult role models. However, work in settings typical to adolescent workers (e.g., fast-food or other service jobs) do not necessarily teach skills useful to the adolescent as an adult worker or provide successful adult role models. Work in some settings may lead to cynicism, poor attitudes toward work, and "premature affluence" (because the youth's basic needs are being provided for by the parents, the youth becomes accustomed to luxury items she will not be able to afford as an independent young adult) (Steinberg, 2002).

One way that many adolescents have of bridging the gap of school and work is through volunteer activities in work environments that they are drawn to as possible career paths. Some adolescents volunteer in hospitals, children's facilities, churches, and work projects such as Habitat for Humanity. As they begin to explore how they might fit into the adult world of work and responsibilities, mentors function as role models, exemplifying the knowledge, skills, and behavior that adolescents hope someday to acquire (Rhodes, 2002).

It is important to note that biological, psychological, social, and economic transitions interact within, and cannot be understood apart from, particular cultural and historical contexts. For example, the changes of puberty initiate a reorganization of the child's social life including changes in the nature of interactions with peers, friends, and family members. Early maturation generally has positive effects on boys, and negative effects on girls. A boy's body image typically remains positive throughout puberty. Furthermore, early maturing boys tend to be leaders and to be viewed as socially and psychologically mature by adults and peers. In contrast, many early maturing girls are embarrassed and dissatisfied with their bodies. They are more likely to enter into sexual relationships in mid-adolescence and experience a decline in academic performance and an increase in problem behaviors (see Cole & Cole, 2001; Anda, 1995).

Cultural-Historical Factors

Cultural and historical contexts can exacerbate or ease the challenges inherent to adolescent development. Gender differences in children's responses to early versus late maturation may be related to cultural ideals for body types (Steinberg, 2002). Muscles and bulk are prized in males, so that boys' physiques become closer to the cultural ideal as they progress through puberty. In contrast, a pubescent body shape may be idealized for women, especially within middle-class North American communities. During puberty, the average girl gains a little over 24 pounds in the form of body fat (Cole & Cole, 2001). Thus, as a girl proceeds through puberty, her body becomes less like the cultural ideal. Indeed, many girls worry about weight gain, and their body images decline. Approximately 53 percent of girls are dissatisfied with their bodies by the age of 13, and many begin a pattern of weight obsession and dieting as early as 8 or 9 (Brumberg, 1997). Girls' responses to early maturation, however, are not uniform. For example, African American girls are less likely than European American and Asian girls to develop a negative body image (Neuman-Sztainer et al., 2002), perhaps because a wider variation of female body types is appreciated in these communities (Steinberg, 2002).

During the Victorian period, the consensus in middle-class and upperclass families was that adolescent girls deserved special attention and consideration because of their biology (Brumberg, 1997). A protective umbrella was created by female community members and spread over middle-class adolescent girls from school to extracurricular activities. Between the 1880s and the 1920s, thousands of girls received mentoring by young women through Girl Scouts, the Camp Fire Girls, the Young Women's Christian Association, Bible study groups, literary societies, and other religious and secular organizations. In her analysis of the diaries of adolescent girls, Brumberg (1997) found that middle-class Victorian girls repeatedly wrote about the informal mentoring they received from their young female teachers and leaders. These women viewed the nurturing of all younger women, not only their biological kin, as their ethical responsibility. Through mentoring in extracurricular activities, girls described enjoyable and meaningful interaction with their female mentors.

Many modern communities do not provide the extended nurturance to adolescent girls as did the Victorian protective umbrella. Yet adolescent girls today are under more pressure and are at greater risk because of a unique combination of biological and cultural forces. Modern girls mature earlier, but there is no parallel increase in their emotional and intellectual development, creating greater vulnerability. Modern fashions and the media sexualize even prepubescent girls and focus on external appearance. In parallel to this trend, Brumberg (1998) documents a heightened concern with physical appearance in the diaries of modern girls. By contrast, in middle- and upperclass Victorian culture, girls' inner beauty—moral character, service to others, and spirituality—was prized (see Brumberg, 1998).

Clearly, there were many problems with the Victorians' protective umbrella. For example, it did not extend over girls from lower-income families, who were sent to be servants in the homes of the wealthy, sent out to work in sweat shops, or forced into prostitution because of poverty. In addition, young women today enjoy greater personal freedom and are able to make more educational, professional, and social choices than their counterparts a century ago.

A lesson that modern school social workers may learn from the Victorian model, however, is the protective value of personal attention and mentoring. Early adolescence can be a period of stress and increased vulnerability for young women due to physical changes and the entrance into teen culture with its new pressures and demands. Yet the educational structure in many communities superimposes additional stress by transferring children from elementary to middle schools. The security achieved in a small, self-contained classroom with a single teacher or stable homeroom can be lost in the transition to middle school, where larger populations of young adolescents are confined together on a larger campus with rotating classes, multiple teachers, and increased academic demands (Germain, 1999). School social workers have responded to the challenge of integrating young adolescents into the middle school environment by advocating for changes in the structure of middle schools, designing transition activities for students finishing elementary school, and through prevention interventions such as mentoring.

The vast majority of adolescents and their families successfully negotiate the complex physical, social, and economic transitions of adolescence. Some adolescents, however, will develop psychological problems, drop out of school, become homeless, or turn to substance abuse, which not only curtails healthy social and emotional development but also presents health risks (see box 4.9).

THE DEVELOPMENT OF MENTORING RELATIONSHIPS

Jean Rhodes, a leading expert on mentoring, once commented that mentoring is "strong medicine": appropriately administered, it can be lifesaving, but administered incorrectly, it can be ineffective or, worse, toxic. Research indicates that not only does the positive impact of mentoring increase over time, but short-term relationships can actually be harmful to youth. It may take up to four months for some adolescents to lower their defenses and develop trust and for mentors and youth to feel an emotional connection (see Morrow & Styles, 1995). In their analysis of data from a national Big Brothers Big Sisters study, Grossman and Rhodes (2002) found that youth who were in relationships that lasted more than four months reported significantly higher levels of self-worth, social acceptance, and scholastic competence; and they reported that their relationships with their parents had improved, that school had become more rewarding, and that both their drug and alcohol use had declined. Yet a significant number of mentors and young people do not sustain their relationships. Only 45 percent of relationships were sustained for one year or more. Furthermore, youth who were in

BOX 4.9 SUBSTANCE ABUSE ACROSS THE LIFE SPAN
Marijuana

In the late 1990s a major study found that approximately 23.1% of eighth-grade students and 39.8% of tenth-grade students reported having used marijuana.

Approximately 25% of young people ages 18 through 21 have used the drug within the last year, and 14% used marijuana in the last 30 days. Young adult males, however, use marijuana at almost twice the frequency for young females.

For many people the most hazardous effect of using marijuana is identical to the carcinogenic and respiratory dangers caused by tobacco. However, marijuana abuse and recreational can result in:

- Psychological dependence
- Cannabis intoxication delirium
- Cannabis-induced psychotic disorder
- Cannabis-induced anxiety disorder

If a person suddenly stops taking high dosages of marijuana, withdrawal symptoms consisting of minor to moderate increases in irritability, restlessness, insomnia, anorexia, and nausea can be experienced.

Malanga, C. J., & Kosofsky, B. E. (2004). Effects of drug abuse on brain development. In D. S. Charney & E. J. Nestler (Eds.), *Neurobiology of mental illness* (2nd ed.). New York: Oxford University Press; Sadock, B. J., & Sadock, V. A. (2003). *Synopsis of psychiatry: Behavioral sciences/clinical psychiatry* (9th ed.). Philadelphia: Lippincott Williams & Wilkins.

matches that terminated within the first three months suffered significant drops in feelings of self-worth and perceived scholastic competence compared to youths without mentors. Because a personal relationship is the heart of mentoring, inconsistencies and terminations can touch the vulnerabilities of youth in ways that less personal youth programs do not (Rhodes, 2002). Generally, adolescence is a life stage during which issues of acceptance and rejection are paramount. Youth who have experienced unsatisfactory or rejecting parental relationships in the past may fear that others will not accept and support them. When adolescents sense that mentoring relationships are not going well, they may readily perceive intentional rejection (Rhodes, 2002).

Understanding the factors that lead to effective mentoring programs can help school social workers establish the best programs possible for adolescents. A major challenge to school social workers involved with mentoring programs is ensuring that matched adults and youth meet long enough and often enough to allow the possibility of establishing a relationship that could generate the life changes that mentoring programs seek to achieve. A developmental-ecological analysis of biological, psychological, social, and cultural aspects of mentoring has a variety of implications for establishing school-based programs to maximize the potential of mentoring and minimize the potential risks.

Biological Factors

Clearly, the teenage years are a period of tremendous biological changes occurring within a social and cultural context. The simple biological fact of age is a consideration of successful mentoring. By middle adolescence, youths' romantic involvements and close friendships may increasingly compete with their relationships with adults. There is some evidence that preteens and young teens are more responsive to mentoring than are older adolescents. Indeed, mentoring relationships with older adolescents are at higher risk for early termination than those with younger adolescents (Rhodes, 2002). Mentors of older adolescents tend to experience their relationships as less close and supportive than do mentors of preteens. These observations suggest the value of establishing mentoring relationships relatively early in adolescence. They also suggest that mentors of younger versus older adolescents need to be prepared for somewhat different roles.

Psychological Factors

Some adolescents struggle with issues of identity, relationships, and self-worth. Mentors can be strong allies and sources of support to youth. For many adolescents, simply sharing enjoyable activities with a caring adult—playing sports, games, eating out, talking, hanging out—can positively affect their sense of self-worth (see Morrow & Styles, 1995). Mentors also can be important sources of support for youth who are experiencing stress. Youth struggling with sexual identity may benefit from a safe, older mentor who has experienced similar struggles (Jucovy, 2000). Mentors may be able to assist adolescents in negotiating the special problems of transitioning to maturity in a society that is often intolerant of sexual identity struggles. Evidence suggests that mentoring programs are not as effective for youth experiencing severe psychological, social, or behavioral problems. For these youth, professional intervention is appropriate. At the other extreme, well-adjusted middle-class youth tend to derive relatively fewer benefits compared to youth who are facing some degree of difficulty in their lives. Youth who fall in the middle of the continuum of psychological and social functioning appear most likely to benefit from mentoring interventions (Rhodes, 2002). These observations suggest that school social workers participating in mentoring programs must support careful screening and assessment not just of potential mentors but of potential adolescent participants as well.

Social Factors

The heart of mentoring is the formation of an interpersonal relationship between a young person and an adult (Phillips, 2003). To be successful, men-

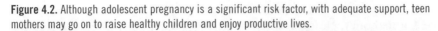

Figure 4.2. Although adolescent pregnancy is a significant risk factor, with adequate support, teen mothers may go on to raise healthy children and enjoy productive lives.

tor and youth must feel connected through mutual trust and a sense of being understood, liked, and respected (Rhodes, 2002). If an emotional bond does not develop, then the youth and mentor may disengage from the match before any positive change has occurred. When adolescents do form close relationships with mentors, their ability to connect with other adults, especially their parents, also improves (Grossman & Tierney, 1988). Interestingly, their relationships with peers also may improve, perhaps as a result of a changing sense of self-worth and improved social and leisure skills (Rhodes, Haight, & Briggs, 1999).

Although interpersonal relationships between the mentor and young person are central, they vary widely in their quality. Morrow & Styles (1995) examined eighty-two mentoring relationships over a nine-month period. They described two types of relationships: developmental and prescriptive. In *developmental relationships*, mentors' goals and expectations varied over time in relation to their perceptions of the adolescent's needs. In the beginning, these mentors devoted themselves to establishing a strong emotional connection with the young person and developing a reliable, trusting relationship. Mentors allowed youth to talk about anything without fear of judgment or reproach, reassuring youth of their availability when difficulties arose, and "just listening." These mentors possessed the ability to listen, understand, and accept the younger person. It was only after the relationship had solidified and strengthened and the youth's receptivity was established that developmental mentors expanded their focus to address other goals such as helping the young person improve in school and be more responsible. Throughout their involvement with the young person, mentors kept the relationships enjoyable and were flexible in their plans, responding to the adolescent's ideas and preferences. In developmental relationships, mentors and young people demonstrated strong attachments to one another. At the end of the nine-month study, 90 percent of developmental relationships continued to meet regularly.

In contrast, *prescriptive relationships* are defined as those in which mentors prioritized their goals for the match rather than the youth's and set the goals and ground rules for the relationship. Mentors' primary purpose was to transform the young people, to guide them toward embracing values, attitudes, and behaviors the mentors defined as positive. There were two subgroups of prescriptive relationships. In the first subgroup, mentors approached the match by setting goals (typically improving school performance) and focusing shared time on achieving these goals. In the second subgroup, mentors required youth to take equal responsibility for maintaining the relationship, a task beyond the capability of most young adolescents. Both subgroups of prescriptive volunteers resisted modifying their high expectations and ultimately felt frustrated. The youth were similarly frustrated, unsatisfied with the relationship, and less likely to share problems or regard their mentor as a source of consistent support. Over the nine-month period of the study, the tension in these relationships grew. At end of nine months, only 33 percent of prescriptive relationships continued to meet, and only 30 percent of those met regularly (Morrow & Styles, 1995).

Given the centrality of the interpersonal relationship to effective mentoring, the question arises as to whether mentoring is effective for adolescents who have experienced problematic relationships with caregivers. In light of their past experiences, adolescents living in foster care may find it relatively difficult to establish close, supportive relationships with mentors. Attachment theory and research suggest that expectations of self and others derived from early, intimate relationships with parents can affect the development of subsequent close relationships (Bowlby, 1988). As a group, foster youth may enter mentoring programs with different relationship histories than youth not living in foster care. Indeed, because most children enter foster care today because of problems in parental functioning, including child abuse and neglect, some foster youth may find it relatively difficult to establish close, supportive relationships with mentors and experience the benefits of mentoring. Other youth who have experienced close relationships with kin or unrelated foster caregivers may welcome the relationship with a neutral adult outside the foster home.

Some evidence suggests that, as a group, foster youth can benefit from mentoring relationships. Rhodes, Haight, and Briggs (1999) examined the influence of a mentoring program (Big Brothers Big Sisters) on the peer relationships of foster youth. Youth were randomly assigned to a mentoring group or a wait-list control group. As a group, foster adolescents appeared to have more difficulty establishing close relationships and trusting adults than youth not living in foster care. Despite the challenges, foster youth in the mentoring group were able to form, and in some cases benefit from, relationships with mentors. Overall, foster youth in the mentoring group reported slight improvement in the support they felt from their peers, while those in the wait-list group reported slight declines.

These data suggest that school social workers and social workers in child welfare can enhance services for some children in foster care by helping them to form a stable relationship with a caring mentor. Research also suggests that social workers recruit and educate mentors as to the centrality of the emotional relationship with the young person in the mentoring relationship. Marketing campaigns to recruit mentors that encourage volunteers to be heroic in a short period of time may be counterproductive, especially to youth who already have experienced disappointing relationships with adults. Volunteers may enter these programs with unrealistic expectations, including fantasies of rescuing a child (Rhodes, 2002). Rather than rely on such heroic images, mentoring programs should recruit adults who value and are skillful at maintaining interpersonal relationships and have the capacity to sustain their involvement over the long term.

Cultural-Historical Factors

Biological, psychological, and social aspects of mentoring are embedded within, and cannot be understood apart from, a larger cultural and historical context. Jean Rhodes (2002) argued that in much of American culture there is generally a suspicion of dependence and close relationships outside of the immediate family. Close relationships tend to be denigrated, and autonomy is viewed as the hallmark of emotional maturity. Trends to valorize independence as evidence of growth while minimizing interpersonal relationships can lead adolescents to devalue adult guidance and emotional support and lead to premature separation from adults.

Beliefs and practices within particular cultural communities in the larger American culture also may render certain youth more or less likely to respond to one-on-one mentoring. Youth from cultures that emphasize collectivism and a deep respect for their elders (e.g., Native Americans) may be uncomfortable in relationships with adults outside their immediate communities. For these youth, more group-oriented approaches (Rhodes, 2002) or recruitment of natural mentors from within the community may be preferable to other formal methods of matching mentor-young person pairs.

Neighborhood and community factors also can affect mentoring relationships. In urban communities with high crime or other dangerous conditions, children and adolescents may remain sequestered at home. They are safe, but their opportunities for contact with adults outside home and school are greatly reduced. Furthermore, when schools, churches, and civic organizations disintegrate, adolescents often have no adults available to offer counsel as problems arise (Rhodes, 2002).

Figure 4.3.
Latino culture is preserved in this *quinceañera* (fifteenth birthday) celebration in a rural farming community.

Family factors also can affect adolescents' mentoring relationships. Parental support of the mentor-young person relationship can be critical to establishing and maintaining relationships. Also, adolescents with more supportive parental relationships tend to have healthy relationships outside the family and to gravitate toward natural mentors. Parents who cultivate connections with well-meaning adults in their neighborhoods and channel their children to community-based recreational and social programs also greatly increase the likelihood that their children will form beneficial relationships with other supportive adults beyond their nuclear family (Rhodes, 2002).

These observations suggest that factors outside the mentor-young person microsystem need to be addressed to establish effective long-term matches. Contextual factors such as community norms for nonfamilial relationships, parental support, and opportunities for adolescents to form relationships with nonfamilial adults need to be considered by school social workers to develop effective mentoring programs for adolescents.

IMPLICATIONS FOR SCHOOL SOCIAL WORK WITH ADOLESCENTS

Mentoring is an example of a prevention intervention suited to the developmental needs of adolescents. Mentoring is not a cure-all for complex psychological problems, but it can assist adolescents in transitioning into resilient adults. Poorly implemented programs, however, can have adverse effects on youth (DuBois, Holloway, Vanentine, & Cooper, 2002). Fortunately, there is empirical literature to guide school social workers in developing effective mentoring programs. This literature has several implications:

1. *Focus on the quality of sustained interpersonal relationships.* For mentors to be effective agents of change, they must have the qualities needed in a meaningful interpersonal relationship. Superficial pairings that do not achieve trust, respect, and closeness are unlikely to be of much value (Rhodes, 2002). Furthermore, the impact of mentoring

---

BOX 4.10 TALKS MENTORING

TALKS is an effective mentoring program serving public school children and adolescents in Illinois and Indiana. TALKS' purpose is to enroll, educate, and facilitate interaction between adults and young people. Mentors are recruited to serve youth in the public schools and trained using the TALKS curriculum. The mentor is asked to commit to one hour per week during the school day to share with one to three young people. In Champaign County, Illinois, there are currently 108 mentors who are serving 302 children. While some mentoring programs target only at-risk youth, the TALKS program serves all children. Children are placed in groups of three incorporating students functioning at several academic levels. The children from diverse racial, cultural, and socioeconomic backgrounds meet weekly with a mentor throughout the school year. Adult mentors provide ongoing support of at least a year's duration to the one to three young people and facilitate the development of a supportive peer group among the three students to assist each other in the school between group meetings.

Davis, O. W. (2001). *Talks my mother never had with me. Mentor's guide.* Champaign, IL: KJAC Publishing.

---

grows as the relationship matures, short-lived relationships are associated with negative outcomes for youth (DuBois, Holloway, Valentine, & Cooper, 2002; Grossman & Rhodes, in press). Mentoring can be harmful when a mentor does not keep her promises to a young person with a history of problematic relationships (Rhodes, 2002).

2. *Screen, recruit, educate, and supervise mentors.* For the safety of the adolescent participants and the effectiveness of the program, it is important that programs carefully screen volunteers. For the best outcomes, it is important to engage and attract volunteers who are willing and able to make long-term commitments, and for program staff

to educate, support, and supervise them (Sipe, 2002). Some mentors manage without training, but mentoring does not come easily to everyone, and difficulties can arise that overtax even the most skilled volunteers. Mentors who are offered continuing support and supervision are more likely to persist. Successful programs also include structured activities for mentors and youth as well as expectations for frequency of contact, mechanisms for the involvement of parents, and monitoring of overall program implementation (Rhodes, 2002; DuBois, Holloway, Valentine, & Cooper, 2002).

3. *Anticipate the challenges of school-based mentoring programs.* There are special challenges to school-based mentoring. Many relationships formed through school-based programs are described as less close than those formed in community-based programs. Perhaps this occurs because the school setting constrains the types of leisure activities mentors and adolescents may engage in to build their relationships, as well as the time they spend together (see Rhodes, 2002). If school social workers anticipate the limitations of school-based pro-

---

BOX 4.11 PRACTICE STORY AND ADVICE

Brenda L., school social worker:
"You really have to have a systems understanding."

Brenda L. is a school social worker with twenty years' direct practice experience. Currently, she is a clinical assistant professor working with masters-level social work students during their field placements in the schools. She has worked in a variety of schools from public elementary schools to alternative high schools. She particularly enjoys the specialization of school social work because of the variety of children she serves, from well-functioning elementary children to adolescents with mental illness. She describes her experiences working in public schools with adolescents who have mental health needs and offers advice for students considering school social work as a specialization.

Practice Story

Well, I think basically that these are kids [adolescents with mental illness] that need a lot of intensive help. They need flexibility, and in a system things are very regimented—the bell rings, you can't go out in the hall unless you have a pass. You know if you have a bad day you can't go and tell someone to f— off, and they're just going to lump it like they would do in a day treatment school, things like that. I had a girl—when I did her background report she had been in so many psychiatric placements that I could not keep track. She was 16 when I first met her. She had tried to kill herself a number of times and she had had a very tragic life. And so she had been in and out of residential placements for quite a while and was being stepped down into the community and, eventually, the plan was that she was going to go home. So the semester before she was supposed to go home, she started transitioning back to a regular high school. And actually that went well. She came for a couple hours in the morning. And then, after a while, we tried her full-time. And it went okay for probably the first six weeks and then things fell apart. And I think what happened is that being the nature of her illness, her mental health issues, is that she just kind of cycled in and out [of depression]. And when she ends up in a bad time what she does is she says that she is going to kill herself. And usually, when she says it, she usually has some kind of a pretty good plan [for how to kill herself]. And one day she was upset about something and brought a knife to school. And you know the rules—zero tolerance. But it was a Swiss Army knife. None of the teachers were afraid that she was actually going to hurt them. But she was going to hurt herself and she wouldn't give it up, and she ended up having to be restrained. These are people that are not used to that on a regular basis and the principal was just like, "We can't have this." We had to wait for the police and an ambulance. They had to shut off the area. They don't allow the kids to pass so the kids won't see all this going on and embarrass her even more—the whole set up was just not conducive to kids like that [with mental illness]. I call the principal just to let him know what's going on, and he says, "You tell her she's suspended for ten days pending expulsion because she brought a knife to school." And I tell her mom that, and her mom is like, "Don't those people understand that she has mental health problems?" So to me that was sort of a typical example of where the school system is just not equipped.

Advice

In school social work, you have to be really good in a lot of different areas. You have to be skilled at clinical issues—you have to be extremely skilled at diagnostic issues. You really have to know what is normal developmental behavior as opposed to abnormal behavior. You also have to be able to interact with people at a lot of different levels. So not only are you going to be doing prevention, [but] you are going to be doing intervention, you are going to do consultation and collaboration where you work with teachers, helping them develop interventions for kids. You also are going to work with parents.

The other thing is that you have to really have a systems understanding. One of the things about school social work is you practice in a host setting. You really have to understand the politics of the organization because as a social worker, you don't do what everybody else does there. You have to understand that even though you think your issues are important—and they are—they are not considered important by everybody else. So you have to really figure out how to work within the system. You have to understand the informal and formal politics. You have to be able to size up who the players are and what their agendas are.

You also have to be flexible, especially when you deal with adolescents. We used to be able to have what was considered an office hour where we could catch up on our reports. And I normally didn't take mine—the one time that I did I probably wasn't in the door five minutes and someone said, "You have an emergency back at your school and you've got to go." I went back, and they said, "We can't believe you weren't here!" A kid had taken an Exacto knife and had sliced his arm in a suicide gesture. And I mean, you can have this plan for the day, but you never know how things are going to work out.

The other thing, I think too, is that you have to be willing to do outreach as a school social worker. I like that; I like home visits. I like seeing people in their environments. But you do have to be comfortable going to places that you wouldn't normally go, and go into neighborhoods where you might—like for me, I am a white—I might be the only white person there. And they [residents] know either she is here for welfare or she is not here because she is visiting for no reason. So you have to be willing to do that. But I like that. I like the challenge of all that.

grams, they may plan compensatory strategies, for example, to support matches through planned events such as special school lunches or outings for mentors and adolescents.

4. *Recognize the limitations of mentoring.* Unfortunately, most interventions have focused on "fixing" at-risk children while ignoring the ecological factors that contribute to their risk. Mentoring cannot make up for years of accumulated failure of the educational system and scars from failures of family, community, and economy. Mentoring alone is not a magic wand. An array of other policies is essential (Rhodes, 2002).

Box 4.10 describes a mentoring program for public school children and adolescents.

SUMMARY

Adolescence is a complex time of biological, psychological, social, and economic transitions. Social workers encounter adolescents in a variety of contexts, including the public schools. School social workers support the well-being and academic achievement of adolescents through the provision of services and advocacy. In recent years, mentoring has gained popularity as a prevention intervention especially suited to the developmental needs of adolescents. Mentoring relationships can result in the formation of mesosystems between other microsystems in the family, school, and community, thus reinforcing and expanding adolescents' values, beliefs, and skills. Empirical evidence indicates that mentoring programs can be highly effective for supporting normally developing adolescents, including those experiencing considerable environmental stress. However, mentoring is not a substitute for adequate social resources and professional assistance for the many complex social, health, and mental health challenges facing adolescents. Furthermore, poorly implemented mentoring programs can be harmful to youth. A developmental-ecological approach to mentoring can guide school social workers in developing and maintaining effective mentoring programs through consideration of biological, psychological, and social factors within a cultural-historical context. Box 4.11 presents the practice story and advice of a school social worker whose clients include mentally ill adolescents with needs that extend far beyond mentoring.

Study and Discussion Questions

1. How do modern developmental psychologists define adolescence? To what extent is it a period of "storm and stress" relative to other periods in the life cycle? What are some stereotypes about adolescents?

2. What are some biological, psychological, and social transitions that adolescents experience? How might these transitions vary across the cultural communities in which you may practice as a social worker (e.g., urban versus rural communities)?

3. What are the psychological consequences of early versus later maturation in adolescence? Why might the outcomes be different for boys versus girls?

4. Describe the goals and the development of mentoring relationships. Jean Rhodes describes mentoring as "strong medicine." How can we ensure that such strong medicine is healing as opposed to toxic?

5. What is school social work? What are some of the challenges a school social worker may face?

6. What are some of the possible advantages and unique challenges of school-based mentoring programs? If you were to implement a school-based mentoring program, what are three program components you would view as essential?

7. Returning to our opening example, what is your position on the use of mentoring programs for vulnerable children in foster care such as Jeremy? Lydia and her husband plan to relocate to the West coast to be with their children and grandchildren. How can Jeremy's relationship with Lydia be terminated? Should Jeremy's case worker be giving more attention to obtaining formal mental health services for him?

Resources

For students interested in learning more about adolescence as a developmental period, Steinberg (2002) and Cole and Cole (2001) are excellent sources. For those interested in deepening their understanding of mentoring, see Morrow and Styles (1995); Rhodes (2002); Tierney, Grossman and Resch, N. L. (1995); and Herrera (1999). For those interested in learning more about school social work, see Constable, Massat, McDonald, and Flynn (2006); Allen-Meares, Washington, and Welsh (2000).

Interested students may also supplement this chapter through a number of excellent Web-based resources.

The American Psychological Association provides an excellent overview of adolescent development. The article is designed to help professionals better understand how teens develop socially, emotionally, cognitively, and behaviorally. Available: http://www.apa.org/pi/pii/develop.pdf

The National Institute of Mental Health provides information for helping teens and children cope with violence and disasters. Available at: http://www.nimh.nih.gov/publicat/violence.cfm

Indiana University's Center for Adolescent and Family Studies provides details about most mental, emotional, and behavioral problems experienced by teenagers. This Web site links with numerous authoritative reports and articles. Available at: http://education.indiana.edu/cas/adol/mental.html

Obesity in adolescents and children causes serious bioecological problems. As a result, the surgeon general of the United States has called for a systematic approach for combating this national health problem. Read "The Surgeon General's Call to Action to Prevent and Decrease Overweight and Obesity in Children and Adolescents" at: http://www.surgeongeneral.gov/topics/obesity/calltoaction/fact_adolescents.htm

The Center for Disease Control outlines the prevalence of adolescent and childhood obesity between 1999 and 2002 and provides additional research reference. Available at: http://www.cdc.gov/nchs/products/pubs/pubd/hestats/overwght99.htm

The use of antidepressant medications with adolescents and adults is discussed by the Federal Food and Drug Administration. Manufacturers of all antidepressant drugs are requested by the Federal Food and Drug Administration to include in their labeling an expanded warning that there is an increased risk of suicidality (suicidal thinking and behavior) in children and adolescents treated with these medications. Available at: http://www.fda.gov/cder/drug/antidepressants/default.htm

The Academy of Child and Adolescent Psychiatry offers suggestions to help parents and clinicians respond to teens who self-injure. Available at: http://www.aacap.org/publications/factsfam/73.htm

References

Allen-Meares, P. (1999). The contribution of social workers to schooling—revisited. In R. Constable, S. McDonald, & J. P. Flynn (Eds.), *School social work: Practice, policy, and research perspectives* (4th ed., pp.24–32), Chicago: Lyceum Books.

Allen-Meares, P., Washington, R., & Welsh, B. (Eds.). (2000). *Social work services in schools* (3rd ed.). Boston: Allyn & Bacon.

Anda, D. de. (1995). Adolescence overview. In R. L. Edwards (Ed.), *Encyclopedia of social work* (Vol. 1, pp. 16–23). Washington, DC: NASW Press.

Anderson, E. (1991). Neighborhood effects on teenage pregnancy. In C. Jencks & P. E. Peterson (Eds.), *The urban underclass* (pp. 375–398). Washington, DC: Brookings Institute.

Annie E. Casey Foundation. (2004). *Kids count data book*. Baltimore, MD: Annie E. Casey Foundation.

Bennetts, C. (2003). Mentoring youth: Trend and tradition. *British Journal of Guidance & Counseling, 31*(1), 63–76.

Berenbaum, S. A., & Snyder, E. (1995). Early hormonal influence on childhood sex-type activity and playmate preferences: Implications for the development of sexual orientation: Sexual orientation and human development [Special issue]. *Developmental Psychology, 31*, 31–42.

Boonstra, H. (2002) Teenage sexual and reproductive behavior. *Guttmacher Report on Public Policy, 5*(1), 1–9.

Bowlby, J. (1988). *A secure base: Parent-child attachment and healthy human development.* New York: Basic Books.

Brumberg, J. (1997). *The body project: An intimate history of American girls*. New York: Random House.

Cole, M., & Cole, S. R. (2001). *The development of children* (4th ed.). New York: Worth.

Cole, S. A. (1993). *Peer education program*. Honolulu, HI: Hawaii Department of Health, School Health Services Branch.

Constable, R., Massat, C., McDonald, S., & Flynn, J. (Eds.). (2006). *School social work: Practice, policy, and research* (6th ed.). Chicago: Lyceum Books.

Curtis, T., & Hansen-Schwoebel, K. (1999). *Big Brothers Big Sisters school-based mentoring: Evaluation summary of five pilot programs.* Philadelphia: Big Brothers Big Sisters of America.

Darroh, J., Frost, J. J., Singh, S., & the Study Team. (2001). *Teenage sexual and reproductive behavior in developed countries: Can more progress be made?* (Occasional Report No. 3). New York: Alan Guttmacher Institute.

Davis, O. W. (2001). *Talks my mother never had with me. Mentor's Guide.* Champaign, IL: KJAC Publishing.

DuBois, D. L., Holloway, B. E., Valentine, J. C., & Cooper, H. (2002). Effectiveness of mentoring programs for youth: A meta-analytic review. *American Journal of Community Psychology, 30*(2), 157–197.

Fisher, A. Q., & Rivas, M. (2001). *Finding fish: A memoir.* New York: W. Morrow.

Freedman, R. I. (1995). Developmental disabilities: Direct practice. In R. L. Edwards (Ed.), *Encyclopedia of social work* (Vol. 1, pp. 721–728). Washington, DC: NASW Press.

Freud, S. (1959). *Group psychology and the analysis of the ego*. London: Hogarth Press (Original work published 1922).

Garmezy, N. (1985). Stress-resistant children: The search for protective factors. In J. E. Stevensen (Ed.), *Recent research in development psychopathology*. Journal of child psychology and psychiatry book (Supplement No. 4, pp. 213–233). Oxford: Pergamon.

Germain, C. (1999). An ecological perspective on social work in the schools. In R. Constable, S. McDonald, & J. P. Flynn (Eds.), *School social work: Practice, policy, and research perspectives* (4th ed.). Chicago: Lyceum Books.

Gladue, B. A. (1994). The biopsychology of sexual orientation. *Current Directions in Psychological Science, 3,* 150–154.

Graber, J. A., & Archibald, A. B. (2001). Psychosocial change at puberty and beyond: Understanding adolescent sexuality and sexual orientation. In A. R. D'Augelli & C. J. Patterson (Eds.), *Lesbian, gay, bisexual identities and youth* (pp. 3–6). New York: Oxford University Press.

Grossman, J. B., & Rhodes, J. E. (2002). The test of time: Predictors and effects of duration in youth mentoring relationships. *American Journal of Community Psychology, 30*(2), 199–219.

Grossman, J. B., & Tierney, J. P. (1998). Does mentoring work? An impact study of the Big Brothers Big Sisters program. *Evaluation Review, 22*(3), 403–426.

Grotevant, H. (1998). Adolescent development in family contexts. In W. Damon & N. Eisenberg (Eds.), *Handbook of child psychology: Vol. 3. Social, emotional, and personality development.* (5th ed., pp.1097–1150). New York: Wiley.

Haight, W. L., Carpenter, B., & Tata, L. (1999). Adult-supported social pretend-play: Strategies for facilitating young children's peer relationships. *School Social Work Journal, 24*(1), 15–28.

Herrera, C. (1999). *School-based mentoring: A first look at its potential.* Philadelphia: Public/Private Ventures.

Hershberger, S. L., & D'Augelli, A. R. (2001). Issues in counseling lesbian, gay, and bisexual adolescents. In R. M. Perez, K. A. DeBord, & K. J. Bieschke (Eds.), *Handbook of counseling and psychotherapy with lesbian, gay and bisexual clients* (pp. 225–247). Washington, DC: American Psychological Association.

Inhelder, B., & Piaget, J. (1958). *The growth of logical thinking from childhood to adolescence.* New York: Basic Books.

Isay, R. A. (1990) *Being homosexual: Gay men and their development.* New York: Avon Books.

Jucovy, L. (2000). *Mentoring sexual minority youth* (Technical assistance packet No. 2). Portland, OR: Northwest Regional Laboratory.

Lefkowitz, B. (1986). *Tough change: Growing up on your own in America.* New York: Free Press.

LeVay, S. (1993). *The sexual brain.* Cambridge, MA: MIT Press.

Levine, A., & Nidiffer, J. (1996). *Beating the odds: How the poor get to college.* San Francisco, CA: Jossey-Bass.

Longres, J. F., & Etnyre, W. S. (2004). Social work practice with gay and lesbian children and adolescents. In P. Allen-Meares & M. W. Fraser (Eds.), *Interventions with children and adolescents: An interdisciplinary perspective* (pp. 80–105). Boston: Allyn & Bacon.

McLearn, K. T., Colasanto, D., & Schoen, C. (1998). *Mentoring makes a difference: Findings from the Commonwealth Fund 1998 Survey of Adults Mentoring Young People.* New York: Commonwealth Fund.

Monkman, M. M. (1999). The characteristic focus of the social worker in the schools. In R. Constable, S. McDonald, & J. P. Flynn (Eds.), *School social work: Practice, policy, and research perspectives* (4th ed., pp. 45-63). Chicago: Lyceum Books.

Morrow, K. V., & Styles, M. B. (1995). *Building relationships with youth in program settings: A study of Big Brother/Big Sister ventures.* Philadelphia: Public/Private Ventures.

Neuman-Sztainer, D., Croll, J., Story, M., Hannan, P. J., Perry, C. (2002). Ethnic/racial differences in weight-related concerns and behaviors among adolescent girls and boys: Findings from Project EAT. *Journal of Psychosomatic Research, 53,* 963-974.

Paterson, C. J. (1992). Children of lesbian and gay parents. *Child Development, 63,* 1025-1042.

Paterson, C. J. (1994). Lesbians and gay families. *Current Directions in Psychological Science, 3,* 62-64.

Paterson , C. J. (1995). Families of the baby boom: Parents' division of labor and children's adjustment: Sexual orientation and human development [Special issue]. *Developmental Psychology, 31,* 115-123.

Paterson, C. J., & Chan, R. W. (1997). Gay fathers. In M. E. Lamb (Ed.), *The role of the father in child development* (pp. 245-260). New York: Wiley.

Phillip, K. (2003). Youth mentoring and the American dream comes to the UK? *British Journal of Guidance and Counseling, 31,* 101-112.

Proctor, C. D., & Groze, V. K. (1994). Risk factors for suicide among gay, lesbian, and bisexual youths. *Social Work, 39,* 504-513.

Rhodes, J. E. (2002). *Stand by me.* Cambridge, MA: Harvard University Press.

Rhodes, J. E., Bogat, G. A., Roffman, J., Edelman, P., & Galasso, L. (2002). Youth mentoring in perspective: Introduction to the special issue. *American Journal of Community Psychology, 30*(2), 149-155.

Rhodes, J., Contreras, J., & Mangelsdorf, S. (1994). Natural mentor relationships among Latina adolescent mothers: Psychological adjustment, moderating processes, and the role of early parental acceptance. *American Journal of Community Psychology, 22,* 211-227.

Rhodes, J. E., & Davis, A. A. (1996). Supportive ties between nonparent adults and urban adolescent girls. In B. J. Leadbetter & N. Way (Eds.), *Urban girls: Resisting stereotypes, creating identities* (pp. 213-249). New York: New York University Press.

Rhodes, J. E., Grossman, J. B., & Roffman, J. (2002). The rhetoric of youth mentoring and reality of youth mentoring. In J. E. Rhodes & G. G. Noam (Eds.), *New directions for youth development: A critical view of youth mentoring* (pp. 9-20). San Francisco: Jossey-Bass.

Rhodes, J., Haight, W., & Briggs, E. (1999). The influence of mentoring relationships of foster youth in relative and nonrelative foster care. *Journal of Research on Adolescence, 9*(2), 185-201.

Rhodes, J. E., & Noam, G. G. (2002). Editor's notes. In J. E. Rhodes & G. G. Noam (Eds.), *New directions for youth development: A critical view of youth mentoring* (pp. 5–8). San Francisco: Jossey-Bass.

Robins, L., Rutter, M., Quinton, D., & Hill, J. (Eds.). (1990). *Straight and devious pathways from childhood to adulthood.* Cambridge: Cambridge University Press.

Ryan, C., & Futterman, D. (1998). *Lesbian and gay youth: Care and counseling.* New York: Columbia University Press.

Schlegal, A., & Barry, H. (1991). *Adolescence: An anthropological inquiry.* New York: Free Press.

Sipe, C. L. (2002). Mentoring programs for adolescents: A research summary. *Journal of Adolescent Health, 31,* 251–260.

Steinberg, L. (2002). *Adolescence* (6th ed.). Boston: McGraw-Hill.

Tasker, F. L., & Golombok, S. (1997). *Growing up in a lesbian family.* New York: Guilford.

Tierney, J. P., Grossman, J. B., & Resch, N. L. (1995). *Making a difference: An impact study of Big Brothers/Big Sisters.* Philadelphia: Public/Private Ventures.

Werner, E., & Smith, R. S. (1982). *Vulnerable but invincible: A longitudinal study of resilient children and youth.* New York: McGraw-Hill.

Wertsch, J. V. (Ed.). (1985). *Culture, communication, and cognition: Vygotskian perspectives.* New York: Cambridge University Press.

Whiting, J. W. M., Burbank, V. K., & Ratner, M. S. (1986). The duration of maidenhood across cultures. In J. W. M. Whiting & M. S. Ratner (Eds.), *School-age pregnancy and parenthood: Biosocial dimensions* (pp. 273–302). New York: Aldine de Gruyer.

Zimmerman, M. A., & Bingenheimer, J. B. (2002). Natural mentors and adolescent resiliency: A study with urban youth. *American Journal of Community Psychology, 30*(2), 221–243.

Zucker, J., & Bradley S. J. (2004). Gender identity and psychosexual disorders. In J. M. Wiener & M. K. Dulcan (Eds.), *The American psychiatric publishing textbook of child and adolescent psychiatry* (p. 813). Washington, DC: American Psychiatric Publishing.

Figure 5.1. Forming lasting intimate relationships is a milestone of development in early adulthood. This young couple has been married for 10 years and they work together as artists and writers.

5

Social Work with Young Adults: Professional Development and Multicultural Education in Schools of Social Work

This chapter considers the young adult as the focal system, emphasizing an important developmental milestone, the acquisition of an occupation, and using the professional development of social work students as an exemplar. Just as it is important to consider the development of the client, so too is it important to consider the development of the social worker, who also is growing and changing. As you read, consider biological, psychological, and social factors of young adult development as they interact within specific cultural and historical contexts. Consider, especially, the macrosystem of the social work profession. How do social work values and ethics relate to the professional development of social work students? How do the values of nondiscrimination relate to experiences students may have had in other cultural settings? What are the implications for multicultural education?

Social work with young adults (approximately 22–35 years) is challenging and important. Young adults typically are at their peak physically and intellectually, ready to take on the many new responsibilities of adulthood. At the beginning of early adulthood, however, young people also are relatively inexperienced. Few have supported themselves through full-time employment, negotiated the complexities of long-term intimate relationships, or held responsibility for the life of a child. Yet many young adults make decisions regarding an occupation or career, marriage, and establishing a family that can affect their lives for decades. By the end of early adulthood, many people have established a more stable niche within society through family, occupation, and community activities. Others, suffering from unmet mental and physical health needs, substance abuse, poverty, and oppression, struggle to meet basic needs for food, shelter, friendship, and belonging. Box 5.1 describes an intervention by Indian social workers to alleviate health threats from HIV-AIDS to impoverished female prostitutes.

An important milestone of development in young adulthood is the assumption of a vocation or profession, typically after an extended period of education or training and apprenticeship (Steinberg, 2002). The transforma-

BOX 5.1 INTERNATIONAL PERSPECTIVES
HIV-AIDS Prevention Efforts in India

HIV-AIDS (human immune deficiency virus/acquired immune deficiency syndrome) has spread to nearly every nation on earth and is the cause of widespread fear and concern. To date, there is neither an effective cure nor a vaccine available for HIV-AIDS. Although new drugs called protease inhibitors prolong the lives of HIV-positive individuals, such medication is unaffordable to people in the developing world. India is one of five countries (along with Russia, China, Nigeria, and Ethiopia) classified by the U.S. National Intelligence Council as representing the second wave of the HIV-AIDS epidemic. Second-wave countries are where the most critical prevention and treatment challenges reside. In 2002, approximately 4 to 4½ million Indians ages 15 to 49 years were infected with HIV, the primary mode of transmission being through heterosexual contact.

The approximately 4 million Indian women engaged in prostitution are particularly vulnerable to contracting and spreading AIDS. Indeed, nearly 50% of these women are already infected with HIV. Many of these women are undereducated and suffer from extreme economic impoverishment, as well as forced exploitation.

To combat the spread of HIV-AIDS, most major Indian cities now have HIV-AIDS prevention programs for women in prostitution. Lakshmi Tata, an Indian social worker, conducted an ethnographic study of prostitution within the red light district of Poona, India, focusing on a peer education program. This program employed former female prostitutes who provided education about HIV-AIDS and distributed condoms to prostitutes to encourage safer sex. Dr. Tata's research indicated that these peer educators were largely successful in transmitting information about HIV-AIDS to women and in distributing condoms. She also found, however, that women's vulnerability and relative powerlessness was an impediment to their acting on this information to protect their health. Some male clients violently resisted the use of condoms. Others chose to take their business elsewhere. As one young prostitute, a mother, explained to Dr. Tata, when her male clients resisted the use of condoms she could not turn them, and the income they provided, away. Her immediate need to feed her desperately hungry children took precedent over worries about her health in the future.

Source: Tata, L. (2003). *HIV-AIDS awareness among sex workers in Poona, India.* Unpublished dissertation, University of Illinois, Urbana-Champaign.

tion of a novice into an expert is a complex process involving more than the acquisition of a technical knowledge base and a set of skills. It involves the acquisition of a culture: a specialized language and way of understanding, norms of behavior, unique customs, rites of passage, and codes of conduct. Professions such as social work are characterized by a prolonged period of adult socialization that powerfully influences novices' knowledge, attitudes, behaviors, and identity. It is this intense process of learning and personal change that transforms students into professional social workers.

SOCIAL WORK EDUCATION WITH YOUNG ADULTS

Social work with young adults occurs in a wide variety of contexts including professional schools of social work in colleges and universities. Social work education developed at the end of the nineteenth century from the concerns of charity organization society members over the quality and consistency of services for poor and dependent people. From their founding, charity societies provided in-service training programs for volunteers (Frumkin & Lloyd, 1995). Skills and knowledge, however, were acquired primarily through an informal apprenticeship system (Brieland, 1995). Over time, the complexity and potential malleability of human problems was recognized and moralistic approaches were replaced with social scientific approaches for assisting those in need. By the end of the century, it was clear that formal education would be necessary to support the development of knowledge, ensure an effective level of services, and supply trained professionals. By the end of World War 1, there were seventeen social work programs in the United States. Soon after, organizations were established to develop and monitor the delivery of an organized quality curriculum. In 1946, the National Council on Social Work Education (CSWE) was established. An important function of CSWE is accreditation. Accreditation involves monitoring the performance of social work educational programs in delivering a quality standardized curriculum (Frumkin & Lloyd, 1995).

Currently, there are approximately 700 accredited social work graduate and undergraduate programs serving over 60,000 students in the United States (CSWE and GADE, 2003). Many of the social work educators working in these programs have their doctorates as well as master's degrees in social work (MSWs) and have spent at least two years practicing social work before entering into social work education. They contribute to the knowledge base of the profession by conducting research and participate in administration within their schools and professional social work organizations. A primary function for most, however, is educating a new generation of social work students to embark on careers as professional social workers.

When she was 30 years old, Lynn entered an MSW program at a large public university. She and her husband (Greg) and 2-year-old son (Jeremy) had recently moved to the East Coast from their home and extended family on the West Coast for Greg to accept a professional position. It was an exciting time of positive change for Lynn, who had put off starting her own career to support Greg and begin their family. In her MSW program, Lynn felt that she had finally found her niche. She excelled in her classes and her interests in social justice were reflected and supported by her classmates and teachers. She was eager to begin contributing to her community through meaningful work. At the same time, Lynn experienced considerable stress in her field placement at a child welfare agency. Although her middle-class European American background was very different from that of her primarily low-income African American and Hispanic clients, she quickly formed supportive relationships with the children. It was their parents with whom she struggled, especially during parenting classes. She viewed the parents as harsh and unloving, and they viewed her as naive and ignorant to the realities of their daily lives. Lynn also experienced anxiety about putting Jeremy in day care, stress within her marriage as she and Greg struggled to develop a new system of shared household chores, and loneliness within the family because she was required to spend increasing amounts of time away from home during her field placements. Over time, with the support of friends and one another, Lynn and her family adjusted to their new home and lifestyle, and Lynn developed a deeper understanding of working with others who lived in very different cultural worlds from her own.

HIGHLIGHTS OF DEVELOPMENT IN EARLY ADULTHOOD

Early adulthood forms the developmental context for many social work students. The beginning and ending of early adulthood are not defined by discrete biological, psychological, and social markers. Instead, early adulthood is marked by the acquisition of new roles, such as employee, spouse, and parent. For many people in the United States, early adulthood involves leaving home, completing an education, beginning full-time work, attaining economic independence, establishing a long-term sexually intimate relationship, and starting a family (Berk, 2001; Sattler et al., 2000). The timing of these milestones varies greatly among individuals, much more so than in childhood or adolescence. Some women bear children in adolescence, while others wait until they are in midlife to begin families or choose not to have children at all. Some individuals discontinue their formal education at 16 years of age, and others pursue advanced degrees into their 30s. In some cultural communities, young adults continue to live with their parents and other family members, whereas in others they are expected to live independently in late adolescence. The timing of development within early adulthood also is affected by the burdens of poverty, violence, and substance abuse (see boxes 5.2–5.5). Development in early adulthood facilitates and is supported by a complex ensemble of biological and psychosocial changes within particular cultural and historical contexts.

> ## BOX 5.2 POVERTY ACROSS THE LIFE SPAN
> ### Household Income
>
> As of 2004, 7.9 million (10.2%) American family households were below the poverty line. This represented a small increase from 2003, when approximately 7.6 million families (10%) experienced constant poverty. During 2002, 7.2 million (9.6%) families lived in poverty. Households headed by females with no male present increased from 3.6 million (26.5%) in 2002 to 3.9 million (28%) in 2003. Poverty also increased for households headed by a single males with no female present. In 2002 there were 560,000 (12.1%) single-male households at or below the poverty line. By the end of 2003, 640,000 (13.5%) male-only households were in poverty. In 2004 there was no change in the poverty rates of female householder, no-husband-present families, and male-householder, no-wife-present families.
>
> ---
>
> Source: DeNavas-Walt, C., Proctor, B.D., & Lee, C.H. (2005). *Income, poverty, and health insurance coverage in the United States: 2004.* U.S. Census Bureau, Current Population Reports (Publication No. P60-226) (p. 6). Washington, DC: U.S. Government Printing Office; DeNavas-Walt, C., Proctor, B. D., & Mills, R. J. (2004). *Income, poverty, and health insurance coverage in the United States.* U.S. Census Bureau, Current Population Reports (Publication No. P60-226) (p. 5). Washington, DC: U.S. Government Printing Office.

Biological Factors

At the beginning of early adulthood (20–30 years), young adults typically are at their peak physically. Toward the latter half of early adulthood (30–35 or 40 years), athletic skills, vision, hearing, and the skeletal system begin to decline gradually, hair begins to gray and thin, basal metabolic rate declines, and gradual weight gain begins. In women, fertility problems increase in the middle 30s. There are, however, vast individual differences in rates of aging due both to genetic and lifestyle differences. Some women conceive and bear healthy children into their early 40s. As long as practice continues, athletic performance drops only slightly—about 2 percent per decade—into the 60s and 70s (Berk, 2001).

Psychological and Social Factors

A number of scholars have contributed to our understanding of cognitive, or intellectual, development in adulthood. K. Warner Schaie (1977, 1978) observed that with the entry into adulthood, the situations in which people must reason become more diverse. The goals of mental activity shift from acquiring knowledge to applying it. Gisella Labouvie-Vief (1980, 1985) argued that in adulthood, reasoning moves from hypothetical thought characteristic of adolescence to pragmatic thought as logic becomes a tool to solve real-world problems. As young adults settle on a specific career or voca-

....

BOX 5. 3 VIOLENCE ACROSS THE LIFE SPAN
Violence and Alcohol

• There is a 5% to 6% suicide rate for people with alcoholism, a significantly higher rate than is found in the general public.

• Fifty percent of all violent deaths in the United States involve the use of alcohol.

• Alcohol was involved in approximately 38.5% of all U.S. traffic fatalities.

• In Eastern European nations alcohol is involved in 33% of all deaths for people ages 15 to 29 years.

Sources: Institute of Medicine, Division of Neuroscience and Behavioral Health (1999). *Workshop summary. The role of co-occurring substance abuse and mental illness in violence*. Washington, DC: National Academy Press; Department of Health and Human Services, National Center for Injury Prevention and Control. (2005). *Impaired driving facts*. [Data file] Available from http://www.cdc.gov/ncipc/factsheets/driving.htm; World Health Organization. (2001). *Global burden of disease 2000*. Cambridge, MA: Harvard University Press.

....

tion, their knowledge deepens and they develop expertise. Toward the end of early adulthood, as family and work lives expand, the cognitive capacity to simultaneously juggle many responsibilities improves, and creativity often peaks (Berk, 2001).

A number of scholars (see Levinson, 1978, and Vaillant, 1977) have made important contributions to our understanding of psychosocial development in early adulthood. Eric Erikson (1964) focused on personality development. He considered intimacy, specifically making a permanent commitment to an intimate partner, to be a critical challenge of early adulthood.

....

BOX 5.4 SUBSTANCE ABUSE ACROSS THE LIFE SPAN
The Cost of Alcohol

• Alcohol abuse costs Americans approximately $166.5 billion annually.

• 100,000 deaths per year in the United States are related to alcohol.

• Alcoholism is the leading risk factor for cirrhosis of the liver.

• Approximately 25% of general hospital admissions involve problems related to chronic alcohol use or withdrawal from alcohol.

Source: Harwood H., Fountain, D., et al. (1998) *The economic costs of alcohol and drug abuse in the United States, 1992*. Washington, DC: National Institute on Drug Abuse and National Institute on Alcohol Abuse and Alcoholism

....

```
..............................................................
:                                                            :
:      BOX 5.5 SUBSTANCE ABUSE ACROSS THE LIFE SPAN          :
:             Animal Studies of Addiction                   :
```

Our knowledge of addiction has been advanced by scientists developing animal models that illustrate how changes in the brain's reward system and environmental learning interact to perpetuate substance abuse. Studies demonstrate that the behavior allowing an animal to gain access to a drug (e.g., pressing a button) is learned and can be triggered by:

- signals from within a brain that has adapted and the substance is needed;

- environmental cues that have been paired with the drug experience—in humans this may be certain peers, going to certain places, or taking part in certain activities;

- perceived stress.

Animal studies have also shown that there are large individual differences that influence the likelihood that drug use will be initiated or inhibited. In both animal and human studies, drug use is highly influenced by stress (deprivation for animals) and a return to environments where a substance was previously consumed.

Source: Wise, R. A., & Gardner, E. L. (2004). Annals of addiction. In D. S. Charney & E. J. Nestler (Eds.), *Neurobiology of mental illness* (2nd ed.). New York: Oxford University Press.

For many people, childbearing and child rearing occurs in the 20s and 30s. Becoming a parent is a major life-changing event. In many families and cultural communities, having a baby is viewed as a joyous event. It also can be a time of stress within a relationship and of vulnerability for young women. For example, 50–85 percent of new mothers experience sadness, fear, anxiety, and loss of energy after the birth (Taylor, 2005). These mothers are experiencing what is known as "the baby blues." The loss of joy occurs almost immediately after delivery and has all the appearances of depression. This sudden change in emotions and loss of confidence most likely results from hormonal shifts and extreme fatigue triggered by the birth process. It may be exacerbated by a woman's perceived failure to experience expected feelings of joy and fulfillment in her baby. For most women, the baby blues disappear spontaneously within a few days, although for some it may last from one to three weeks. Once the baby blues are gone, the mother's normal affect, motivation, self-perceptions, and psychological outlook on motherhood return. The baby blues seldom prevent women from leaving the hospital or caring for their babies. Nonetheless, assistance at home and with child-care tasks and emotional support can be extremely meaningful for the new mother.

During the first twelve months after childbirth, some mothers develop postpartum depression. Unlike the baby blues, this can be a disabling, dangerous disorder that is less likely to disappear spontaneously. Although the illness often is not highlighted in the press or professional literature, it is not a rare disorder. Research indicates that up to 15 percent of mothers will experience postpartum depression (Taylor, 2005). Mothers who develop severe postpartum depression are best treated with psychiatric medications and may require inpatient hospitalization. Box 5.6 describes facts about postpartum depression important for social workers.

The many critical life choices and decisions surrounding careers, relationships, and families are complex even in the best of circumstances, let alone to adults facing challenges such as cognitive or physical disabilities, poor mental or physical health, poverty, or oppression. Marriage and children can bring great pleasures, but also great vulnerability, challenge, and responsibility. How does one meet a prospective mate and make the decision to marry? How does one raise healthy children within a racist society, or within divorced families? The answers to these and other questions are neither simple nor obvious.

Establishing families can be especially challenging for individuals in the sexual minority. Because homosexual couples are not sanctioned as legal families, it is an important social work issue. Their inability to marry legally makes couples, children, and family units vulnerable to harassment and physical danger, unnecessary emotional stress, and economic hardships. Research has documented that most gays and lesbians, like heterosexuals, desire long-term, caring, and lasting relationships (Patterson, 1992; Flaks, Fischer, Masterpasqua, & Joseph, 1995). The development of children raised by gay and lesbian parents does not differ from that of children raised by heterosexual parents (Patterson, 1992; Flaks et al., 1995). Young adults raised by gay or lesbian parents report high satisfaction with their family life, and close relationships with their parents (Garner, 2004; Patterson & Chan, 1997). When viewed as a whole, research findings discredit the logic of withholding civil liberties and penalizing homosexuals and their families.

Cultural-Historical Factors

The biological, psychological, and social changes of young adulthood emerge and are shaped within specific cultural-historical contexts. These contexts may hasten or delay employment, financial independence, or establishment of intimate relationships such as marriage and children. An American baby born in 1900 had a life expectancy of just less than 50 years. In 1997, as a result of improved nutrition, medical treatment, sanitation, and safety, life expectancy rose to 76.5 years (Berk, 2001). The gains in life expectancy in the twentieth century allow for longer periods of education and the delay of marriage and childbearing.

BOX 5.6 POSTPARTUM DEPRESSION

Social workers need to be aware of the following facts about post-partum depression:

- Postpartum depression is real depression and not simply a state of sadness that can be willed away.

- Mothers suffering from postpartum depression require mental health treatment as quickly as possible.

- As the illness increases in severity, the mother may neglect, abandon, or physically abuse the baby.

- Mothers with postpartum depression often report doubting whether they can meet the child's needs, obsessively worrying about the baby's well-being, and having recurring fears that they are going to accidentally injure the baby.

- Other mothers report they lost all interest in the baby or became upset when their child cried and could not be satisfied.

- Having had one or more children without a depressive episode does not ensure that postpartum depression will not occur sometime during the first year after the next child is born.

- In addition to child-focused symptoms, mothers experiencing postpartum depression also report problems routinely seen in people with mood disorders such as changes in sleeping and eating patterns, increased guilt, thoughts of hopelessness, and loss of interest in things that previously provided enjoyment or satisfaction.

- Having had an episode of depression, bipolar disorder, or other major mental disorder in the past places the mother at a higher risk for postpartum depression.

- Many mothers have unknowingly suffered from mild depression, anxiety, or other disorders and are also at a greater risk.

- All prospective mothers and their families need preventive education and written information telling them how to identify and get professional help quickly for postpartum depression. Like other mood disorders, postpartum depression increases the risk for suicide. In rare cases the depression can shift into a psychosis causing the mother to lose sight of reality and to develop delusions and hallucinations. Postpartum psychosis only occurs in about 1 out of 1,000 births, but it requires an immediate response from the helping communities.

Source: Taylor, E. H. (2005). *Atlas of bipolar disorders*. London: Taylor & Francis.

FACILITATING THE PROFESSIONAL DEVELOPMENT
OF SOCIAL WORK STUDENTS

It is within the context of early adult development that many individuals begin their social work educations. As with any profession, becoming a social worker involves both the acquisition of a knowledge base and technical skills and the acquisition of a set of values and ethics that inform practice. The knowledge base, type, and depth of skills that social workers need are extensive. Social work draws upon various disciplines (e.g., biology, psychology, sociology, anthropology, political science, and economics), professions (e.g., law, psychiatry, education), and contexts of practices (e.g., hospitals, schools, community mental health centers). Furthermore, social work is shaped in relation to the larger social and historical context, including fiscal constraints; increases in poverty, drug use, and violence; changes in family structure; demographic transitions, including the proportion of elderly and people of color in the population (Hopps & Collins, 1995); health threats from HIV-AIDS; and fear of terrorist attacks.

Along with an extensive knowledge base and technical skills, social work students acquire a set of attitudes and beliefs. In his first-person account, *Becoming a Doctor: A Journey of Initiation in Medical School,* Melvin Konner (1987) observed that student doctors acquire much more than a knowledge base and technical skills from their teachers. They carefully watch, and in some cases imitate, the attitudes and behaviors of their physician teachers toward patients and issues of illness, death, and dying. This socialization into the medical culture profoundly affects both the quality of patient care and students' abilities to cope with the stress of becoming a physician, for example, students' ability to respond with empathy toward a dying patient and to recover, emotionally, from the experience of the patient's death.

Social work students, like student doctors, also learn through observations and participation in the culture of their profession. Students observe not only the content but the apparent attitudes and behaviors of their teacher toward course material and clients. Are teachers comfortable discussing issues of childhood sexual abuse, or do they resort to inappropriate humor? Is the field instructor dismissive and condescending or respectful to parents in the child welfare system?

As in medicine, the scope and complexity of professional social work have led to specialization. As a consequence, the student specializing in child welfare will acquire a somewhat different knowledge base from the student specializing in medical social work. Each specific practice setting will have its own set of skills, relationships, and practices. Underlying this diversity, however, is a common culture: a set of values, ethics, and standards for professional conduct that distinguish and unify the social work profession.

Social work values include service, social justice, respect for the dignity and worth of each person, respect for diversity, and the importance of human relationships. Like other professions such as law, medicine, and engineering, social work has developed from its values ethical standards and guidelines for professional conduct. Ethical standards in social work appear in various forms, but the NASW (National Association of Social Workers) Code of Ethics is the most visible compilation of the profession's ethical standards (Reamer, 1995). The code of ethics begins by making explicit core social work values. According to the preamble, "The primary mission of the social work profession is to enhance human well-being and help meet the basic human needs of all people, with particular attention to the needs and empowerment of people who are vulnerable, oppressed, and living in poverty" (p.1).

From the core values emerges a set of ethical principles. First, social workers' primary goal is to help people in need and to address social problems. Service to others is elevated above self-interest. Second, social workers challenge social injustice and pursue social change, particularly on behalf of vulnerable and oppressed individuals and groups of people. Third, social workers respect the inherent dignity and worth of each person. Social workers treat each person in a caring and respectful fashion, mindful of individual differences and cultural and ethnic diversity. Fourth, social workers recognize the central importance of human relationships and understand that relationships between and among people are an important vehicle for change. Fifth, social workers are continually aware of the profession's missions, values, ethical principles, and ethical standards and practice in a manner consistent with them. Sixth, social workers practice within their areas of competence, develop and enhance their professional knowledge and skills, and strive to contribute to the knowledge base of the profession.

These ethical principles inform social work practice and guide social workers' conduct. The NASW Code of Ethics addresses social workers' responsibilities to clients and to other social work professionals to perform the job an agency hired the worker to do, to enhance the well-being of society at large, and to support and promote the social work profession. Although the code provides a brief guide for dealing with ethical dilemmas in social work practice, it offers no set recipe. Simple answers are not available for many complex ethical issues involving, for example, confidentiality and conflicts of interest. Instead, the code offers a set of values, principles, and standards to guide decision making and professional conduct. It also is intended to educate members and to help socialize new members into the profession.

The culture of social work, with its distinct set of professional values, ethics, and standards for conduct, is transmitted to the social work student during the course of formal education, fieldwork, and early professional practice. An individual student's acquisition of the social work culture will be profoundly influenced by a variety of factors including personal characteristics, level of development, support systems, and past experiences. Relatively little systematic research has explored the professional development of social work students. A developmental-ecological analysis draws our attention to a variety of biological, psychological, social, and cultural-historical factors when we consider how to best support the professional development of social work students.

Biological Factors

Biological factors that can affect the social work student's professional development are nutrition, adequate rest, and stress management. Medical education provides a good illustration of the importance of attending to physical health during professional socialization. Critics of socialization practices in medical schools and patient advocates have long noted that poor eating habits, sleep deprivation, and intense stress experienced by student doctors can interfere with their technical competencies as well as their abilities to empathize with and support patients (Black, 1993). Like student doctors, social work students also experience stress during their professional development. MSW students who have been academically successful as undergraduates may struggle to succeed on challenging exams and paper assignments. Students also may experience pressure during field placements where they encounter emotionally and professionally challenging cases involving, for example, child abuse, death, serious and persistent mental illness, or substance abuse. During their field placements, students may experience stresses endemic to the United States workplace, such as sexual harassment, discrimination, or other abuses of power.

In addition, students may be attempting to balance multiple responsibilities of adulthood, including work and family obligations, with social work education. Unlike the young adult population involved in medical education, social work students also include middle-aged adults in dual career relationships, parents, single parents, and adults caring for aging parents. These students have substantial components of their lives outside social work school to which they must attend and nurture. The multiple stressors experienced by social work students can lead to inadequate rest and poor eating habits, which, in turn, can lead to illness and psychosocial problems.

Psychological Factors

Psychological factors that affect and are affected by professional development include the adequacy of the student's intellectual skills and preparation and emotional readiness to succeed in school and the profession. Social work students and professionals must reflect on how their own psychological needs relate to their relationships with clients. For example, social workers avoid entering into *dual relationships* with clients. Dual relationships fulfill a psychological need of the professional and hence shift the focus of the helping relationship from the client's needs. Such relationships can lead to an abuse of power harmful to the client, for example, when professionals have sexual relationships with clients. They also can lead to stress and possible burn-out of the social worker.

Joshua Miller's (2001) reflections on his loneliness and needs for family during his first professional social work job illustrate the complicated issues of dual relationships. After graduating with his MSW from the University of Washington, Mr. Miller moved to London to begin his first job. One of his first clients, Violet, came to him for help after leaving her abusive husband. Several weeks later, Violet's husband forced his way into her home and murdered her in front of their children. Far from family and friends, Mr. Miller threw himself into supporting Violet's traumatized children and their grandparents. Soon, his life became intertwined with theirs, and he recognized that just as he was meeting their needs for professional support during this traumatic period, they were meeting his own needs for family. Questions soon arose: Was he the best professional to provide services to this family? How would they be affected by his eventual departure? Lacking professional supervision, Mr. Miller wrestled with these issues on his own. A young and inexperienced social worker, he did not know to address complex personal issues related to his own *secondary trauma*: guilt, overwhelming emotions, rescue motifs, nightmares, social isolation, and persistent sadness. From his current perspective as a social work educator more than twenty years later, Mr. Miller advises students in similar circumstances to get professional and personal help, think carefully about what they realistically can offer the family, and be cautious about dual relationships.

Social Factors

A student's professional development also affects and is affected by social factors. These factors include the student's interpersonal relationships (microsystems) with family, friends, neighbors, employers, coworkers, other students, professors, field instructors, and clients. Relationships with family members can provide invaluable support to the student. On the other hand, relationships with partners and children can be harmed through neglect stemming from the pressing and sustained demands of professional training (Black, 1993). Balancing family with professional training is challenging, as one young medical student described:

When I'm involved in training, the house goes to hell, my husband complains that his needs are not being met, the kids complain. And the experience of tending to a lot of pressure at school, and then coming home and finding pressure there—I just feel like everywhere I turn I'm inadequate. (Broadhead, 1982, as referenced in Black, 1993).

On the other hand, the student's professional success can provide security, status, and satisfaction to the entire family. Balancing the pressures of professional training with the needs of partners and children can be challenging. A university mental health counselor related:

At the clinic, many graduate students came to us when their marriages were falling apart, often around transition points like orals, preliminary exams, or graduation. The stresses in their relationship stay buried until these milestones come along that bring a couple to a crisis.

(Scheinkman, 1988, as referenced in Black , 1993).

Social factors beyond those of interpersonal relationships also affect students' professional development. Characteristics of university and field placement mesosystems can be critical to a social work student's success. Annie Houston's (2001) reflections on ethical conflicts during her social work field placement at a women's jail illustrate the importance of the formation of strong relationships between universities and field placements. As a beginning graduate social work intern, Houston worked as an advocate for incarcerated women. Although the prison refused to supply safe sex paraphernalia, widespread lesbian relationships raised serious concerns about the spread of sexually transmitted diseases, including HIV-AIDS. Houston found herself looking the other way as dams were illicitly passed to prisoners, raising complex ethical dilemmas. Was it ethical for a social work student to break the rules of the prison, thereby modeling the very same type of behavior that resulted in her clients' incarceration? Or was she obligated as a social worker to break unjust rules to help protect the physical well-being of her clients? There are no easy answers, but an important question raised by Janet Black (2002) is: Where was the university faculty field liaison? Faculty field liaisons are employed by universities as liaisons between the field placement and the university. They serve as resources for students in creating a strong mesosystem between the university and field placement. As Black argues,

An interdependent relationship must exist between the university and the agency providing field education. The behaviors and interactions of each partner are related; one individual's disregard for the partnership may result in unsuccessful learning experiences and disruption of service and education. (p. 57).

Cultural-Historical Context

Students' professional development is embedded within and affected by the larger cultural-historical context, including the economic, political, and cultural characteristics of the larger society (macrosystem). The level of funding available for community mental health care can affect the type of interventions students may be exposed to during field placements. Chronic underfunding of community mental health as well as the social stigmatization of individuals with chronic mental illness can result in field placements that focus on case management and do not offer opportunities for supervision in diverse therapeutic approaches.

The cultural-historical context can critically affect students' field placements and first job experiences. Katherine Van Wormer's (2001) narrative describing her first experiences as a social worker in Norway, where she served for two years as a treatment director at a private alcoholism treatment, illustrate the impact of larger societal factors on social work practice.

In Norway, alcoholism treatment usually is provided free of charge by the state. Because of the hostility toward privatization in Scandinavia with its strong socialist tradition, private centers such as the one described by Van Wormer operated independently, without state regulation. The director-owner, a self-described "chief alcoholic," answered to no one and allowed questionable, corrupt, and flagrantly unethical practices to flourish. The director-owner pursued sexual relationships with former clients and staff members, alcoholics with as little as two months' sobriety were hired as staff, staff got reluctant individuals very drunk and then "kidnapped" them into treatment, and trainees were instructed to pretend that they were not working in order to qualify for sick-pay money from the state. Van Wormer went on to blow the whistle on this treatment center, bringing the unprofessional practices in private centers to the attention of the deeply shocked Norwegian social work community and, ultimately, helping to bring change to the system.

For purposes of discussion, biological, psychological, social, and cultural-historical factors in professional development have been discussed separately and at a single time point. It is important to remember, however, that the factors interact in a complex fashion over time. The BSW, MSW, or PhD degree is only the beginning of a social worker's professional development. As the dean of a large social work school once commented, the MSW is merely a learner's permit. Ideally, development will continue throughout their professional careers as social workers learn through experience and continuing study. One of the contexts in which social work educators continue their professional development is through participation in the Council on Social Work Education (CSWE). Best known for its role in setting the standards for BSW and MSW programs through accreditation, CSWE also provides programs and resources to promote the professional development of social work educators. For nearly fifty years it has sponsored the Annual Program Meeting (APM), the largest national conference of undergraduate and graduate social work educators. This meeting offers more than 500 presentations, meetings, and receptions. CSWE also publishes the *Journal of Social Work Education* to help educators develop their skills and curricula.

IMPLICATIONS FOR SOCIAL WORK EDUCATION

A developmental-ecological framework has a number of more general implications for enhancing social work education. First, adequate attention must be paid to biological factors. Some stress is inherent as students such as Lynn strive to achieve higher levels of competence. How a student responds to the challenges of professional development depends on a variety of complex contextual factors. It also depends, very simply, upon biological factors such as nutrition, adequate rest, and stress management.

Figure 5.2. Many critical life choices, including which occupation to pursue, are made in early adulthood. This young woman is visiting with a family as part of her preparation for a career in social work.

Second, adequate attention must be paid to social and emotional factors. Forming and maintaining supportive relationships with others such as spouses can prove to be invaluable during the process of professional socialization. As Lynn testified, emotional support from family, friends, and peers can reduce stress and provide perspective. Professional supervision from experienced faculty and field supervisors can help the student reflect upon professional conduct and complex ethical issues in social work practice. The absence of such support can lead to difficult and complex situations that ultimately may present obstacles to professional development.

Social factors beyond the interpersonal also affect the socialization of social workers. Strong ties between the university and field placement can result in consistent guidance to students struggling to behave professionally in the ethically complex situations that are routine in social work practice. The absence of strong ties can lead to students' confused and unprofessional conduct, and risk to clients. When entering into field placements, students should consider the broader social context of their education. In particular, what is the quality of communication between the prospective field placement and their school of social work?

Third, attention must be paid to the cultural-historical context in which biological and social factors are embedded. Do women such as Lynn have adequate familial and societal support to develop their own skills and talents to the fullest? Is day care available? Do adult men participate in child care and household chores?

BOX 5.7 PRACTICE STORY AND ADVICE FROM THE FIELD

Dean W.: "Our function in society starts fundamentally from a moral paradigm."

Dean W. has worked in social work education for 25 years and is currently the dean of a school of social work. She spoke about her experiences as a woman within social work education and higher education administration as well as the characteristics of successful social work administrators.

Practice Observations

Human service is moral work. I think this applies to educational institutions as well. Our function in society is to socialize students into certain professional roles. That is moral work. And because we are the social work profession, there are things in our mission and how we teach that differ from other units on campus. We are talking about social and economic justice. I just photocopied an editorial from the *Journal of Social Work Education* about access to higher education that I am going to send around to the provost and chancellor because I think it raises economic justice issues that are important in a university. That sort of moral work—and moral voice—is important to how I see our particular unit in higher education.

Human service is gendered work. [In] higher education institutions, of course, there are gender issues. I am constantly aware of those in dynamics of various meeting I am in. And I think I have to talk about race as well. This school, since 1980, has had two African American deans, including an African American woman. I am not sure if there have been any or many other members of the Council of Deans who are African American or African American women. And that's still the case. You know, I look around at my peers and I don't see a group that very much mirrors the diversity that we have in society, and certainly that we hope to have on this campus. And that's a concern of mine—there are many more woman in administrative roles on campus, but I still think that if you look at the larger units, they all have men as deans—liberal arts, engineering, business, the largest units on campus all have men as deans— and that makes for some interesting issues. When you have the issue of the larger units, which tend to be more powerful, being led by men, and woman in the smaller units its harder to get the issues voiced that need to be voiced. Although the group has been pretty good overall about listening and so on, there is still this sort of large-small split and when you combine that with gender, it raises some issues for me. I think it also combines with the social and economic justice issues—their graduates make a lot of money and so they can raise tuition, so they are getting more money to run the different units.

Advice on Teaching in Higher Education

First about the teaching side. If you go out in the practice world and supervise [social work] interns, think about what it is in the internship situation that you are teaching, how you are drawing on what you learned in social work education—theories, research—and be able to convey that in frameworks that help an intern. You have to start moving up a level in your thinking; in other words, you have to be reflective enough to be aware of the frameworks you are using so that you can teach about them. There is a whole knowledge base about how to teach, so you need to begin to look at that knowledge base.

Advice on Administrative Careers in Higher Education

I think the thing that our (MSW) students don't realize is that within two years most of them will be in supervisory level positions. They need to be paying attention to those aspects of theory and practice that relate to role theory and organizational theory. And then there are administrative skills that apply across organizations. Yes, you need to know some things about higher education as opposed to service agency, but some of the things are the same. So what you are learning about administration and organization and supervision is all the way along, and you just also need to learn a little bit about what the issues are in administration.

Flexibility is key, both intellectually and emotionally. I can come in with a to-do list, with two or three things started in my mind as the things that I would like to do today, and if somebody walks into my door and says that there is a problem, it has to be resolved now. Basically, for example, I had two to three weeks earlier this summer where we were negotiating with our major founders and everything else went off my plate for a little over two weeks. Your own life must have the flexibility you need—shifting concentration from one thing to another instantly, yet keeping everything moving forward.

Information management is huge for all of us. E-mail will instantly triple, and triple is an underestimation. On the other hand, getting the information you want can be difficult, so information-retrieval skills are important, and not only for me, but for my staff. My administrative assistant has to be a good administrative retrieval person and has to know some sets of university policies, and my business manager has to know another set of university policies, so that they can support me in my role in carrying out the mission of the school.

Strategic and pragmatic thinking—you have to have a vision and you have to be able to convey that. What I must do is convey with enormous clarity my vision for the school. Every time I am outside of this building interacting with anybody on campus, I have to be able to present the school—whether I am on this campus, in the national social work scene, or in the accreditation meeting or deans and directors meeting, I am the face of the school. I need to be constantly presenting us in a way that makes sure everybody out there on campus or in the social work world knows that we are a top ten school, and this is why.

Working with the campus budget committee or the campus commercial and tenure committee or the council of deans, we have to put forward a certain face. And yet you have to be yourself, you can't be anybody other than who you are. And the feedback I have received from people in committees is that I do an excellent job. I do not pretend to be somebody other than who I am and that's important to me.

Finally, social workers continue to develop long after they receive their degrees. Some will enter into administrative roles, including in schools of social work. Box 5.7 addresses social work education and administration.

Implications for Multicultural Social Work Education

Understanding the complex interaction of biological, psychological, and social factors embedded within particular cultural-historical contexts over time has important implications for social work education. Nondiscrimination is a central social work value with which social work educators grapple. Social work students come from diverse cultural backgrounds. Many, like Lynn, are able-bodied, heterosexual, European American middle-class women from the suburbs. Others grew up in urban or rural communities; come from working-class homes; are black, Hispanic, or Asian; are challenged by disabilities; are gay or lesbian; or are male. However, given the nature of social work, as well as our increasingly pluralistic society, *all* will serve clients with experiences, values, and practices different from their own. How can educators facilitate students' understanding, empathy, and openness to others who are different from them because of age, gender, sexual orientation, ability/disability, race, or culture?

A developmental-ecological approach to social work education suggests attention to a variety of factors. First, in order to learn, social work students must feel physically safe. A young, white, male middle-class student initially made good strides in his understanding of children participating in an after-school program for inner-city African American children. During a misunderstanding with several adolescent boys in which he felt physically threatened, he regressed to racist thinking. As he wrote in his reflection journal:

They [older boys] were trying to act tough with me, so I wrestled with them for fun, but not enough to scare or hurt them. Suddenly one of them took a shot at my groin. I luckily dodged it and ended up with a bruise on my thigh. I did not feel comfortable with the boys' aggression that night. My personal reaction is that the African American culture cannot be as aggressive and tough. If these boys' parents and culture are teaching them to always be tougher than someone else then there is no way they can learn to cooperate within their community in the United States. These kids have to stop their tough image because in this world it pays to be intelligent and not tough. No wonder there are so many African Americans and Hispanics in gangs. I think toughness and machismo might be part of their culture. (Haight, 2002, p.189)

Clearly, in this context more professional supervision was needed. A supervisor might have asked the student to consider why these boys might feel threatened. Are they really being socialized to be tough? If so—why? Is being tough incompatible with being intelligent? With closer supervision, the conflict between this student and the adolescent boys would not have escalated to the point that all participants were anxious for their physical safety and racist beliefs were reinforced rather than challenged.

Second, successful professional development addresses complex psychological factors, including students' feelings and values. In a study of European American university students (Haight, 2002), the majority of students described intense and complex mixed emotional reactions to their work with African American children in a computer club. One student expressed loving feelings toward a child but antipathy toward the child's parent. Such intense emotional responses, including guilt and defensiveness in relation to issues of oppression (see Garcia and Van Soest, 1997), can interfere with learning (see King, 1991; Tatum, 1992) through distortion of the "facts" and dampened motivation for continued multicultural learning. With adequate supervision, reflection, and interaction with peers, professors, and field supervisors, students will gain the perspectives necessary to function professionally with diverse clients in various settings.

Third, attention must be paid to social factors. Social work students, as members of particular communities, enter social work school with social representations, cultural models (Goodnow, 1988), or folk psychologies (Bruner, 1990) of human behavior and diverse cultural communities. The cultural models of European American students may contain omissions and inaccuracies regarding people of color. Thus, students' initial frame of reference within which they interpret cross-race experiences, assess problems, and formulate goals and strategies may be inadequate, as well as discrepant with that of their future clients. Through exposure to the professional social work literature, as well as face-to-face interactions with diverse students, professors, field instructors, and clients, students will acquire information about a variety of cultural communities.

A developmental-ecological approach also directs attention to the variety of contexts in which professional development occurs. Haight (2002) found that European American middle-class students' responses to multicultural education varied markedly with context. Students were relatively unchallenged by multicultural materials presented in books and lectures, but more challenged by face-to-face interactions with African American adults.

Some students were distressed and angered by the disciplinary practices (spanking) of some adults that varied from their own preferred strategies (time-out). Fortuitously, face-to-face interactions with members of culturally diverse communities are increasingly characteristic of field placements in social work. The challenge is to use such experiences systematically to enhance students' understanding of emotionally difficult interactions. With adequate supervision, guided reflections, and planned debriefings, social work students can develop the perspective-taking skills to function as effective professionals even within socially and emotionally complex contexts.

A developmental-ecological approach also suggests attention to professional development as an active process that continues over time. The ways in which students actively interpret diversity relates to their own unique life experiences—including past and ongoing interactions with members of particular groups—and to their individual interests and strengths. Haight (2002) found marked changes over time in students' reported emotional reactions to their multicultural field placements, including an increased comfort in interacting with African American children and adults and an increased sadness for the plight of individual children living in poverty. In short, students' understanding, and hence the impact of the field placement on their development, changed over time.

SUMMARY

This chapter has applied the developmental-ecological approach to understand an important area of development in early adulthood, the acquisition of an occupation or career. In social work, a common denominator in professional development is the socialization and acquisition of a core set of social work values, and the ethical principles and standards of professional conduct that emerge from these values. Nondiscrimination is a central social work value with which social work students and educators grapple. Research on multicultural education suggests that the student's successful socialization into the professional social work culture requires an adequate knowledge base, attention to affect, and experiences that occur over time and in a variety of social contexts. A developmental-ecological analysis of social work students' professional development suggests a variety of ways in which professional development may be enhanced. Although professional development may be most rapid during the initial years of education, it does not end with graduation. Social workers continue to develop as they take on new roles throughout their careers, and as practice and policy evolve over time.

Study and Discussion Questions

1. Early adulthood (approximately 22–35 or 40 years) is a major life transition often involving the establishment of economic independence,

a marriage, a family, and a career. What are some challenges that individuals may face in this transition, and how might social workers address these issues?

2. What is professional socialization, and what does it entail? How might becoming a professional social worker be similar or different from professional socialization in other professions such as medicine or law?

3. Describe the NASW Code of Ethics, its content areas, goals, and guidelines.

4. Considering biological, psychological, social, and cultural factors, how might social work students facilitate their own professional development?

5. What are some of the challenges to multicultural education? How might these challenges be successfully resolved?

6. Returning to our opening example, how might the multiple transitions of young adulthood experienced by Lynn affect one another (e.g., the transition into a profession, parenting, intimate relationships, and emotional and financial independence from family of origin)? How might socialization into the social work profession be experienced by an adult in midlife?

Resources

For students interested in learning more about development in middle adulthood, Berk (2001) is an excellent place to begin. For those interested in learning more about the history of social work, we recommend Brieland (1995). Those interested in exploring social work education, should see Frumkin and Lloyd (1995). Those interested in social work values and ethics should see Abels (2001), Reamer (1995), or Gambrill and Pruger (1997). The student interested in multicultural education should see Tatum (1992).

Interested students also can supplement this chapter through a number of excellent Web-based resources.

The *Alan Review* addresses how young adults perceive, use, and understand spirituality. The electronic journal is sponsored by ALAN, an organization dedicated to promoting a better understanding of late adolescents and young adults. Available at: http://scholar.lib.vt.edu/ejournals/ALAN/spring 96/mendt.html

A discussion of Erikson's young adulthood stage of development is available at http://web.cortland.edu/andersmd/ERIK/stage6.HTML

A National Institute of Health news release demonstrates that maintaining cardiorespiratory fitness in early adulthood significantly decreases the chance of developing high blood pressure and diabetes in middle age. Available at: http://www.nih.gov/news/pr/dec2003/nhlbi-16.htm

In 2005, the Annie E. Casey Foundation published a comprehensive report detailing the characteristics of individuals age 18 to 24 years and how they transition into adulthood. The complete report is in PDF format and is located at http://www.prb.org/Template.cfm?Section=PRB&template=/ContentManagement/ContentDisplay.cfm&ContentID=12562

The Young Adult Cancer Resource Site offers information, support, and resources for young adults and older teenagers with cancer. Available at: http://wableyer.oncologymail.com/index.html

The National Cancer Institute of Canada provides information about the epidemiology and treatment of young Canadian adults who develop cancer. Available at: http://www.ncic.cancer.ca/ncic/internet/standard/0,3621,84 658243_85787780_91035800_langId-en,00.html

A study funded by the U.S.Agency for International Development investigated the psychosocial and cultural factors that influence sexuality of young adults in Nicaragua. An overview of the study is available in PDF format at: http://www.agi-usa.org/pubs/journals/2917403.pdf

The Rand Corporation compared smoking trends among four racial/ethnic groups. Researchers collected data from 6,259 individuals ages 13 through 23 years. Available at: http://www.rand.org/publications/RP/RP1124

References

Ashfold, J. B., Lecroy, C. W., & Lortie, K.L. (2001). *Human behavior in the social environment: A multidimensional perspective* (2nd ed.). Belmont, CA: Wadsworth/Thomson Learning.

Berk, L. E. (2001). *Development through the lifespan* (2nd ed.). Needham Heights, MA: Allyn & Bacon.

Black, J. E. (1993). In praise of families. In H. M. Swartz,. & D. L. Gotteil (Eds.), *Education of physician scholars* (pp. 235–249). Rockville, MD: Beth Press.

Black, J. E. (2001). Between the agency and the university. In S. L. Abels (Ed.), *Ethics in social work practice: Narratives for professional helping* (pp. 57–60). Long Beach, CA: Love.

Brieland, D. (1995). Social work practice: History and evolution. In R. L. Edwards (Ed.). *Encyclopedia of social work* (Vol. 3, pp. 2247–2254). Washington, DC: NASW Press.

Bruner, J. (1990). *Acts of meaning*. Cambridge, MA: Harvard University Press.

Council of Social Work Education (CSWE) Retricved May 2005 from http.//www.cswe.org

Erikson, E. H. (1964). *Childhood in society*. New York: Norton.

Flaks, D. K., Fischer, I., Masterpasqua, F., & Joseph, G. (1995). Lesbians choosing motherhood: A comparative study of lesbian and heterosexual parents and their children: Sexual-orientation and human development [Special issue]. *Developmental Psychology, 31,* 105–114.

Frumkin, M. & Lloyd, G. A. (1995). Social work education. In R. L. Edwards (Ed.), *Encyclopedia of social work* (Vol. 3, pp. 2238–2247). Washington, DC: NASW Press.

Gambrill, E., & Pruger, R. (Eds). (1997). *Controversial issues in social work ethics, values and obligations.* Needham Heights, MA: Allyn & Bacon.

Garcia, B., & Van Soest, D. (1997). Changing the perceptions of diversity and oppression: MSW students discuss the effects of a required course. *Journal of Social Work Education, 33,* 119–130.

Garner, A. (2004). *Families like mine: Children of gay parents tell it like it is.* New York: Perennial Currents.

Goodnow, J. J. (1988). Parents' ideas, actions, and feelings: Models and method from developmental and social psychology. *Child Development, 59,* 286–320.

Group for the Advancement of Doctoral Education (GADE). (2003). Retrieved September 2005 from http://web.uconn.edu/gade

Haight, W. L. (2002). *African-American children at church.* New York: Cambridge University Press.

Hopps, J. G., & Collins, P. M. (1995). Social work profession overview. In R. L. Edwards (Ed.), *Encyclopedia of social work* (Vol. 3, pp. 2266–2282). Washington, DC: NASW Press.

Houston, A. L. (2001). Do the right thing. In S. L. Abels (Ed.), *Ethics in social work practice: Narratives for professional helping* (pp. 27–33). Long Beach, CA: Love.

King, J. (1991). Dysconscious racism: Ideology, identity, and the miseducation of teachers. *Journal of Negro Education, 60,* 133–146.

Konner, M. (1987). *Becoming a doctor: A journey of initiation in medical school.* New York: Penguin.

Labouvie-Vief, G. (1980). Beyond formal operations: Uses and limits of pure logic in life-span development. *Human Development, 23,* 141–160

Labouvie-Vief, G. (1985). Logic and self-regulation fron youth to maturity: A model. In M. Commons, F. Richards, & C. Armon, (Eds.), *Beyond formal operations: Late adolescent and adult cognitive development* (pp. 158–180). New York: Praeger.

Levinson, D. J. (1978). *The seasons of a man's life.* New York: Knopf.

Miller, J. (2001). Violet's seeds. In S. L. Abels (Ed.), *Ethics in social work practice: Narratives for professional helping* (pp. 111–129). Long Beach, CA: Love.

Paterson, C. J. (1992). Children of lesbian and gay parents. *Child Development, 63,* 1025–1042.

Paterson, C. J. (1994). Lesbians and gay families. *Current Directions in Psychological Science, 3,* 62–64.

Paterson, C. J. (1995). Families of the baby boom: Parents' division of labor and children's adjustment: Sexual orientation and human development. [Special issue]. *Developmental Psychology, 31,* 115–123.

Paterson, C. J., & Chan, R. W. (1997). Gay fathers. In M. E. Lamb (Ed.), *The role of the father in child development* (pp. 245–260). New York: Wiley.

Reamer, F. (1995). Ethics and values. In R. L. Edwards (Ed.), *Encyclopedia of social work* (Vol. 3, p. 893–901). Washington, DC: NASW Press.

Schaie, K. W. (1977/1978). Toward a stage theory of adult cognitive development. *Aging and Human Development, 8,* 129–138.

Shatter, D. N., Kramer, G. P., Shabatay, V., & Bernstein, D. A. (2000). *Lifespan development in context: Voices and perspectives.* Boston: Houghton Mifflin.

Steinberg, L. (2002). *Adolescence* (6th ed.). New York: McGraw-Hill.

Tatum, B. D. (1992). Talking about race, learning about racism: The application of racial identity development theory in the classroom. *Harvard Educational Review, 62*(1), 1–24.

Van Wormer, K. (2001). Doing alcoholism treatment in Norway: A personal reminiscence. In S. L. Abels (Ed.), Ethics in social work practice: *Narratives for professional helping* (pp. 95–103). Long Beach, CA: Love.

Vaillant, G. E. (1977). *Adaptation to life*. Boston: Little, Brown.

Figure 6.1. In middle adulthood, many individuals reach the peaks of their careers. This social worker is a leader in supporting adults with major mental illnesses. The client was recently released from prison and is on probation, living in temporary housing. The client has been diagnosed as having schizophrenia, anxiety, depression, and alcohol abuse issues.

6

Social Work with Midlife Adults in Mental Health Contexts: Understanding and Treating Depression

This chapter considers the midlife adult, aged approximately 35 to 65 years, as the focal system. For many individuals, midlife brings increased responsibilities including rearing and launching children, caring for aging parents, taking on leadership roles at work, and preparing for retirement. These responsibilities can bring great joy, but also considerable stress. For many other individuals, midlife brings the accumulated stresses of a lifetime of poverty, violence, substance abuse, and unmet health and mental health needs. In vulnerable individuals, stress from positive and negative life changes can lead to mental health problems such as depression. As you read, consider how biological, psychological, and social factors interact within particular cultural and historical contexts to influence mental health in middle adulthood.

In the United States, the majority of mental health services are provided by social workers in settings ranging from community mental health centers to private psychotherapy practices. As you read, consider how the normal blues may be distinguished from depression in midlife, and how effective intervention for depression triggered primarily by environmental stress is similar to or different from intervention for depression triggered primarily by genetic vulnerability. What unique roles do social workers play within a team of psychiatrists, psychologists, nurses, and others involved in care for those suffering from mental illness?

Social work with individuals in middle adulthood is as varied as the experience of midlife itself. In midlife, many adults are functioning at their peak as they continue to enjoy good health and assume positions of responsibility at work and within their families. Others may be struggling with the burdens of decades of unemployment, poverty, and/or substance abuse (see boxes 6.1-6.3). Some adults in their early 40s are new grandparents as the children they produced in their late teens and early 20s begin their families, while other adults who delayed having children until they established professional careers are new parents. Some adults in careers within academia, law, or medicine, which require lengthy periods of formal education and apprenticeship, are just beginning to assume leadership roles in their 40s.

BOX 6.1 POVERTY ACROSS THE LIFE SPAN
American Indian and Alaska Native Median Income

The two-year average (2003-2004) median income for American Indian and Alaska Native households was approximately $32,510. This represented a 3.7% loss of household income between 2003 and 2004. Comparatively, the incomes of American Indian and Alaska Native households were higher than those of African American households ($30,288), almost equal to those of Hispanic households ($34,062), and substantially lower than the median incomes of Asian ($57,357) and white ($49,019) households.

Source: DeNavas-Walt, C., Proctor, B. D., and Lee, C. H. (2005) *Income, poverty, and health insurance coverage in the United States: 2004.* U.S. Census Bureau, Current Population Reports (Publication No. P60-226). Washington, DC: U.S. Government Printing Office.

Those who entered the military in their late teens, may be enjoying retirement or launching a new career in their 40s. With this diversity of experience comes a wide range of challenges. Not surprisingly, social workers encounter midlife adults in a variety of contexts, including educational institutions, mental health centers, domestic violence shelters, and medical settings. In this chapter, we consider social work in mental health contexts.

MENTAL HEALTH CARE WITH MIDLIFE ADULTS

Mental health care has been a special concern of social workers since the beginning of the twentieth century. In the late 1980s, social workers' commitment to serving those with mental illness gained momentum, clarity, and direction. Social workers began to consider mental illness primarily as a disease, a disease that affects and is affected by the individual's social and

---

BOX 6.2 POVERTY ACROSS THE LIFE SPAN
The Poor Get Poorer

People in the lowest 20% of household earnings (twentieth national income percentile) saw their incomes decline 1.9% in 2003 from a median of $18,326 to $17,984. People in the top twenty percentile enjoyed a 1.1% increase from $85,000 to $86,867.

Source: DeNavas-Walt, C., Proctor, B. D., & Mills, R. J. (2004). *Income, poverty, and health insurance coverage in the United States.* U.S. Census Bureau, Current Population Reports (Publication No. P60-226). Washington, DC: U.S. Government Printing Office.

BOX 6.3 SUBSTANCE ABUSE ACROSS THE LIFE SPAN
Substance Dependence, Genetics, and Environment

- Substance dependence results from a gene-environment interaction.
- The following environmental factors are believed to interact with genes and increase the probability for addiction:

    Family dynamics (especially if addiction is part of the family system);

    Peer interactions;

    Individual temperament and social climate fit;

    Socioeconomic factors (low income and poor education);

    Cultural norms and beliefs.

- The risk for developing a drug disorder is eight times more likely for people with substance-abusing relatives compared to individuals from families with no history of a substance disorder or mental illness.
- Twin studies indicate that the heritability for substance disorders range from:

    48% to 87% in males;

    21% to 73% in females.

- If a person is genetically predisposed to substance dependence but never uses a substance, an addiction cannot occur. Further, a person who is not genetically predisposed for addiction can learn to abuse substances.
- In both abuse and addiction, environment plays a shifting and differential role. Within the same person, environment can shift a number of times between having a major and a minor influence.
- When one is addicted, the brain actually changes and can independently create the need for the intake of substances.
- The close relationship between genes, brain adaptation, and environment has made sorting out gene and environmental influences difficult. This question will be answered more specifically as scientists learn to decode DNA.

Sources: Merikangas, K. R., Stolar, M., Stevens D. E., Goulet, J., Preisig, M., Fenton, B., et al. (1998). Familial transmission of substance use disorders. *Archives of General Psychiatry, 55* (11), 973–979. Merikangas, K. R., & Stipelman, B. (2004). Genetic epidemiology of substance use disorder. In D. S. Charney & E. J. Nestler (Eds.), *Neurobiology of mental illness* (2nd ed.). New York: Oxford University Press.

cultural context. Initiatives for improving social work interventions and research with those suffering from mental illness were sponsored by clinical treatment facilities, academia, NASW, and the National Institute of Mental Health (NIMH). In 1988, NIMH funded a planning committee to develop recommendations for increasing social workers' knowledge, involvement, and research of individuals suffering from mental illness. One result of this work was a series of federally sponsored training seminars and financial assistance for developing research centers within selected schools of social work (Taylor, 1996, 1997).

Today, mental health is the single largest field of concentration for MSW students. Mental health social workers confront a wide range of issues with clients (see box 6.4 for a discussion of antisocial personality disorder). Individuals experiencing depression, anxiety, or psychosis require a range of medical, psychotherapeutic, and social services to promote their well-being and to alleviate mental disorders. Social workers specializing in mental health have important roles on a team of medical professionals (psychiatrists, nurses) and social service and psychotherapy providers. Within this team, social workers provide a unique ecological perspective, for example, how the individual's living circumstances (housing, relationship with family members) upon discharge from the hospital affect long-term mental well-being. Social workers are also leaders in developing culturally competent mental health training and education, for example, how attitudes and beliefs about mental illness within the family and community affect compliance with psychotropic medication or participation in psychotherapy.

Currently, social work is second only to nursing as the largest occupational group staffing mental health facilities. Within the mental health field, social workers are nearly twice as prevalent as either psychiatrists or psychologists (Lin, 1995). This chapter elaborates on how a developmental-ecological analysis can inform social work practice with depressed individuals in middle adulthood. Two cases illustrate the complexity of recognizing and appropriately intervening with individuals experiencing depression in midlife. As the following cases illustrate, depression takes complex and various forms in midlife and affects not only the individual, but family and community as well.

I Need a Change

Joe is a 56-year-old white executive who has been married for thirty-three years. He and his wife have two successful adult children. Joe has a large almost-paid-for suburban home; a secure moderately high-paying job; money saved for retirement; manageable monthly bills; an ability to buy personal luxuries, including short annual vacation trips; respect from peers; strong religious faith and values; and routine invitations from friends to play golf. What Joe does not have is a sense of peace, control over his destiny, and, most of all, happiness. Joe and his wife argue and have sex only occasionally and in a perfunctory manner. The relationship problems started about six

---

BOX 6.4 VIOLENCE ACROSS THE LIFE SPAN
Antisocial Personality Disorder

Professionals debate how antisocial personality disorder should be defined. Currently most mental health professionals use the definition and criteria provided by the American Psychiatric Association's (2000) text revision of the *Diagnostic and Statistical Manual of Mental Disorders (DSM-IV-TR)*. The disorder is described as starting in childhood or early adolescence and continuing into adulthood. Symptoms can generally be traced to the person's childhood. The diagnosis should not be made in a child because many children and adolescents who break social norms and fail to learn from experience do not demonstrate antisocial behaviors as adults. People with an antisocial personality disorder have a long pattern of failing to conform with social norms, are extremely irresponsible, disregard the rights and concerns of others, violate the civil rights of others, and often are aggressive. It is not unusual for people with this disorder to get into physical fights, fail to learn from experience, and blame the victim rather than accept responsibility for their behaviors. Community studies show that about 3% of men and 1% of women meet the criteria for antisocial personality disorder diagnosis. There is a ray of hope for people who fall into this diagnostic category. Even though psychotherapy and most rehabilitation efforts are not effective, with time many improve. When the young adult reaches midlife, criminal and other antisocial behaviors decrease. No one is certain why this happens, but researchers hypothesize that as the person ages, the brain changes and allows new insights and improved impulse control.

Sources: American Psychiatric Association. (2000). *Diagnostic and statistical manual of mental disorders* (text revision, pp. 701–714). Washington, DC: Author; Black, D. W. (1999). *Bad boys, bad men. Confronting antisocial personality disorder.* New York: Oxford University Press.

---

months ago and have increased over the last six weeks. For months, work has seemed mundane and Joe's ability to concentrate has decreased. It seems hard to focus on or care about tasks. This is especially true at work but also occurs in almost every sphere of his life. Joe still performs all the necessary or required tasks, but with less interest, pride, and motivation. Joe often finds it difficult to get out of bed in the morning; he often feels numb and tired. He used to have no problem sleeping at night and getting up early. Now, he goes to sleep at his regular time but often awakens after a few hours and cannot get back to sleep. As a result, during the past few months he has been using more and more sick leave. Unlike earlier in his career, he now says his work is just a job allowing him to limp toward retirement. Even his interest in golf has plummeted. He plays but tires more easily, loses more often, and gets into disputes with other golfers. In the past, he seldom argued or became upset when playing golf. Joe explains these difficulties away by telling people his life is in a rut that needs change.

More than anything, Joe blames his wife. He explains that she has changed and seems to have completely lost interest in their sex life. Joe realizes that at his age divorce would be costly to both him and his wife. He would lose at least 50 percent of the equity in their home, retirement, and savings accounts, and other community property. He also knows the idea of divorce will not be supported by his adult children or aging parents. There is no other person in his life, and he is not having any extramarital relationships. Life as presently arranged is just not working, and in Joe's mind there is no solution other than ending the marriage. As a result, Joe has an appointment with a lawyer and he intends to start divorce proceedings immediately. Joe and others may see his situation as a midlife crisis. However, there may be an alternative way for understanding his behavior and how he perceives his world.

How Can This Be Happening?

Maria is a 47-year-old Mexican American professional woman who resides in a middle-class neighborhood. An internal medicine physician has placed Maria on an antidepressant and referred her for psychotherapy. Although she has no psychiatric history and does not consider herself an anxious or depressed person, she nonetheless has developed major depressive symptoms. Maria describes herself as a strong person who can take care of herself, her children, and other family members without help. Therefore, it is difficult for her to tell a stranger, especially a mental health social worker, that for the past three weeks she often cries, has problems sleeping, vacillates between having no appetite and gorging food, and has little enjoyment, even from activities that used to be rewarding. At first Maria minimizes her difficulties, insisting that she simply has been emotional and came in to see the social worker because her doctor asked her to but now has things under better control. However, after slowing the interview down, joining with Maria, and winning a degree of trust, the social worker listens as details of Maria's life unfold.

Maria has been a strong, productive person. She is the oldest of six children who grew up traveling rural America harvesting crops with her migrant farm-laboring parents. She has many stories of the hardships involved in working the fields, caring for siblings, always living with inadequate medical care, and trying to piece together an education while on the move. Maria states she really never had a childhood. She was always either helping raise the younger children or helping harvest crops. As an older teenager she worked part-time in the fields, attended school, helped care for her siblings, and worked on weekends at fast-food restaurants. In spite of these hardships, Maria excelled academically and won a scholarship to a small liberal arts college. After completing a bachelor's degree in accounting, she passed the CPA exam, joined a nationwide firm, married, and moved to suburbia. As an upwardly mobile person, she considered herself to have no major financial or emotional difficulties throughout her young adulthood. With great pride she states, "I have passed every test life has given me, at least until now." Over the past nine months, Maria's life has had one major setback after another.

After working nineteen years for a nationwide firm, she lost her job three months ago when the company declared bankruptcy and laid everyone off. Although no criminal accusations were directed toward Maria, federal auditors have questioned the company's bookkeeping practices. As a result, she feels her trustworthiness and professional integrity have been questioned. She also strongly believes the company's bad publicity has played a major role in her inability to find new employment. Maria is presently without health insurance, and her doctor wants her to have a lump in her breast examined by a specialist. Along with these stressors, less than two months ago a flood destroyed Maria's aging parents' home. Everything was lost and their homeowners' insurance did not cover floods.

The parents, who have only a small Social Security income, are now living with Maria. In a moment of anxiety while arguing with Maria last week, her mother declared that the family's problems are occurring one after another because Maria no longer attends Mass, is no longer religious, has forsaken her heritage, thinks she is better than everyone, and has caused someone with power to give her and the family the "evil eye." Maria is embarrassed to tell this part of the story. She feels certain a social worker could not understand and that an educated person would not believe that her problems are caused by a mystic spell placed by a "witch." These were the beliefs and explanations she left in the strawberry and lettuce fields years ago. She is now 47 years of age and an uncertain financial future, worry about what the doctor will find and how to pay the bill, the fear of spirits, embarrassment for a rural uneducated family, and her mother's never-ending advice are all back! Every thought, anxiety, feeling, and person are once again crammed together in a house no longer financially affordable. Maria cries but expects no answers, no help. She just hopes that once again she can reach in and find the inner strength that used to be her hallmark, but, at this point in time, Maria is not sure she has the ability to face the problems. Her energy, drive, and self-belief are momentarily gone.

In the first case, Joe has been highly successful in his work, family, and social life. His current difficulties were not precipitated by any specific crisis or set of stressful events. He demonstrates behaviors that fit the popular press stereotype of midlife crisis. However, he also has behaviors that signal the onset of major clinical depression. According to the American Psychiatric Association's text revision (2000) of the *Diagnostic and Statistical Manual of Mental Disorders (DSM-IV-TR)*, major depression is a genetically determined biochemical disorder manifested by inability to experience pleasure and cope with everyday events. As Joe described his childhood, he identified symptoms of depression in his father and paternal grandfather. Joe, like his father and grandfather before him, is not only unhappy but seems to have lost interest in most or all of his activities and relationships. He performs only necessary tasks at work; golf is no longer enjoyable; he is upset with his

Figure 6.2. Historically, social workers have served as leaders in supporting individuals struggling with poverty.

spouse and finds it easier to give up part of his financial security than resolve his marital issues. Solving these problems will require great energy, but Joe has difficulty even getting out of bed. Depression may be a cause of Joe's sleeping problem; it can cause people to routinely awaken after falling asleep and then be unable to return to sleep. Joe identifies his marital, work, and even golf problems as stemming from someone else. Furthermore, he is easily agitated in these environments and finds problem solving difficult. Depression often narrows peoples' perspectives and causes them to think in a very concrete manner.

Maria, like Joe, has experienced considerable success in her life but is currently experiencing symptoms of depression. Unlike Joe, Maria has no family history of depression, and her difficulties are clearly linked to current stressful events. Maria is suffering from *reactive depression* occurring in response to adverse life events (loss of job, illness, family problems). Three important facts are illustrated by this case example. First, Maria's environmentally triggered symptoms, emotions, and thought processes mirror the biologically triggered depression experienced by Joe. This occurs because Maria's neural chemical system is temporarily out of balance. Maria is not psychologically or unconsciously willing the depression; her brain has simply started to function in a depressed mode.

Second, Maria finds both strength and tribulation from her culture of origin. Maria's heritage can provide valuable hope and support necessary to overcome the current crisis. It also can cause stress, for example, her return to concerns about mystic evil powers and embarrassment about these concerns. Despite an individual's formal education or acculturation, cultural beliefs learned early within the family and home community can resurface during a crisis. Maria is caught in a mental struggle between beliefs, roles, and goals learned from two differing and conflicting cultures.

Third, Maria's story underscores that macrosystem policies and economic stability can cause an individual's situation to change. Social workers must be prepared to identify when a person's problems are caused more by environmental factors than by internal psychological structure or brain disorder. As discussed in this chapter, the causes of depression have important implications for which a combination of intervention strategies will be most effective.

HIGHLIGHTS OF DEVELOPMENT
IN MIDDLE ADULTHOOD

Human development is shaped in relation to accumulating biological, psychological, and social factors operating within particular cultural and historical contexts. Common biological characteristics, for example, changes associated with aging, may form a basis for common psychological and social characteristics. In addition, as individuals inch toward the senior years, their increasingly diverse developmental pathways lead to varied biological, psychological, and social characteristics.

Although considerable development does occur in midlife, there are wide individual differences. Levinson (1978, 1980, 1986, 1990, 1996) characterized midlife as the most difficult developmental era to describe in general terms. Midlife changes and tasks are shaped by each individual's culture, health, genetics, economics, politics, empowerment, and environmental opportunities. How biological aging in midlife affects individuals is dependent upon numerous social and cultural factors. Ashford, LeCroy, and Lortie (2001) point out that "Midlife is different from other developmental phases in that it is less affected by biological maturation. Indeed, adults are most affected by their own experiences" (p. 470).

Biological Factors

Biological changes, however, do occur as individuals age. Most adults in middle adulthood are healthy and energetic, but they may begin to notice gradual physical changes such as hair loss or graying, wrinkling of the skin, decreased sight and hearing, weight gain, and lessening of muscular strength and physical stamina. These changes are universal, but their timing and degree vary. This variability is related to a number of factors, including genetics, diet, health care availability, health history, and risk taking.

Individuals in midlife also may develop troubles sleeping due to biological changes, mental health problems, and/or environmental factors. Based on a cross-sectional survey of 1,506 adults, approximately 40 percent reported sleeping less than seven hours each night during the work week. Furthermore, 24 percent reported having only a few good nights of sleep each week, and 26 percent reported that they get a good night of sleep only a few evenings per month (National Sleep Foundation, 2005).

While the trend for less rest is reported by men and women, it appears to be more prevalent in younger and middle-aged women. This may result from physiological changes occurring from menstruation, pregnancy, and menopause. It also may occur because of mental health problems. About 20 percent of individuals reporting sleep difficulties suffer from depression, and up to one-third have an underlying mental disorder of some type (Cummings & Mega, 2003; Hales & Hales, 1995). Unfortunately, the less individuals sleep, the more they "learn" not to sleep. An interaction can occur between bodily changes or pain keeping a person awake and developing a "habit" or learned response of not sleeping. Approximately 15 percent of people seeking help for chronic insomnia have primarily learned not to sleep (Hales & Hales, 1995).

Environment can greatly affect sleeping patterns. Many of us have developed poor eating and exercise habits and consume substances like caffeine, nicotine, or alcohol that can induce insomnia. Additionally, work-related stress can have a negative impact on a person's physical health and sleep patterns. Women working late shifts, for example, are at a higher risk for having irregular menstrual cycles, problems becoming pregnant, and higher rates of miscarriages, premature births, and low birth-weight babies (Hales & Hales, 1995; National Sleep Foundation, 2005). Because a wide range of physiological, psychological, neurological, and environmental factors can cause sleeping problems social workers can best serve their clients by:

- screening for sleeping problems;

- identifying environmental factors that can trigger insomnia;

- understanding that sleeping difficulties may stem from both physical problems such as breathing difficulties while asleep (sleep apnea), pain, and menstruation, and learned habits;

- knowing that some people, but not the majority, cannot sleep because of a mental disorder;

- recognizing that the inability to sleep may be a symptom of a more serious physical illness;

- referring clients to appropriate sleep clinics and experts for a complete assessment.

Most social workers are not trained to independently assess and treat primary sleep disturbances. Once the diagnosis has been correctly made, under expert supervision social workers can assist some clients with relaxation and cognitive interventions. We can also directly help individuals learn to improve their sleeping environments and overcome habits that interfere with gaining a restful night's sleep. Surveys indicate that as we age, quality sleep increases if one's lifestyle includes:

- ongoing routine and trusting relationships;
- hopeful and positive attitudes;
- regular and appropriate exercise;
- commitments for volunteer work or other organizational activities.

An important biological milestone for women in middle adulthood is menopause. Menopause is triggered by a decrease in ovarian function and consists of three stages. The first stage, premenopause, normally begins at about 40 years of age, but may appear for some women in their early 30s. Throughout the first stage, the ovaries slowly decrease hormone production. The erratic ovarian functioning causes changes in the woman's menstrual cycle and flow. Premenopausal hormone changes can also trigger weight gain and premenstrual breast tenderness and water retention. As a result, doctors often recommend women restrict their salt intake and routinely exercise during the premenopausal stage.

BOX 6.5 HEART ATTACK WARNING SIGNS

Although most individuals experience good health in middle adulthood, those with genetic vulnerabilities to illness and/or stressful lifestyles may experience ill health or the beginning of chronic disease. Heart attacks may be sudden and intense or start slowly and in the beginning cause only mild discomfort. More often the onset is slow and less dramatic. This can cause a person to be uncertain about what is happening and about the need for immediate medical care. Common signs and warnings of a heart attack are:

- mild pain or discomfort in the center of the chest lasting more than a few minutes, or pain that goes away and comes back which can be described as pressure, squeezing, fullness, pain, or heartburn;
- mild pain or discomfort in other upper body regions such as one or both arms, the back, neck, jaw, or stomach;
- shortness of breath which can occur before chest pain/discomfort, or simultaneously with chest discomfort;
- the person may or may not break out in a cold sweat, become nauseated, or experience lightheadedness

Sources: American Heart Association. (2003). *Heart attack, stroke and cardiac arrest warning signs.* Retrieved December 12, 2003, from http://www.americanheart.org/presenter.jhtml; Ashford, J., LeCroy, C.W., & Lortie, K. (2001). *Human behavior in the social environment A multidimensional perspective* (2nd ed.). Belmont, CA: Wadsworth/Thomson; Seifert, K. L., & Hoffnung, M. (2000). *Lifespan development* (2nd ed.). Boston: Houghton Mifflin.

The second stage, menopause, begins a year after a women has her last period and is no longer able to become pregnant. The average age at which women reach menopause is 51.4 years, and the majority of women reach menopause between 45 and 55 years of age. Hot flashes and inability to sleep through the night are common menopausal complaints that result from falling levels of estrogen. Hormonal depletion also causes fat to increase in the abdomen, breasts to be less firm, and skin to thin. Women and their spouses or partners also need to know menopause can cause breaks in the vaginal skin, dryness that makes sex uncomfortable, urinary tract infections, and for some women unpleasant and embarrassing urinary leakage. More importantly, hormonal imbalance caused by menopause can affect women's hearts, bones, and brains. Without proper treatment, the cardiovascular system is at risk for hardening of the arteries, bones lose calcium and become brittle, and the brain becomes vulnerable for memory loss, depression, and disrupted sleep patterns (Shumaker, Legault, Rapp, et al., 2003; Rap, Espeland, Shumaker, et al., 2003; Seifert & Hoffnung, 2000). Most of these problems disappear as a woman enters postmenopause (third stage) and hormonal levels become more stable. However, periodic medical exams for loss of bone density and cardiovascular changes should continue throughout life.

Responses to the biological changes of menopause vary, depending on cultural context and women's individual expectations. In societies where a woman's role is largely reproductive, the inability to bear more children may result in a loss of status. In cultures where the wisdom and experience of older women is valued, menopause is seen as a more positive life event (Borysenko, 1997; Northrup, 1994). Margaret Lock (1993) studied menopause and the symptoms experienced by thousands of women, ages 45 through 55 years, in Japan, the United States, and Canada. Lock hypothesized that Japan's history of war, poverty, and traditional societal rules and roles would cause Japanese women to experience more menopausal symptoms than North American women. To the researcher's surprise, Japanese women reported significantly fewer symptoms than the American and Canadian research participants. Shoulder stiffness (52%) followed by headaches (28%) were the leading Japanese complaints. In the North American sample, shoulder stiffness was hardly mentioned, but more than 33 percent of the Canadian sample and 37 percent of the American women had experienced headaches. Only 10 percent of the Japanese women reported symptoms of depression, whereas 23 percent of the Canadians and almost 36 percent of the Americans indicated that menopause caused them to feel blue or depressed. These findings illustrate culture's role in determining how individuals experience some but not all of the body's biochemical changes. One wonders whether future generations of North American women will find the physical appearance changes caused by menopause to be an ever-increasing stressor. The popular print media and television document our continuing interest in anti-aging creams, plastic surgery, and an endless search for the fountain of youth. Regardless of the cultural lens, menopause will continue to be a midlife event women must experience. The social worker's role is to provide education and support to help the woman, her spouse or partner, and her family to reduce psychological stressors and maintain positive interpersonal and intrafamily communications as the woman moves through the menopausal stages.

Psychological and Social Factors

Individuals in midlife also continue to experience psychological changes and development. Erikson characterized midlife as a period when thought and activities focus on moving from personal concerns to providing meaningful and creative care for others. A central challenge of midlife, according to Erikson, is generativity, a concern with improving or contributing to the well-being of future generations (Lachman & James, 1997). Santrock (2002) documented that middle adulthood is a relatively productive and emotionally healthy period for women and men. Most people traverse midlife without developing major physical and mental health problems. Many middle-aged adults experience a period of feeling safe, secure, and settled. With this sense of security comes a greater commitment and interest in nurturing the next generation, assumption of the role of carrier and transmitter of culture and knowledge, as well as a review of one's own past commitments (Lachman & James, 1997).

Less optimal psychological outcomes in midlife may include feelings of boredom and bitterness regarding opportunities foregone. Common psychological issues include an increased concern about future health, possibly a result of the inevitable physical changes associated with aging. Hooker and Kaus (1994) found that people in midlife are aware of their increased vulnerability for major illnesses, decreased motor skills, hearing loss, decreased vision, reduced sexuality, and other physical and psychological issues. Indeed, the prospect of developing heart disease, cancer, or having a stroke can be frightening (see box 6.5 for a discussion of heart attack warning signs).

Although a popular topic in the media, the phenomenon of a midlife crisis is not widespread. Research has generally failed to support the idea that by simply entering midlife one becomes vulnerable for an emotional or identity crisis (Lachman & James, 1997; Andreasen & Black, 2000). Labeling a person as being in a midlife crisis does not inform the social worker how to treat the client. The concept of midlife crisis is overly broad and highly influenced by culture, social class, and personal beliefs. Perspectives and experiences of midlife are affected by basic survival and health factors.

Midlife takes on a different meaning for individuals who face decreased life expectancy and increased probability of developing a potentially fatal illness. Within the United States, life expectancy varies across ethnic groups.

For example, American Indians and Alaska Natives die from tuberculosis at a rate 750 percent higher than the rest of the nation and from diabetes at a rate 420 percent higher than other American citizens. They also die from accidents and suicide at an increased rate of 280 percent and 190 percent respectively. American Indian deaths from alcoholism are 770 percent higher than those of the general population (U.S. Indian Health Service, 2002).

People in middle adulthood also experience social changes. They have been described as the "sandwich generation," caught between obligations to their partners, children, and aging parents. Nonetheless, many of these relationships continue to play an important supportive role in the lives of most individuals in middle adulthood. Many adults in midlife experience greater affection and love, especially in lasting partnerships. More people in midlife than in early adulthood report that their marriages are good or excellent. Furthermore, individuals who divorce during midlife have a less emotionally volatile relationship with former spouses than people who divorce at a younger age. Most parents in middle adulthood continue to feel close to their children and may regret not having spent more time with them. The experience of children's leaving home, resulting in an empty nest, often increases rather than decreases life satisfaction; however, many children return home because of economic factors. Friendships are highly valued by most middle-aged people and can be a source of great joy and support. As during other periods of life, relationships with siblings vary widely; some middle-aged siblings grow closer, while others drift farther apart (Santrock, 2002).

Cultural-Historical Factors

The meaning and purpose of middle adulthood vary across cultural and historical contexts. In Asian, African, and Native American societies midlife is viewed as preparation to becoming a more powerful and respected elder. In United States and Western European cultures, midlife is often viewed as a period of work and community productivity, consolidation of economic worth, and preparation for retirement. In terms of authority and power, midlife in America is what later adulthood is for people, particularly men, in Asian, African, and Native American communities. The United States culture values its members more in midlife as expert parents, workers, and community leaders than in later adulthood as retired senior citizens. In the United States, having adult status, expertise, and full-time employment is not only empowering, but difficult to achieve before midlife, and even harder to maintain in later life. It is during midlife that one often achieves prestigious social titles, such as foreman, supervisor, chief, grandparent, senior clinical social worker; gains practical knowledge and is at least partially sanctioned by society to give advice; gains increased assets; and is perceived as wiser than younger, less experienced adults.

There is, however, significant individual variation in how one understands and responds to middle adulthood. People do not live only within the context of macrosystems, but within particular communities and families. We develop our own "place-in-culture," or niche, that personalizes and reflects macro- and microsystems. Therefore, people, may come from identical macrosystems, but because of their place-in-culture they experience personal and societal events differently. For some people, becoming a grandparent stirs warm emotions, a positive identity, parental validation, and a link to their historical culture, whereas others worry about aging, unwanted responsibilities, and economic concerns. Midlife attitudes and perspectives become individualized by health and physical changes, life experiences, beliefs, personality factors, genetics, and, for some, psychiatric disorders.

DEVELOPMENTAL-ECOLOGICAL ANALYSIS OF DEPRESSION IN MIDDLE ADULTHOOD

Depression is one of the most frequent psychiatric problems faced by individuals throughout the life span. Approximately 5 percent of North Americans suffer from depression (Baldwin & Birtwistle, 2002; DePaulo, 2002; Taylor, 1997). Depression occurs in both genders but occurs more than twice as frequently in women than in men *(DSM-IV-TR)*. Depression also occurs at all ages, but the most vulnerable period for the onset is between 20 and 40 years of age (Stahl, 2000). Depression can limit people's ability to control not only their mood, but also energy, social perceptions, problem solving, information processing, motor coordination, and decision making. Depression is more than simple sadness, a lack of hunger, or an inability to sleep. While these are all possible symptoms of depression, the terms fail to convey an illness that captures, controls, and limits a person's mind, emotions, and range of possible behavioral responses (Taylor, 2005). Depression affects neurological, emotional, and body systems. The depressed individual may find it extremely difficult to understand abstractions, identify islands of hope, and develop alternative perspectives or solutions (Taylor, 2005; Taylor, 2003; DePaulo, 2002).

Symptoms of major clinical depression usually develop over days or weeks. A major depressive episode occurs when there is depressed mood or the loss of interest or pleasure in nearly all activities, and four additional symptoms including changes in appetite or weight, sleep, and psychomotor activity; decreased energy; feelings of worthlessness or guilt; difficulty thinking, concentrating, or making decisions; and recurrent thoughts of death or suicide *(DSM-IV-TR)*. These symptoms persist for at least two weeks and are new or worse than before the episode. Depressed individuals may describe feeling down-in-the-dumps, sad, hopeless, and discouraged. They may report a loss of interest in hobbies or work. Appetite may be reduced or increased with a craving for sweets and carbohydrates. Depressed individuals may suffer from insomnia or may oversleep. They may experience agitation or slowed speech and have difficulty thinking, concentrating, or making decisions. Decreased energy, decreased libido, and fatigue are common, as are feelings of guilt and worthlessness. Frequently, they may think of death or suicide and may attempt suicide. The degree of impairment with an episode of major depression varies, but there must be clinically significant distress, or interference with social, occupational, or other important areas of functioning.

Fortunately, depression is a treatable illness and 75 percent to 80 percent of individuals who receive psychotherapy and/or medications experience substantial improvement within three to four months (Stahl, 2000). Left untreated, however, an episode of depression typically lasts for six months or longer before abating. Tragically, as many as 15 percent of people who suffer from major depression will commit suicide (Stahl, 2000). In the United States, suicide is the eighth most frequent cause of death, and sixth in the United Kingdom. Among Americans ages 15 to 44, suicide is the second leading cause of death (Baldwin & Birtwistle, 2002). Individuals with depression must be screened on a regular basis for suicidal thoughts and behavioral indicators. Social workers should not hesitate to ask a client if he or she has thoughts or plans for taking his/her life when symptoms or signs of suicidal behavior are observed. Some of the key risk factors for suicide often reported by clinicians and researchers include:

- a history of one or more suicidal attempts;
- family history of suicide;
- feelings of hopelessness;
- statements about life not being worth living;
- statements indicating that there is no solution, or that a situation will not improve;
- increased risk taking or impulsiveness;
- written suicide notes, or obsessive writing, reading, or talking about death;
- alcohol and substance abuse;
- severe mental health symptoms, with particular attention to hopelessness, sleep disturbance, anxiety, and agitation;
- increased isolation;
- recent or increased life stressor;
- preparation for death (e.g., giving away personal items and money);
- poor response to psychotropic medications, or refusal to take medications (Taylor, 2005).

Some individuals experience episodes of depression associated with *bipolar disorder* (also known as *manic-depressive* disorder). During manic phases individuals experience unusually high levels of exuberance, grandiosity, feelings of invulnerability, and extremely fast thinking. In this phase, an individual demonstrates poor judgment and decision making. The individual may vastly overspend his financial resources, exhibit hypersexuality, and engage in risk-taking behavior that can result in death (e.g., running across a highway, trying to dodge speeding cars). The individual also may display low tolerance, with frustration that leads to arguments and physical fights (Taylor, 2005).

Biological Factors

Research indicates that major depression is a biologically based illness caused by structural and functional problems occurring in the brain

---

Box 6.6 THE ASSESSMENT PROCESS
An Overview Using the
Developmental-Ecological Perspective

Assessment is a critical first step in the development and implementation of an appropriate, effective social work intervention. As used in this book, assessment refers to the systematic collection of information guided by valid and appropriate theories of human development that are linked to empirical research findings. Social workers in all practice fields routinely assess the ever-changing challenges, skills, and resources of individuals, families, communities, and other social systems. The types of information we collect, as well as how we evaluate, interpret, and use this information, is guided by our theoretical or conceptual perspectives.

The first steps in the assessment process are to determine what information is relevant to collect and how to go about collecting it. From our developmental-ecological perspective, information collected should include a description of biological, psychological, and social factors within cultural-historical contexts. The focus of this assessment is determined by the problem we hope to address through systematic interventions, for example, problems of living stemming from major depression.

Once information collection is completed, clinical assumptions are made, that is, certain facts are accepted with little or no challenge. It is a reality of social work that we will never have all the relevant information. Budgets are tight and we often rely on reports from clients and others that may or may not be accurate and complete. Making clinical assumptions is one of the most risky and potentially dangerous parts of the assessment. Bias, lack of experience and knowl-

---

edge, or inability to see beyond the expected can lead us to accept incorrect or incomplete assumptions. If our assumptions are wrong, then we may misunderstand the person's behaviors and environments. Social workers must always question whether the "obvious" is camouflaging reality, and if our professional beliefs and assumptions are conceptually and empirically sound.

Given assessment information and clinical assumptions, the next steps in the assessment process are to form and then test clinical hypotheses. A clinical hypothesis explains an observed behavior, problem, or social interaction (Rubin & Babbie, 1993). The hypotheses we form and test, like the clinical assumptions we make, are guided by our theoretical perspectives. From our developmental-ecological perspective, hypotheses typically include specific biological and social factors as contributing to the issues we hope to address through intervention.

The clinical hypothesis must always be tested and proved by multiple sources to be contextually valid. From a developmental-ecological perspective, contextual validity means that the clinical hypotheses used for explaining observed behaviors are not only theoretically true, but apply the correct weight and meaning to reciprocal exchanges occurring among environmental settings and the client. Contextual validity requires behavior to be assessed in context with the environment, current and historical culture, and time and place. In isolation, behaviors have little meaning.

The assessment process of collecting information, making clinical assumptions, and forming and testing clinical hypotheses is a continuous process. Assessments are never final because change can occur from multiple interacting physical and social contexts at any time. Thus, developmental-ecological assessments are always tentative and must be subjected to ongoing analysis. The developmental-ecological perspective provides an analytic framework, a heuristic, for approaching complex problems within social work, including assessment.

(Goodwin & Jamison, 1990; Jamison 1999; DePaulo, 2002; Stahl, 2000; Taylor, 1997, 2005). Major depression is biologically determined (i.e., family history). Examination of identical twins separated at birth (i.e., individuals who share the same genetic code, but not the same environment) reveals strong associations between genetics and mental illness (Jones, Kent, & Craddock, 2002; Sadock & Sadock 2003; Torrey et al., 1994). Depression has a much higher probability of occurring in a pair of identical twins, who share the same genes, than in a pair of fraternal twins, who do not share the same genetic codes. In major depression, concurrent rates for identical twins are twice that of fraternal twins (Jones, Kent, & Craddock, 2002; Kalidindi, McGuffin, & McGuffin, 2003). Several brain chemicals, called *neurotransmit-*

ters, play important roles in mood disorders such as depression. Neurotransmitters conduct communications between different brain cells. Neurotransmitters implicated in major depression include norepinephrine, serotonin, acetylcholine, and gamma-aminobutyric *(DSM-IV-TR)*. Advances in technology provide further evidence of the biological basis of major depression. They include the ability to image neurological structures and measure the brain's metabolic rate and numerous differences in the brain's structure and function that occur between individuals with and without mental illness (Taylor, 2005).

The biological basis of depression is sensitive to, and interacts in complex ways with, psychological, social, and cultural factors. The stress caused by economic problems, interpersonal difficulties, and other hardships can trigger major depression in vulnerable individuals. In addition, severe hardships and trauma also can trigger the biological symptoms of depression in individuals who are not particularly genetically vulnerable (DePaulo, 2002; Taylor, 2003).

Psychological Factors

Major depression has profound psychological consequences that can block interpersonal development and positive growth (DePaulo, 2002; Gotlib & Hammen, 2002). A major depressive episode can rob a person of hope, limit information-processing skills, slow and narrow cognitive abilities, distort social perceptions, cause paranoia, block empathy and social insights, and spark unexplainable agitation, anger, and social withdrawal (Gotlib & Hammen, 2002). Furthermore, individuals suffering from depression and other mood disorders may develop substance abuse disorders through their efforts to self-medicate and achieve temporary relief from their profound psychological pain (Mueser, Noordsy, Drake, & Fox 2003; Taylor, 2005). For individuals with bipolar disorder, the drug of choice is most often alcohol, but they may also abuse street and prescription drugs during a depressive or manic episode. In the United States, 46 percent of individuals with bipolar disorder, compared to 13 percent of the general population, either abuse or are addicted to alcohol. Additionally, 41 percent of people with bipolar disorder, compared to 6 percent of the general public, abuse street drugs (Taylor, 2005).

Temporary drops in psychological functioning caused by environmental factors may produce reactive symptoms. Changes in mental clarity may not stem from a neurobiological disorder like major depression, but rather from real and perceived environmental stressors. People become tired, grief stricken, anxious, or overwhelmed by obligations and events that appear to be beyond their control. Usually environmental and perceived problems decrease a person's mental wellness rather than cause a mental illness. The brain's physical structure has not been injured or changed, but the perceptual, emotional, and cognitive responses stimulated by upsetting environ-

BOX 6.7 PRACTICE STORY AND ADVICE FROM THE FIELD

Susan C., mental health social worker:

**"This has never been just a job for me.
It's been the living out of my spiritual values."**

Susan C. has been involved in social justice issues since the 1960s, and has more than 20 years' experience as a social worker. She has practiced social work in a wide variety of cultural contexts, including Hawaii and the Marshall Islands. Currently, she is a professor of social work at a large university, where she conducts research and teaches.

Practice Story

Many of the Vietnamese clients that I saw [at a health center in Hawaii] were dealing with depression that was the result of PTSD from the Vietnam War. This was at the time when the U.S. government was recognizing and allowing Vietnamese children of U.S. service men to come to the United States. These were children who were outcast [in Vietnam] mainly because they were biracial. They couldn't walk on the street—it was very problematic. And many of them [parents] had experienced the loss of numerous children, spouses, parents, all of that. I worked with one mother over a period of time. As things were going along, she really wasn't feeling better and even the meds she was receiving for depression were not working. Some of us because of our experiences have a great sadness. So I said, "What would you do in Vietnam?" She told me, "The women would get together and we would sit under a blanket and boil herbs. And we'd have a fire and we had certain herbs and it would be a process of helping us to put our sadness aside." So I said, "Why don't we do this?" And it was the first time that she laughed and she said, "We can't do this in here!" I said, "I am willing to do that with you." And she said, "No, no, I don't think that's necessary." And I said, "Well let's talk about what would happen during that ceremony," and then we went off of that and we tried to deal with some of those issues. [The therapy did] validate something from her culture, and brought it over here and she could say, "I can do this in this way here." People were bombarded with, "This is the way we do things here," and so they started to feel like nothing that was helpful there [Vietnam] could be helpful in the new culture. In therapy, clients realized, "Oh yeah, there may be things that I did before that I can use here and how can I do that?" So it was the beginning of trying to integrate her past and her present in a positive way and to go on and not feel so isolated and sad. You know, no matter how bad things are in the country of origin, they weren't like that 24/7. And it's still their family and it's still their home.

Advice

I think we make the mistake of overgeneralizing. I am thinking about the number of Vietnamese clients that I have had. They fled along with U.S. troops because they had money. And their experience of Vietnamese culture was very different than [the experience of] this woman [client described above]. She was illiterate in her own language and had very limited resources in a lot of ways. Clients need to tell you what it means to be from their culture and what role that plays in their lives presently.

Often I worked with folks who were not very respected by some people. I always took a posture of respect for the person. That was very helpful for me. I felt my role was to help them see what those strengths were and how those allowed them to survive. I think that allowed me to be successful.

The other thing is that over the years, I realized that I was just one person in a lifetime of the person. What was there then, when I saw them, had been the result of many years. But I was optimistic because they could choose a different path.

Sometimes as a social worker, I had to go outside some of the established norms, not outside the ethical norms, and I think it made a difference. It made a difference when I was a student and one of the parents was seeing me after she came off a midnight shift. She was exhausted, and I brought in cookies for her, and that was a clincher. And that was only because I said, "Look, I made these for my family and for you. Have some cookies. You know you are really tired when you come in here and it is hard to focus." And it shifted the relationship.

This has never been just a job for me. It's been the living out of my spiritual values. I was raised a Catholic. And so, my being a pacifist and all of that is a result of really examining what it means to be committed to spiritual values. So, I've struggled to make those consistencies in my life.

mental events have temporarily decreased the person's mental wellness. Another way of explaining this is that stressful interactions with the environment restrict the brain temporarily from functioning at its fullest and healthiest potential. Even though personal problems may not stem from a brain disease or major mental disorder, decreased mental health can trigger hazardous behaviors, inappropriate affect, and reduced problem solving. An inability to cope with personal losses, high anxiety, or uncontrolled emotions can stimulate irrational thoughts or prevent a person from considering alternative solutions and problem-solving methods. As thinking is restricted, behaviors and decisions can be triggered that are extremely destructive for the individual, family, and community.

As social workers, we must always be mindful of temporary decreases in mental wellness, which, like neurobiological disorders, can cause internal pain, poor decisions, and behaviors resulting in economic hardships, family break-ups, physical abuse, and suicide. Therefore, it is extremely important to intervene therapeutically with people facing problems of living and decreased mental wellness. Such interventions, however, may place greater emphasis on environmental manipulation, support, case management, crisis intervention, and advocacy rather than on long-term psychotherapy or psychiatric medications. Severe symptoms resulting from grief, personal crisis, environmental factors, or other psychological issues may require medication and psychotherapy. Before treatment can start, however, accurate assessment of the problem is required (see box 6.6).

Social Factors

Psychological symptoms of depression have profound social consequences. The middle-aged person experiencing depression will find it difficult to hold a job, maintain family obligations, and sustain extended social networks. Problems of this nature create major problems at any age but are particularly devastating in midlife. Losing a job may end realistic hopes for a secure retirement, force children to drop out of college, and jeopardize the long-term investment made in a home. Further, middle-aged people in mainstream United States culture are generally expected to reach out and care for others and to demonstrate mature behavior, knowledge, self-reliance, and civic responsibility. Depression makes these tasks practically impossible.

Individuals suffering from major depression often face family members, communities, and sometimes even mental health professionals who interpret their lack of activity as willful defiance and a considered decision to remain incapacitated. Depressive symptoms may be viewed as psychological choices, not biologically driven signs of illness. Unvoiced suicidal thoughts can be validated by social interactions that directly or indirectly (1) blame the individual for not improving; (2) provide little empathy for emotional pain; (3) deny that some family, social, or work tasks cannot be performed; and (4) fail to acknowledge that the accomplishment of any routine task requires deliberate physical energy and painfully difficult or slow cognitive processing (Bongar, 2002; Jamison, 1995, 1999; Taylor, 2005).

The National Alliance for Mental Illness (NAMI), founded in 1979, is an important grassroots support and advocacy group that helps to combat the stigma of mental illness. NAMI is comprised of people with serious mental illnesses and their friends and family members. It works to achieve equitable services and treatment for individuals with mental illness and their families. Hundreds of thousands of volunteers participate in more than 1,000 local affiliates and fifty state organizations to provide education and support, combat stigma, support increased funding for research, and advocate for adequate health insurance, housing, and jobs for people with mental illness.

Cultural-Historical Context

Throughout recorded history, scholars in science, philosophy, and religion have attempted to define and understand serious mental illness. Hippocrates described symptoms resembling schizophrenia and theorized that the illness was a form of organic dementia. As Western civilization struggled to develop, these early insights were lost or replaced by myths, religious hypotheses, and dehumanizing stigma. Not until the late 1800s, with the advent of European psychiatry, was the organic nature of serious mental illness again emphasized (DePaulo, 2002; Taylor, 2005).

Despite evidence of a biological basis for depression, numerous societal myths about depression persist. Symptoms of depression are often interpreted by community members as anger, lack of motivation, poor personal choices, or immaturity. As a result, the community not only rejects and withdraws from the depressed person but removes the assigned roles and status normally given to a person who has reached full adulthood. As social workers, our responsibility is to help the depressed person obtain psychiatric treatment, educate the community, advocate for the family and client, and help restore the person's place in society. Box 6.7 describes cultural components of social work with depressed clients

IMPLICATIONS FOR SOCIAL WORK

Social workers often work as part of a team to help individuals suffering from major depression. This team may include a psychiatrist, nurse, psychologist, and/or psychotherapist. Interventions for depression try to reduce symptoms, often with medication, and treat psychological and social problems through psychotherapy or family therapy. In addition to providing therapy, social workers may contribute to treatment using wellness techniques. Wellness techniques provide support, increase intact skills, and empower clients and their families. The goals and emphasis of wellness techniques vary depending on the origins, history, and severity of the depression. For individuals with long-standing major mental illness that originates in a biopsychiatric brain disorder, interventions will be medically focused (e.g., identification of the most appropriate and effective psychotropic medication). For individuals who have stabilized on their medications, or whose depression stems primarily from stress and trauma, intervention may focus on wellness techniques in conjunction with psychotherapy or family therapy.

When working with depressed individuals, social workers need to remember that depression is a deadly illness. Depression is a significant risk factor for suicide. As stated earlier, approximately 15 percent of individuals with major depression commit suicide. Additionally, 25 percent of people with bipolar disorder will make a serious suicide attempt, and at least 10 percent succeed (Torrey & Knable, 2002). The probability that people will take their lives also increases if there is a history of previous suicide attempts; alcohol or other substances are abused; the person is an aging white male living alone; a family member committed suicide; or thoughts of suicide occur and an actual plan for killing oneself is developed (Jameson, 1999). Therefore, it is important that medical and community social workers are well-trained for conducting suicide assessments. Social workers may feel awkward asking people if they have had thoughts about taking their own lives, but this discomfort will disappear with practice and knowledge about mental disorders and suicidal risks. It is helpful to understand that professionals and the public have, for far too long, incorrectly framed or spoken of suicide as a personal choice. Social workers should instead remember that when a person is depressed, suicide is not an existential choice, but an overwhelming obsession or drive produced by an ill brain (Taylor, 2005). As explained by Bongar (2002), depressed clients often are more focused on using suicide for stopping unbearable emotional pain rather than on the issue of death. However, depression can cause clients to obsess about death, and experience unexplained impulses or urges to kill themselves (Taylor, 2005). Therefore, social workers have an ethical and professional responsibility to help people live through depression, overcome suicidal thoughts, regain a personal direction in their lives, and reclaim the right of free choice. Depression is extremely treatable. Although medication, psychotherapy, support, and environmental manipulations will not cure depression, they can lessen symptoms, shorten the length of episodes, and delay or prevent future episodes (American Psychiatric Association, 2002; DePaulo, 2002; Taylor, 2003, 2005).

SUMMARY

Midlife, like all periods of life, has the potential for major life challenges. As a person ages, the probability increases for experiencing major health problems, family deaths, bodily changes, loss of peer relationships, and unreachable goals. However, the person also faces these challenges with increased life experiences, stronger self-efficacy, improved problem-solving skills, and an increased understanding of the environment and ability to make sense of difficulties that cannot be resolved. Additionally, at midlife many individuals face challenges with more power and status than they held as younger women and men. How midlife is lived and experienced depends on the individual's genetics, health, life experiences, economics, support, beliefs, perceptions, culture, and macropolicies. Age represents only one factor in determining how the person develops and behaves.

Mental health settings are one context in which social workers encounter middle-aged adults. This chapter has applied the developmental-ecological approach to understanding depression in middle adulthood. In middle adulthood, major depression can prevent an individual from taking leadership roles within the family, profession, and community. This lack of fit between individual functioning and social and cultural expectations can be demoralizing to the individual and devastating to the family and can result in social stigma. Self-help and advocacy groups such as NAMI have played important roles in educating the public and advocating for adequate interventions for individuals suffering from mental illness. With appropriate treatment, most individuals with major depression can experience significant relief from their symptoms and lead healthy, happy lives. Such treatment usually involves both medication and therapy. Untreated depression can have devastating consequences, including suicide.

Study and Discussion Questions

1. Ashford et al. state that "Midlife is different from other developmental phases in that it is less affected by biological maturation. Indeed, adults are most affected by their own experiences" (p. 470). To what extent do you agree or disagree? In responding, consider developmental changes in biological, psychological, and social factors within cultural and historical context.

2. What is menopause? How might culture affect a woman's experience of menopause?

3. What is depression? In responding, consider diagnostic criteria, as well as discussion of biological, psychological, and social characteristics.

4. What are some of the consequences of major depression during midlife?

5. What are some of the roles of the mental health social worker in intervening with depressed clients?

6. To return to our opening examples, what are some options for intervention with Joe and Maria? What are some of the roles that social workers might assume?

Resources

For students interested in learning more about development in midlife, good sources include Kail and Cavanaugh (1996); Lachman and James (1997); Lock (1993); Masters, Johnson, and Kolodny, (1994); Pearson, Hunter, Ensminger, and Kellam (1990); Staudinger, Hezber, & Bluck (2003). For students interested in learning more about depression, see Baldwin and Birtwistle (2002); Gotlib and Hammen (2002). Students interested in learning more about social work in mental health should see Bentley and Walsh (2005); Lin (1995); and Wasow (1995).

Interested students can further supplement this chapter with the following Web-based resources:

The John D. and Catherine T. MacArthur Foundation's Research Network on Successful Midlife Development offers readers authoritative information and suggestions for improved quality of life based on research findings. Available at: http://midmac.med.harvard.edu

Geriatrics Medicine for Midlife and Beyond is a journal designed to inform physicians and allied health professions who work with midlife adults experiencing health problems. The journal also addresses preventative research and other important health issues. Available at: http://www.geri.com/geriatrics

Planned Parenthood offers sound information for understanding and living with menopause. Their Web site also provides links to other Web resources for women. Available at: http://www.plannedparenthood.org/pp 2/ portal/files/portal/medicalinfo/femalesexualhealth/pub-menopause.xml

The Medscape Web site offers a wealth of information on physical and mental well-being with articles by leading researchers and clinicians. Readers will also find an article reviewing the importance of exercise during midlife. Available at: http://www.medscape.com/viewarticle/514204?rss

Time magazine weaves a large amount of information into an article on whether women have a midlife crisis. Students are reminded that popular press publications are rich sources for ideas, references, and brief overviews of complex subjects, but they may fail to present a complete and accurate scientific perspective. Popular press articles seldom stand alone or are viewed as a strong reference for term papers and other academic writing. Available at: http://www.time.com/time/covers/1101050516

An excellent site for women's health during midlife is the Melbourne Women's Midlife Health Project. This is a large sample study using an excellent research design for investigating women's health during midlife and menopause. The University of Melbourne initiated the study because of Australia's lack of adequate information about this important period of a woman's health. Available at: http://www.psychiatry.unimelb.edu.au/midlife

References

American Psychiatric Association. (2000). *Diagnostic and statistical manual of mental disorders* (text revision). Washington, DC: Author.

Andreasen, N. C., & Black, D. W. (2000). *Introductory textbook of psychiatry.* Washington, DC: American Psychiatric Publishing.

Ashford, J., LeCroy, C. W., & Lortie, K. (2001). *Human behavior in the social environment: A multidimensional perspective* (2nd ed.). Belmont, CA: Wadsworth/Thomson Learning.

Baldwin, D. S., & Birtwistle, J. (2002). *An atlas of depression.* London: Parthenon.

Bentley, K. J., & Walsh, J. F. (2005). *The social worker and psychotropic medication* (3rd ed.). Belmont, CA: Wadsworth/Thomson Learning.

Bongar, B. (2002). *The suicidal patient. Clinical and legal standards of care* (2nd ed.). Washington, DC: American Psychological Association.

Borysenko, J. (1997). *A woman's book of life.* New York: Penguin.

Cummings, J. L., & Mega, M. S. (2003). *Neuropsychiatry and behavioral neuro-*

science. New York: Oxford University Press.

DePaulo, J. R. (2002). *Understanding depression: What we know and what you can do about it*. New York: Wiley.

Dozois, D. J. A., & Dobson, K. S. (Eds.). (2004). *The prevention of anxiety and depression*. Washington, DC: American Psychological Association.

Germain, C. B., & Gitterman, A. (1996). *The life model of social work practice* (2nd ed.). New York: Columbia University Press.

Goodwin, F. K., & Jamison, K. R. (1990). *Manic depressive illness*. New York: Oxford University Press.

Gotlib, I. H., & Hammen, C. L. (Eds.). (2002). *Handbook of depression*. New York: Guilford.

Hales, D., & Hales, R. E. (1995). *Caring for the mind: The comprehensive guide to mental health*. New York: Bantam Books.

Hooker, K., & Kaus, C. R. (1994). Health-related possible selves in young and middle adulthood. *Psychology of Aging, 9*(1), 126–133.

Jamison, K. R. (1995). *An unquiet mind*. New York: Vintage Books.

Jamison, K. R. (1999). *Night falls fast*. New York: Vintage Books.

Jones, I., Kent, L., & Craddock, N. (2002). Genetics of affective disorders. In P. McGuffin, M. Owen, & I. I. Gottesman (Eds.), *Psychiatric genetic and genomics* (pp. 211–246). New York: Oxford University Press.

Kail, R. V., & Cavanaugh, J. C. (1996). *Human development* (pp. 337–442). Pacific Grove, CA: Brooks/Cole.

Kalidindi, S., & McGuffin, P. (2003). The genetics of affective disorders: Present and future. In R. Plomin, I. W. DeFries, C. McGuffin, & P. McGuffin (Eds.), *Behavioral genetics in the postgenomic era* (pp. 481–502). Washington, DC: American Psychological Association.

Lachman, M. E., & James, J. B. (Eds.). (1997). *Multiple paths of midlife development*. Chicago: University of Chicago Press.

Levinson, D. J. (1980). Toward a conception of the adult life course. In N. J. Smelser & E. H. Erikson (Eds.), *Themes of work and love in adulthood* (pp. 265-290). Cambridge, MA: Harvard University Press.

Levinson, D. J. (1986). A conception of adult development. *American Psychologist, 41*, 3–13.

Levinson, D. J. (1990). *The seasons of a woman's life: Implications for women and men*. Paper presented at the meeting of the American Psychological Association, Boston.

Levinson, D. J. (1990). A theory of life structure development in adulthood. In C. N. Alexander & E. J. Langer (Eds.), *Higher stages of human development* (pp. 35-54). New York: Oxford University Press.

Levinson, D. J. (1996). *The seasons of a woman's life*. New York: Knopf.

Levinson, D. J., Darrow, C. N., Klein, E. B., Levinson, M. H., & McKee, B. (1978). *The seasons of a man's life*. New York: Knopf.

Lin, A. (1995). Mental health overview. In R. L. Edwards (Ed.), *Encyclopedia of social work* (Vol. 2, pp. 1705–1711). Washington, DC: NASW Press.

Lock, M. (1993). *Encounter with aging: Mythologies of menopause in Japan and North America*. Berkeley and Los Angeles: University of California Press.

Masters, W. H., Johnson, V. E., & Kolodny, R. C. (1994). *Heterosexuality*. New York: Harper Collins.

Mueser, K. T., Noordsy, D. L., Drake, R. E., & Fox, L. (2003). *Integrated treatment for dual disorders. A guide to effective practice.* New York: Guilford. National Alliance for Mental Illness (NAMI). Available from NAMI Web site, http://www. nami.org

National Sleep Foundation. (2005). *2005 Sleep in America Poll.* Washington, DC: National Sleep Foundation.

Northrup, C. (1994). *Women's bodies, women's wisdom.* New York: Bantam Books.

Pearson, J. L., Hunter, A. G., Ensminger, M. E., & Kellam S. G. (1990). Black grandmoth ers in multigenerational households: Diversity in family structure and parenting involvement in the Woodlawn community. *Child Development, 61,* 434-442.

Rapp, S. R., Espeland, M. A., Shumaker, S. A., Henderson, V. W., Brunner, R. L., Manson, J. E., et al. (2003). Effects of estrogen plus progestin on global cognitive function in postmenopausal women. The women's health initiative memory study: A randomized controlled trial. *Journal of the American Medical Association, 289*(20), 2663-2672.

Sadock, B. J., & Sadock, V. A. (2003). *Synopsis of psychiatry* (9th ed.). Philadelphia: Lippincott Williams & Wilkins.

Santrock, J. W. (2002). *Life-span development* (8th ed.). New York: McGraw-Hill.

Seifert, K. L., & Hoffnung, M. (2000). *Lifespan development* (2nd ed.). Boston: Houghton Mifflin.

Shumaker, S. A., Legault, C., Rapp, S. R., Thal, L., Wallace, R. B., Ockene, J. K., et al. (2003). Estrogen plus progestin and the incidence of dementia and mild cognitive impairment in postmenopausal women. The women's health initiative memory study: A randomized controlled trial. *Journal of the American Medical Association, 289*(20), 2651-2662.

Stahl, S. M. (2000). *Essential psychopharmacology of depression and bipolar disorder.* Cambridge: Cambridge University Press.

Staudinger, U. M., Hezber P. Y., & Bluck, S. (2003). Looking back and looking ahead: Adult age differences in consistency of diachronous rating of subjective well-being. *Psychology and Aging, 18*(1), 13-24.

Taylor, E. H. (1997). Serious mental illness: A biopsychosocial perspective. In R. L. Edwards (Ed.), *Encyclopedia of social work* (Supplement, 19th ed., pp. 263-273). Washington, DC: NASW Press.

Taylor, E. H. (2003). Practice methods for working with children who have biologically based disorders: A bioecological model. *Families and Society, 84,* 39-50.

Taylor, E. H. (2005). *Atlas of bipolar disorders.* London: Taylor & Francis.

Taylor, E. H., & Edwards, R. L. (1996). The role of social work in psychiatry and mental health. In B. B. Wolman (Ed.), *The encyclopedia of psychology, psychiatry and psychoanalysis* (pp. 539-541). New York: Holt.

Torrey, E. F., Bowler, A. E., Taylor, E. H., & Gottesman, I. I. (1994). *Schizophrenia and manic depressive disorder: The biological roots of mental illness as revealed by the landmark study of identical twins.* New York: Basic Books.

Torrey, E. F., & Knable, M. B. (2002). *Surviving manic depression. A manual on bipolar disorder for patients, families, and providers.* New York: Basic Books.

U.S. Indian Health Service. (2002). *Facts on Indian health disparities.* Washington, DC: Author.

Wasow, M. (1995). *The skipping stone. Ripple effects of mental illness on the family.* Palo Alto, CA: Science and Behavior Books.

Figure 7.1. This older woman living with Alzheimer's disease can become confused and disoriented even with her family in the context of her home.

7

Medical Social Work with Older Adults: Alzheimer's Disease

This chapter considers older adults, from approximately 65 years until death, as the focal system. During the twentieth century, the number of people ages 65 and older in the United States rose dramatically from 3 million in 1900 to 34 million in 1998. By the middle of the twenty-first century, older adults are expected to comprise 23 percent of the United States population (U.S. Department of Health and Human Services, 1999).

In later adulthood, everyone experiences the inevitable physical changes of aging, dying, and death. Most individuals also experience significant loss of a loved one, of physical health, or of prestige. As life expectancy increases, more individuals will live for extended periods with disabilities and chronic illness. Nevertheless, for many individuals, late adulthood brings a sense of fulfillment in life, continued curiosity about the world, engagement in meaningful social and individual activities, and a desire to leave a legacy. For others, the later adult years are marked by poverty, illness, loneliness, and despair.

Dementia is a set of medical disorders that occur almost entirely in late adulthood and are characterized by cognitive and intellectual impairment sufficient to disrupt everyday activities. It rises sharply with age, affecting approximately 1 percent of people in their 60s; doubles in rate every five years, and stabilizes at 30 percent of persons affected in their 90s (see Berk, 2001). Following an overview of development in late adulthood, this chapter elaborates a developmental-ecological analysis of the most common form of senile dementia, Alzheimer's disease, which accounts for 50 to 60 percent of all cases of dementia and affects approximately 15 percent of those older than 80 years. Alzheimer's disease is a leading cause of death in late adulthood accounting for 100,000 deaths per year in the United States (see Berk, 2001).

Medical social workers assist older adults and families in the contexts of hospitals, assisted living and nursing homes, and community health and mental health centers. As Alzheimer's disease progresses, the medical social worker plays an important role within a team of physicians, nurses, caregivers, and others. As you read, consider how biological, psychological, and social factors interact within specific cultural and historical contexts to influence physical health in later adulthood. What unique role does the medical social worker play in supporting individuals with Alzheimer's disease and their families?

At age 82 years, Edith Hudley, a great-grandmother with a tenth-grade education, published her first book, a social work text (Hudley, Haight & Miller, 2002). At age 70 years, former president Jimmy Carter climbed Japan's Mount Fuji (Carter, 2000). These two very different people illustrate a common but often forgotten fact—later adulthood need not signal an end to productivity, potential, or quality of life. The senior years do introduce never-before experienced limitations that require adjustment, but they also can provide new opportunities. President Carter was more strategic in planning his ascents than in his younger years, but the retirement years allowed him the leisure time to pursue active hobbies. Although Mrs. Hudley's stamina for work was less than in her younger years, the wisdom she had gained over her lifetime was passed down to subsequent generations through her book. Advancing age forces people to make sense and meaning of new challenges and limitations. Western societies often link aging with disabilities, inactivity, and the inevitability of death. For social workers, it is more helpful to think of aging as another period of a person's life in which developmental change creates new avenues for growth and rewards, as well as hazards and limitations. While passing through the life span, we build meaning, understanding, and satisfaction by living productively within our limitations. Healthy aging requires the same process and has the same potential of rewarding individuals with new self-knowledge, relationships, and achievements. Boxes 7.1 to 7.4 illustrate how substance abuse, violence, and poverty can continue to threaten healthy development in later adulthood.

BOX 7.1 VIOLENCE ACROSS THE LIFE SPAN
Elder Abuse

The U.S. Administration on Aging (2005) states that elder abuse includes physical abuse, sexual abuse, emotional or psychological abuse, financial exploitation, neglect, and self-neglect (when an older person's life, health, or safety is jeopardized by personal behaviors). A committee for the National Academy of Science has developed the following broad criteria for researchers and clinicians to identify elder mistreatment/abuse. It occurs when (1) intentional behaviors and actions cause harm, (2) actions or behaviors place the person at risk of serious harm, (3) a caregiver fails to provide or satisfy basic care needs, or (4) an older adult is not protected from harm (National Research Council, 2003). The definition places violence by strangers in a separate category but includes abuse, neglect, exploitation, and abandonment of aged individuals by others (Fulmer et al., 2004).

Elder mistreatment and abuse occur in many contexts, not only in nursing homes and assisted-living residences. Elder mistreatment and abuse also occur in poorly managed housing for older adults, in the homes of relatives and neighbors, and in public places. Furthermore, it is a national problem. The National Elder Abuse Incidence Study (U.S. Administration on Aging, 1998) reports that:

- in a one-year period, approximately 551,011 people ages 60 and older experienced abuse, neglect, and/or self-neglect;
- elder mistreatment and abuse are highly underreported. There may be as many as four times as many mistreated and abused older people as currently reported;
- people ages 80 years and older are abused or neglected approximately two to three times more often than their younger peers;
- approximately 90% of mistreatment or abuse is perpetrated by a family member. In approximately 66% of cases, the perpetrator is an adult child or spouse.

Vulnerable elders can be purposefully targeted by professional criminals, neighborhood gangs, and people who find pleasure in harassing others.

Identifying elder mistreatment and abuse is difficult and it is often overlooked by professionals (Fulmer at al., 2004). Clients often fear disclosing and have difficulty reporting abuse by family members and significant others. The process of identification is complicated because there have been few reliable and valid assessment instruments developed. As a result, social work assessments must often depend on interviews with the client, family, and community members; review of medical and emergency room reports; and expert consultation from medical personnel. Doctors and other specialists can often ascertain from X-rays and laboratory reports that an injury, illness, or death did or did not occurr by accident.

Sources: Fulmer, T., Guadagno, L., Dyer, C. B., & Connolly, M. T. (2004). Progress in elder abuse screening and assessment instruments. *Journal of the American Geriatrics Society, 52,* 297–304; National Research Council. (2003). Elder mistreatment: Abuse, neglect, and exploitation in an aging America. In R. J. Bonnie & R. B. Wallace (Eds.), *Panel to review risk and prevalence of elder abuse and neglect. Committee on national statistics and committee on law and justice, division of behavioral and social sciences and education* (pp. 34–59). Washington, DC: National Academies Press; U.S. Administration on Aging (1998). *The national elder abuse incidence study.* Washington, DC: Department of Health and Human Services.

As the nation and world ages (see box 7.5), social workers must become stronger advocates for older adults (e.g., securing and protecting retirement income, disability benefits, and health insurance for low-income people). Although many adults older than 65 continue to live active, productive lives,

BOX 7.2 SUBSTANCE ABUSE ACROSS THE LIFE SPAN

Prescription and Over-the-Counter Drug Abuse by Older Adults

Abuse of prescription medication occurs when one knowingly or unknowingly takes a drug in a manner that deviates from the prescribed dose, medical instructions, or purpose approved for the drug. It includes underuse as well as overuse of a medication. Epidemiologists have estimated that between 3% and 33% of older adults overuse prescription drugs (Patterson, Lacro, & Jeste, 2005). Overuse of prescription drugs can result in addiction, medical crisis, and even death. Abusing benzodiazepines can increase an older adult's risk for falling, automobile accidents, and experiencing memory and cognitive problems. Underuse of prescription drugs can result in an acceleration of the disease process, or chronic pain. Problems resulting from the under- or overuse of prescription drugs are serious and can reduce the older adult's quality of life as well as drain economic resources.

The abuse of prescription drugs by the elderly can be framed, in part, as a failure of public policy. Consider the underuse of prescription drugs. When feeling better, to save money, some older adults will forego one or two doses in order to ensure having the drug when more severe symptoms occur. Others underuse drugs to reduce or avoid drug-induced side effects. This may appear to be an older adult's lapse of responsibility, but consider how few public health nurses and person-to-person information programs are available to the public, the amount of time that is actually spent with medical professionals during outpatient office visits, how quickly medical instructions and explanations are given, and the short-term memory challenges of many older adults. Think about the difficulty some older adults have in getting to the doctor or paying for the services. The medical system, payment responsibility, transportation availability, and patient teaching methods work against many older adults and result in mismanaged geriatric medical care.

It is important for social workers to actively address the issue of prescription and over-the-counter drug abuse. Social workers can play important roles in helping educate older clients about their medications—developing ways for clients to remember how to take medications, linking them with public health services, attending doctor appointments with them and ensuring that they receive full medical insurance benefits. It is also important for social workers to actively advocate for universal health coverage. When a nation fails to provide universal health and prescription drug insurance and willingly allows older citizens to live below or at the poverty line, it is certain that medications will continue to be improperly used.

Sources: National Institute on Drug Abuse. (2005). *Trends in prescription drug abuse. Research report series. Prescription drugs:Abuse and addiction.* Bethesda, MD: National Institutes of Health. Retrieved May 2005 from http://www.nida.nih.gov/Research Reports/Prescription/prescription5.html; Paterson, T. L., Lacro, J. P., & Jeste, D. V. (1999). Abuse and misuse of medications in the elderly. *Psychiatric Times, 16*(4). Retrieved May 2005 from http://www.psychiatrictimes.com/p990454.html

---

BOX 7.3 POVERTY ACROSS THE LIFE SPAN
Older Americans and Poverty

As one ages, poverty becomes a greater risk. In 1998, the poverty rate was 9% for people ages 65 through 74. This rate increased to 12% for people ages 75 through 84, and to 14% for people older than 84. Older women and people of color run the highest risk of living in poverty. In 1998, 47% of single African American women aged 65 through 74 years lived in poverty.

In 1995, 38% of households headed by African American women, and 33% headed by Hispanic women ages 75 and older, had incomes below the poverty level. In contrast, 15% of white female-headed households and 8% of white male-headed households ages 75 years and older were below the poverty level (U.S. Bureau of Census, 1997).

Source: Federal Interagency Forum on Aging Related Statistics. (2000). *Older Americans 2000: Key indicators of well-being. Federal interagency forum on aging related statistics.* Retrieved May 2005 from http://www.aging stats.gov/chart book 2000/economics.html

---

many people experience health problems that limit their functioning. Epidemiological studies indicate that 80 percent of Americans ages 65 and older have at least one chronic medical disorder, and 50 percent suffer from two or more serious long-term illnesses. Nearly 25 percent of North Americans older than 65 have diabetes, and this rate is expected to increase because of dietary choices, increased obesity, and reduced exercise habits (Centers for Disease Control and Prevention, 2003). Because of the hardships of poverty and racism, older people of color generally experience more health problems, as well as more difficulty accessing medical services, than do older middle-income adults who are white. For example, American Indian and Alaskan Native peoples face death 4.4 years earlier than all other North American ethnic groups (Grim, 2002; U.S. Indian Health Service, 2002; U.S. Indian Health Service, 2001), signaling a need to attend to the health needs of these and other vulnerable older adults.

BOX 7.4 POVERTY ACROSS THE LIFE SPAN

Social Security

The AARP (American Association of Retired People) reports that only 19% of African Americans ages 65 and older receive a private pension, and only 29% have personal assets providing all or part of their income. The largest provider of income for aging African Americans is Social Security. Approximately 88% of African Americans receive Social Security payments. For one in three African Americans age 65 and older, Social Security is the only source of income. Almost 57% of income for African American women and 44% of income for all older African Americans comes from Social Security payments.

Source: AARP. (2004). *Social Security and African Americans: Some facts. AARP research*. Retrieved May 10, 2005, from http://research.aarp.org/econ/fs94_ss.html

MEDICAL SOCIAL WORK WITH OLDER ADULTS

Given their increased vulnerability to disease, disability, and poverty, it is not surprising that social workers encounter many aging adults in health-care settings such as hospitals, assisted-living facilities, and nursing homes.

BOX 7.5 CHANGING DEMOGRAPHICS

United States and world demographics are changing so that older adults comprise an increasingly large segment of the population. In 2000, it was estimated that worldwide there were 420 million people older than 65. Based on current trends, by 2030 the number will increase to 973 million. Experts believe that global aging is occurring as a result of increased life expectancy, coupled with decreased international fertility rates. In industrialized nations, the twentieth century ushered in the highest life-expectancy gains for newborn infants ever recorded, as well as effective birth control. Today, Americans and Canadians have a life expectancy of 76 to 80 years. Since 1950, life expectancy for citizens in emerging nations has also increased.

By 2030, the number of United States households with people ages 65 years and older will increase from 35 million to approximately 71 million. By this date, people of color will increase from 11.3% to 16.5%. Between 1990 and 2050, the number of African American older adults is projected to increase by 234%. While the number of older adults in almost all ethnic and majority populations is growing, the distribution between males and females is expected to remain approximately the same. In 2000, 59% of people ages 65 and older were women; by 2030, the number will decrease slightly to 56%.

In the next 25 years, the world's developing counties will experience the largest increase of older adults. If migration patterns do not change dramatically, industrial developing nations will have nearly triple the number of people older than 65. The growing number of older people will be slowed only in the poorest parts of the world. Sub-Saharan Africa currently has, and is projected to continue to have, less than 4% of its population ages 65 and older. Sadly, mortality rates caused by disease, poverty, poor sanitation, inadequate diets, unavailability of medical services, wars, and other problems are not projected to decrease.

An aging population has implications for human development, research, policies, and social work practice. Social workers need to be aware of the ways life-threatening illnesses have changed, the impact of illness on, the quality of life of an older adult, who in North America dies before reaching the national expected age, and the importance of advocating for policies to increase and improve the lives of people living in the world's poorest nations. As a result of wars, poverty, and other global factors, a growing number of aging political refugees and immigrants find their way to North America and other industrialized countries. Illegal immigrants entering the United States to work will remain into their later adulthood. Specialized social work skills are required to help undocumented aging persons to traverse ever-changing immigration regulations, health and mental health-care systems, Social Security requirements; to locate affordable housing and transportation; and to meet other social welfare needs.

Sources: Kinsella, K., & Velkoff V. (2001). *An aging world: 2001*. U.S. Census Bureau (Publication No. P95/01-1). Washington, DC: U.S. Government Printing Office; U.S. Census Bureau International Database. (2004). *Midyear population, by age and sex* (Table 094). Retrieved May 10, 2005, from http://www.census.gov/population/wwwprojects/natdet-D1A.html

Medical social work is a specialization that focuses on the impact of disease and disability on individuals of all ages, their families, and communities. The specialization emerged in the beginning of the twentieth century when Richard Cabot and Ida Cannon introduced medical social services at Massachusetts General Hospital. Here, professionally trained social workers helped patients and their families deal with personal and social factors that affected disease onset and recovery (Poole, 1995). Today, much of what medical social workers do still involves helping patients and families cope with and adapt to changes brought about by illness, medical treatment, and disability. Hospitals remain a major context for medical social work. Medical social workers also practice in out-patient primary care settings, home health care, long-term care facilities, public health departments, community

Figure 7.2. Medical social workers help individuals to adapt and cope with illness and treatment.

health-care clinics, school-based health clinics, and associations focused on specific illnesses (e.g., HIV and AIDS consortia) (Berkman & Volland, 1997).

To be successful in a medical setting, social workers must develop knowledge specific to diseases or populations at risk, including knowledge of various diseases, treatments, and their outcomes. It is equally important to understand the individual's and the family's perception of the disease, its causes and its cures, and the family's resources for coping. How will the individual and family handle the stress of illness? How will the individual and family obtain necessary follow-up health care? Social workers use bio-psycho-social-spiritual assessments to understand how individuals adjust to illness and medical treatment and to define what social health-care needs must be addressed. Services provided by medical social workers may be preventive, developmental, or remedial (e.g., social risk screening, discharge planning, psychosocial intervention, health education and referral, and advocacy) (see Berkman & Volland, 1997; Poole, 1995).

In the following case, a medical social worker practicing in a city hospital tackles the complex task of assisting an elderly woman suffering from senile dementia and her family.

Mrs. P., an 85-year-old African American woman, was taken by ambulance to an emergency room in Missouri following complaints of dizziness and difficulty staying awake. She was accompanied by a middle-aged friend with whom she was visiting. Mrs. P., who was visiting from her home in Texas, could not remember where she lived, which city or state she was in, how long she had been with her friend, the time or day of the week, or the sea-son. She could not remember the name of her primary care physician, or if she was on any medication. Mrs. P. was hospitalized for three days with dehydration and kidney failure. The friend reported that she had driven to Texas for Mrs. P. because Mrs. P. was deeply depressed and isolated living alone with her husband of twenty years in a low-income inner-city apartment. Her mood had improved greatly since coming to Missouri, and she did not wish to return to Texas. Her friend reported that Mrs. P. currently was taking no medication and provided the name and phone number of Mrs. P.'s husband and of an adult son in Iowa. The social worker called Mrs. P.'s husband and learned that he, too, was ill and living with dementia. She then called the adult son, who reported that Mrs. P. had been diagnosed with dementia three years ago and, at that time, was placed on medications for high blood pressure and glaucoma. He had not visited her in the past three years and was unaware of the extent of her current dementia or his stepfather's illness. The social worker talked with Mrs. P.'s son regarding a long-term plan for her health care. He agreed to make arrangements for Mrs. P. and her husband to move into an assisted-living facility near his home where he could monitor their care. Prior to discharge, a medical social worker met with Mrs. P. and her friend to develop a plan for short-term care following release from the hospital. The friend agreed to take Mrs. P. to follow-up health-care appointments the following week and to drive her to Iowa to meet her son. Ten days later, however, the medical social worker received a call from Mrs. P.'s friend, who was very concerned. Although follow-up health care was uneventful, Mrs. P. had had an argument with her son and was refusing to go to Iowa. Instead, she wanted to return to her husband in Texas. It was clear, however, that Mrs. P. could not remember to take her medicine and was having difficulties with basic tasks of everyday living. The medical social worker arranged to meet with Mrs. P. and her friend that afternoon. The social worker then researched services in Houston and contacted an agency providing home care and transportation services for seniors, as well as arranging volunteer opportunities to alleviate social isolation and depression. That afternoon, Mrs. P. resisted the need for services, expressing the opinion that "When I can no longer do for myself, God should just carry me away." The social worker spoke with her at length, and Mrs. P. agreed to allow a home-care provider into her home once a day to monitor her medicine and to help her get to doctor's appointments. She expressed interest about participating in volunteer opportunities with children. Unfortunately, Mrs. P. and her husband chose not to follow through with the referrals. At last contact, they were living alone in a low-income inner-city apartment in Houston.

As this vignette illustrates, medical social workers play an important role in the health care of older adults. Mrs. P. urgently needed to be stabilized medically. During her hospital stay, however, it became clear that her dementia had become a barrier to independent living. An intelligent, independent, and strong-willed woman with a largely intact long-term memory, her short-term memory presented serious problems to everyday living, including taking necessary medications. The medical social worker assisted Mrs. P. and her family in developing a plan for her to maintain as much independence as possible for as long as possible while meeting her medical and safety needs. The reality, however, is that it ultimately is the decision of the client to accept or refuse services. Mrs. P., despite her emerging mental impairments, retained her power of attorney. Her life and sense of self had been built upon being a leader and teacher of younger generations, and, at last contact, receiving assistance with daily living was not acceptable to her or her husband. The medical social worker, although unsuccessful in initiating services, did successfully alert Mrs. P.'s relatives to her deteriorating state as well as to the availability of services when her needs become urgent.

OVERVIEW OF DEVELOPMENT IN LATE ADULTHOOD

As life spans increase, the period of later adulthood can range from 20 to 30 years. During this time, much change and development can occur. Clearly, the healthy 65-year-old working full-time to support grandchildren has very different needs from the frail, dependent 85-year-old. To more clearly represent this diversity, some scholars argue that later adulthood should be divided into periods (e.g., Charness & Bosman, 1992; Santrock, 2002). Individuals ages 65 through 74 may be considered "young-old." They may be active within their community and with their families and friends. Many are employed part- or full-time. During this period, however, more and more individuals will begin to experience chronic illness, and the phenomenon of women outliving their spouses emerges. Individuals ages 75 through 84 may be considered "middle-old." They typically live more constricted lives; experience more physical impairments such as decreased hearing, vision, and response time; and have more chronic diseases, such as arthritis and cardiovascular disease. They also experience more stress due to loss of spouses, relatives, and friends. Some, however, continue to contribute to the arts, literature, science, and politics. The "old-old," ages 85 and older, are a growing segment of the population. They are the most dependent and frail and experience more disabilities and chronic illnesses.

As this general overview suggests, social workers cannot depend entirely on chronological age but must retain a dual focus on chronological age and level of functioning. There is considerable variation in characteristics of individuals during each period of later adulthood because of genetics, environmental factors, diseases, nutrition, and availability of medical care. The aging process can be conceptualized as consisting of chronological, biological, psychological, and social age (Santrock, 2002). If these components are assessed separately, but understood as a gestalt, a person's functional age can be determined. Under this system the importance of a person's birth age decreases, while strengths, such as emotional control, cognitive problem solving skills, memory, mobility, social network, economic stability, and physical health gain importance. For example, a socially isolated, depressed 65-

year-old suffering from several chronic medical conditions may be functionally older than a person who is 80 and is healthy and active in community and family. It is important to keep in mind that all components of the functional assessment are not equal. An older adult may have a high level of emotional and cognitive functioning, and good economic stability, but be in the final stage of congestive heart failure. Unfortunately, the person's strengths—

BOX 7.6 PHYSICAL PROBLEMS WITH ADVANCING AGE

- Motor and sensory responses become slower caused by changes in cardiovascular and peripheral nervous systems.
- Skin wrinkles; pigmentation is irregular.
- Bones weaken and have less mass—osteoporosis can develop.
- Muscle strength and speed decreases.
- The respiratory system is less effective.
- Sight and hearing decrease.
- After 70 years of age, ability to detect odors decreases rapidly.
- Arthritis is the most common chronic problem reported by older adults.
- Accidents cause greater injuries and disabilities than in young adults.
- 75% of older adults die of heart disease, cancer, or stroke.

---

intact cognitive, emotional, and economic systems—cannot compensate for an aged circulatory system. Social workers need to determine an older adult's functional age to avoid making decisions about service needs and capabilities from a biased and stereotypical perspective of aging.

Biological Factors: Physical Aging, Death, and Dying

Physical aging begins early in adulthood. By 30 years of age, a person's bones have reached their maximum growth, and the process of slow deterioration toward brittleness has started. After 30 years of age, internal body organs decrease their ability to function by approximately 1 percent per year, resulting in a 25 to 40 percent loss of peak organ functionality between 30 and 80 years of age. This slow, ongoing erosion places people at a higher risk for debilitating and life-threatening diseases such as diabetes, heart disease, and arthritis (Smith, 2003). Box 7.6 lists a number of health problems that affect older adults.

Although physical aging is inevitable, good prevention efforts can enhance the quality of life in later adulthood. For many, aging is more difficult than necessary because illness prevention is not emphasized until people are between 40 and 60 years of age. However, prevention for major physical disorders needs to begin no later than 30 years of age (Smith, 2003). The possibility of good health throughout the life span can be increased by routinely sleeping seven to eight hours; consistently eating a healthy breakfast; rarely snacking; keeping body weight no more than 20 percent above or 10 percent below what is medically recommended; routine, systematic, and safe exercise; no more than moderate use of alcohol; and no use of tobacco (Smith, 2003).

Despite the quality of prevention efforts, the final stage of physical development is death. These are several outward physical signs of the process of dying. Beginning one to three months before death, the person may sleep more and eat less. One or two weeks before death, the person may become mentally disoriented, confused, or agitated; sleep more; and eat very little. The dying person also may experience increased perspiration, changes in skin color to pale yellow with bluish hands and feet, and irregular breathing and pulse. Days or hours before death, these signs intensify. The dying person may experience a surge in energy and be more alert, eat and socialize, and then slip into a coma. Hands, feet, and legs become blotchy and purplish, pulse is hard to find, and breathing becomes very irregular with long pauses between breaths. Eventually, the dying person becomes unresponsive and breathing stops.

Psychological and Social Factors: Coming to Terms with Death

The actual process of aging and dying is a psychological and social as well as a physical process. Individuals, their families, and friends are confronted with and respond to mortality and loss. In her classic work, *On Death and Dying,* Elisabeth Kubler-Ross (1969) describes the psychological aspects of dying based upon years of interviewing and observing people dealing with their mortality:

- *Denial.* The person attempts to convince her or himself that the situation is not hopeless, that death is not certain. Often denial results in an emotional explosion of energy in an attempt to prove the medical reports are incorrect or search for alternative treatments.

- *Anger.* It is not unusual for persons facing death to experience periods of anger. They may feel cheated, alone, and lacking understanding. They may be angry at people in general or specifically at family members, the medical profession, or God. Sometimes, the dying person is simply angry, unable to identify or label whom the anger targets.

- *Bargaining.* This is the negotiation step of dying. The person may try to bargain with God, promising if spared from death to live in ser-vice of the most needy. Others may try bargaining with medical personnel for experimental treatments or illegal medications believed to have curing powers. For others, the bargaining is in the form of requests and hopes to live long enough for a special event, such as a birth or marriage or a child's graduation.

- *Depression.* When there is no hope, the person may experience an overwhelming sense of depression and hopelessness. The depressed person may think obsessively about past events, recalling and wishing things had been different, or focus on feeling embarrassed because self-care and personal dignity have slipped away. Depression can also appear as grieving the lost future. Individuals may become sad and anxious that their dreams and relationships are ending. They also may worry about the future well-being and financial care of loved ones.

- *Acceptance.* The sting and fear of death primarily disappear. The person at a minimum acknowledges that death cannot be escaped, and has made existential sense and meaning of the situation. If a person fights until the end, this stage may not be reached.

Originally, these issues were presented by Kubler-Ross as progressive stages. Today, most professionals recognize that stages may occur in any order, and may be repeated or retriggered numerous times, and that some people never experience all these issues. Furthermore, certain issues may be more prominent at various phases in the lifecycle (e.g., acceptance may be more difficult to achieve when death occurs at a younger age). Later adulthood seems to be a time when many individuals come to terms with their inevitable death. Compared to middle-aged adults, older adults generally have less fear of death. Perhaps this is because older adults have experienced the death of friends and family members (Ashford, LeCroy, and Lortie, 2001), and their own death may be perceived as relatively normal and expected. An individual's psychological experience of death and dying may be profoundly affected by social relationships (e.g., a surviving spouse, child, or friend) and how significant others respond to the dying person and their own imminent loss.

When social workers support clients who are facing life's end, or their grieving families and friends, confirming and discovering each individual's unique emotions, rationalizations, fears, and beliefs related to death can be extremely important. To prepare for this role, it is helpful to reflect upon how our own beliefs about death and dying relate to those of our clients. Beliefs shape the very tone, goals, and motivations that direct our behavior and emotional responses. Beliefs can make us try to embrace or hide from death, view it as a natural process or an enemy. Understanding how our own beliefs are similar to or different from those of our clients can minimize hurtful conflict and facilitate appropriate, effective support during what, for many, is an emotionally charged time of transition. The following observations and belief statements are provided to help social workers establish a framework and tone for guiding individuals who are in the process of dealing with death. These statements, while not comprehensive, provide basic boundaries and ideas for counseling and talking with clients about the end of life. While reading the statements, consider (1) the extent to which the statement matches your own observations and beliefs; (2) the emotions, anxieties, and thoughts each statement stirs; (3) whether you agree or disagree with these statements; and (4) what you would add, leave out, or change.

1. Death is final, the end of dreams, plans, and personal and social development.

2. People across all cultures deal with loss of life within both established social norms and their personal private psyches; reflecting that death is both universal and yet markedly unique for each individual and family.

3. The issues of spirituality, life after death, meaning of death, and use of religious and spiritual leaders and artifacts are highly charged beliefs and concepts that can cause pain and hardships if they are not addressed within the needs and belief systems of each client—if you do not understand the cultural or religious practice, do not fake it.

4. It is the social worker's responsibility to identify the client's beliefs and provide appropriate cultural and religious leaders, rather than trying to personally bridge all of the clients needs.

5. The reality of death often changes how a person previously predicted that she/he would respond when faced with death, and the new perceptions may change how the person chooses to use her/his fleeting time, and final wishes or directives.

6. Cultural norms, expectations, and death-related ceremonies may or may not help an individual make sense and meaning of the loss and resolve grief.

7. Grieving is both linked to culture and personal perceptions, beliefs, and realities.

8. No matter how well planned, there are concrete legal, personal, financial, and emotional tasks that must be completed before death, at the time of death, and after the funeral is over.

9. Unexpected death may or may not create a greater level of crisis and shock for the survivors than an expected death.

10. It is the social worker's responsibility to provide as much or as little assistance, support, and crisis intervention as needed.

11. Regardless of the available support, each person must individually explore, confront, and resolve the pain and void created by death.

12. Death is emotionally painful. There are no words, symbols, beliefs, or interventions that erase the pain or reduce the magnitude of the event.

13. Some mourners need attention for an extended period after the funeral, while others require respect, space, and time away from professionals.

14. The person does not have to grieve or accept death the way others expect.

15. Many, but not all, surviving family members would benefit from social work assessments repeated over months and even years or more to identify and prevent them from spiraling into economic poverty or a major mental disorder such as depression.

Clearly, counseling individuals facing their own death or the death of a loved one is a challenge. To be effective, professional social workers must understand themselves and know how to handle difficult interpersonal communications before intervening with clients about death. Spend a little time thinking about how you would handle requests that go against your own values or ethics. For example, you believe that a person must believe in Jesus to reach heaven, and a Jewish client states, "His suffering is done, today he is with God." Do you validate the grieving person, remain silent, or gently explain your beliefs? What do you do if you do not believe in God and prayer, and your client asks you to lead the family in a prayer for the dying person?

Recent research underscores the complexity of individuals' diverse responses to grief, and hence of grief counseling. There is no one correct way to grieve, and so no one correct strategy for counseling the bereaved. Some people openly express their emotional pain and benefit from talking. Traditional grief counseling assumes that this pathway (talking about, processing, and working through the grief) is necessary to a healthy recovery. Recent research, however, questions this generalization. Many people do not require formal grief work to overcome a loss, and insisting on processing grief may actually worsen symptoms, trigger rumination, and increase or induce depression in some people (Bonanno & Kaltman, 1999; Bonanno, Keltner, Holen, & Horowitz, 1995; Wortman & Silver, 1989). Bonanno and Kaltman (1999) present an alternative to traditional grief counseling in which the social worker helps the client to:

1. Evaluate or define how the death has created major life difficulties (i.e., help clients determine and examine life's realities created by the loss).

2. Regulate the conscious processing of and emotional reaction to the loss by employing relaxation methods (e.g., thought-stopping techniques, distraction, or other cognitive-behavioral methods).

3. Learn how an attachment and connection with the deceased can be continued rather than severed (e.g., through memories and rituals).

4. Break up extended periods of negative thoughts or feelings during the bereavement (e.g., with laughter and positive emotions).

Lindstrøm (2002) concurs that grief counseling should not push people into an extended process, rumination, and long review of negative emotions. However, some people may expend considerable energy avoiding thought about the loss and diverting or avoiding their feelings. Lindstrøm suggests that counselors take a middle-of-the-road perspective that validates sadness and distressed thoughts but does not encourage clients to become overwhelmed or lost in negative emotions and behaviors.

Cultural-Historical Context: Caring for the Elderly and Dying

As with other developmental processes, cultural and historical contexts shape our interpretation and experience of aging and death. Western society generally places responsibility for adapting on the aging person; that is, public opinion and professional assessments focus on the aging individual's physical health and psychological adjustment. Yet an individual's negative perceptions, motivation problems, and reduced activity may stem more from environmental than psychological or neurological deficits. Within the community, workforce, and family the person can face age bias, stigma, and a lack of meaningful opportunities. Physiological changes occurring with age can come into conflict with cultural priorities and values (e.g., values emphasizing youthful appearance, energy and productivity over wisdom and experience). When this occurs, older adults are tempted to deny the realities of their physical condition. Furthermore, older adults are devalued by society, and care for the elderly and dying may be compromised.

In contemporary Western society, the care of many elderly and dying people has become depersonalized. Before 1940, families in the United States generally cared for older adults at home (Kaplan, 1995). Today, 80 percent of all deaths in the United States take place in hospitals, nursing homes, or other institutions (DeSpelder & Strickland, 2002). Because of our mobile society, key family members and friends often cannot be present when death occurs. Professionals also play a role in the depersonalization of death. Almost immediately after a person dies, medical, police, emergency-care providers, and others stop referring to the deceased by name. Bobby Jones becomes the "corpse," the "body," or an assigned morgue identification number.

The way in which we experience our final days is affected not only by practices within a broader cultural and historical context, but by our particular position within that context and our interpersonal relationships. In her beautiful and moving portrayal of her mother's dying and death, Simone de Beauvoir (1965) draws our attention to the importance of personal care, and to the role of social class in the experience of dying. Prior to the following passage, Beauvoir described the horror of her mother's final hours. Responding to Beauvoir's distress, a nurse commented, "But, Madam, I assure you it was a very easy death" (p.88). Beauvoir goes on to reflect:

For indeed, comparatively speaking, her death was an easy one. "Don't leave me in the power of brutes." I thought of all those who have no one to make that appeal to: what agony it must be to feel oneself a defenseless thing, utterly at the mercy of indifferent doctors and over-worked nurses. No hand on the forehead when terror seizes them; no seda-tive as soon as pain begins to tear them; no lying prattle to fill the silence of the void. . . . Even today—why?—there are horrible agonizing deaths. And then in the public wards, when the last hour is coming near, they put a screen round the dying man's bed: he has seen this screen round other beds that were empty the next day: he knows. I pictured Maman, blinded for hours by the black sun that no one can look at directly: the horror of her staring eyes with the dilated pupils. She had a very easy death; an upper-class death. (pp. 94–95)

Global Perspective on Death and Dying

Simone de Beauvoir's memoir draws our attention to political and soci-etal factors that affect death and dying. If we expand our perspective, simi-lar factors may operate at a global level. Demographers have documented that the leading causes of death for older people living in the industrialized world has shifted from infectious diseases and rapid-onset severe illnesses to chronic and degenerative physical and mental disorders. In North America and Europe, death more often occurs from cardiovascular diseases and can-cer, followed by respiratory diseases and injuries. In contrast, infectious and parasitic diseases cause the most deaths in Africa (World Health Organization, 2002; Kinsella K. & Velkoff V, 2001). With the exception of HIV, which rages in many parts of Africa, existing medical science, manufacturing technology, sanitation knowledge, and modern distribution methods could erase much of the human suffering and premature deaths across the conti-nent of Africa and other impoverished regions. In a global society, silence is not acceptable when people are dying from preventable illnesses like diar-rhea, malaria, common childhood diseases, poor prenatal care, and treatable infections. For people in poor nations, the probability that life will be ended because of an acute, but treatable, illness is greatly increased. In industrial-ized nations, the odds are greater that individuals will reach an advanced age and be forced to learn to live for an extended period with chronic disorders, various levels of pain, and disabilities (World Health Organization, 2002; Kinsella & Velkoff, 2001).

ALZHEIMER'S DISEASE: DEVELOPMENTAL-ECOLOGICAL ANALYSIS

Among the various physical changes associated with aging, many peo-ple find changes in cognitive functioning most frightening, especially the possibility of developing dementia (National Council on Aging, 2002). Therefore, it is important and comforting to note that a variety of intellectu-al functions remain intact or continue to develop into late adulthood. These intellectual functions include comprehension, vocabulary, verbal skills dependent on word knowledge, and verbal reasoning. There is no denying, however, that brain changes do occur with aging and that these changes do affect some aspects of cognitive functioning, particularly information processing speed, accuracy, flexibility, memory, and verbal fluency (Raz, 2002).

Some older adults will develop dementia. *Dementia*, an umbrella term that covers a set of disorders, is a progressive loss of cognitive and intellectual functions. It includes the diminishing of intellectual abilities such as short-term memory, judgment, and language. Personality changes also may occur; for example, a formerly outgoing person may become withdrawn, a well-groomed person disheveled, a socially sensitive person prone to angry outbursts (Tobin, 1997). It is important that individuals experiencing what appear to be early signs of dementia receive a thorough medical exam. A variety of medical conditions can result in confusion and other cognitive problems in older adults that are not dementia and that respond to proper medical care. There is some evidence that memory difficulties can increase because of poorly regulated blood sugar or reduced glucose tolerance (Convit, Wolf, Tarshish, & de Leon, 2003).

Alzheimer's disease is the most common and well-known type of dementia. Behaviorally, Alzheimer's disease is characterized by a slow progression from "islets of confusion to total confusion" (Tobin, 1997, p. 17) and eventually results in death in anywhere from three to twenty years. Alzheimer's disease was identified in 1907 by Alois Alzheimer, a German neurologist. He described a case of a 51-year-old woman whose intellectual functioning progressively deteriorated. Over a period of four years she became bedridden, incontinent, and eventually died. An autopsy showed that her brain tissue contained neurofibrillary tangles and amyloid plaques (described below), features recognized today as neuropathologic indicators of Alzheimer's disease (Tobin, 1997).

In the United States, Alzheimer's disease is a major cause of disability among older adults (Tobin, 1997), and a leading cause of death in later adulthood (Berk, 2001). Alzheimer's disease almost always begins after 50 years of age, and most cases are genetically linked (Cummings & Mega, 2003). Only 2 to 3 percent of 65-year-olds have Alzheimer's disease, but after 65 years of age, the number of cases doubles every five years (Turner, 2003). In 1990, there were approximately 4 million people in the United States with the disease. In 2050, if life span and population growth continue to increase and effective medical interventions are not developed, social work and medical services will be needed for approximately 14 million North Americans living with Alzheimer's disease (Turner, 2003).

Biological Factors

Alzheimer's disease results from major structural and chemical changes in the brain. Many neurofibrillary tangles develop inside of neurons. These are bundles of twisted threads that are the product of collapsed neural structures. Outside the neuron, amyloid plaques develop. These are deposits of material surrounded by dead neurons that destroy surrounding neurons and their communication networks. Although some neurofibrillatory tangles and amyloid plaques are present in the brains of healthy middle-aged and older people, they are much less abundant and widely distributed. In additional to structural changes in the brain, Alzheimer's disease is characterized by chemical changes, specifically lowered levels of neurotransmitters necessary for communication between neurons (see Berk, 2001). These brain changes progressively rob the person of memory, problem-solving skills, insight, control of moods, and, finally, life itself.

Psychological Factors

Alzheimer's disease advances in three behavioral stages, with each new stage marked by an increase in symptom severity and new problems. Alzheimer's disease may first appear as a personality change. The person may become indifferent and apathetic toward events, situations, and people that previously created a variety of emotions and behavioral responses. The person may become anxious and prone to angry outbursts. These personality changes are triggered by emerging cognitive deficits that cause uncertainty and compromise social behavior.

Cognitive deficits in the early stages of Alzheimer's disease involve language, memory, visual spatial skills, abstract thinking, and calculations. Early language problems often appear as difficulties in naming known people and objects *(anomia),* and conversational speech that is empty of content. Memory problems first look more like carelessness or inattentiveness. The people may periodically forget to make appointments, complete tasks, or turn stove burners on or off. As the illness progresses, they forget well-rehearsed information. During the early stage of Alzheimer's disease, people may misplace their eyeglasses and other items. As the disease progresses, they may completely forget they even need and use glasses. Calculation skills at first are slow then partially disappear and may deteriorate until even simple counting can no longer be mastered. As these changes progress, the people are often indifferent to mounting personal, family, and social problems.

Depression may appear in the early stages of Alzheimer's disease. Depression may be part of the disease process, and it also may reflect the person's awareness of cognitive deterioration. Some people have articulated the devastation of a loss of self. Cohen and Eisendorfer (1986) quote from the diary of James Thomas, "Help me be strong and free until my self no longer exists. . . . Most people expect to die some day, but who ever expected to lose their self first?" (as quoted in Tobin, 1997, p. 19.) This experience of the dissolution of the self can be catastrophic for the person who is still aware and self-reflective (Tobin, 1997, p. 19).

In the second stage of Alzheimer's disease, symptoms become more severe and new problems appear. The neuromotor system becomes dysfunctional, causing people to experience extreme restlessness, and safety problems (e.g., roaming at night) may occur. The third stage is marked by increased severity of all symptoms and extreme problems with language, memory, abstraction, motor and visuospatial skills, and personality. Neurological deterioration results in *palilalia* (repeating over and over one's own words), *echolalia* (repeating over and over words spoken by someone else), or *mutism* (Cummings & Mega, 2003). Motor coordination difficulties, myoclonus (sudden uncontrolled contraction of muscles causing a jerking motion, often in the legs), seizures, and incontinence appear late in the disease (Kaufer & DeKosky, 2004). In the final stage, the person loses not only mental competency but also control over coordination, muscle groups, and flow of movement.

Social and Cultural Factors

Caring for a loved one with Alzheimer's disease can be overwhelming to family members. Compared with caring for older adults with physical disabilities, caring for older adults with Alzheimer's disease requires substantially more time in caregiving tasks and results in more stress (see Berk, 2001). Education of caregivers about Alzheimer's disease (e.g., how to optimize communication with the person who has Alzheimer's disease) and social support are vital. Even with such education and support, caring for a loved one with Alzheimer's disease is stressful. The diary of Carol Swenson (2004) describes the profound impact of caring for her mother-in-law on her and her husband, David, her family, and work. In a particularly moving passage, Swenson writes:

One night Mother became really upset, crying to Dave, "Am I losing my mind?" He told me about it later; he was shattered. I remember my reaction the day she couldn't remember my sister-in-law's name. These things keep shocking us, no matter how "prepared" we are. (p.458).

Many caregivers and family members have found support and information through the Alzheimer's Association. The Alzheimer's Association consists of a nationwide network of eighty-one chapters. It provides a wealth of community programs and services including help lines, telephone services to provide emotional support, and information. Information includes community resources such as home care, adult day care, assisted living, skilled nursing facilities, elder-care lawyers, and transportation. Chapters of the Alzheimer's Association also provide peer and professionally led support groups for caregivers and a wealth of educational materials on topics related to Alzheimer's disease. (Alzheimer's Association, 2006).

INTERVENTION

As in all major disorders, there is no single treatment or intervention approach that fits all Alzheimer's clients and families. Treatment for Alzheimer's disease requires (1) specific medical supervision, (2) behavioral management and control of symptoms, (3) prevention of additional physical and emotional problems, and (4) family support (Cummings & Mega, 2003). Social workers provide a number of social services for Alzheimer's clients and their families. Most families need help developing a plan to prevent accidents and successfully maintain the Alzheimer's client at home as long as possible. Many families also expect professionals to help them limit or stop the client from driving a vehicle. In the first stage, some Alzheimer's clients are able to continue driving but are usually limited to traveling on well-known, highly practiced routes on roads that require less speed and are less congested and hazardous. In an assessment of driving skills of twenty-one participants with very mild dementia and twenty-nine participants with early Alzheimer's disease, fourteen of the very mild dementia group and twelve of the early Alzheimer's disease group were scored as safe drivers (Duchek et al., 2003). When Alzheimer's disease progresses from the first to the second stage, however, all driving must end.

As a general rule, discussions and education about driving and other lifestyle changes always include the Alzheimer's client and family. In order for clients to be successfully maintained at home, dangerous behavioral symptoms must be controlled through appropriate use of medications, humane behavior modification techniques, cognitive training, social support, and environmental manipulations (Wise, Gray, & Seltzer, 1999). A standard treatment goal for social work interventions is to help clients maintain and use as much personal control, self-empowerment, and dignity as possible. Alzheimer's clients must not be treated as if they have no voice and no ability to comprehend information. In most cases cognitive skills dissipate slowly and unevenly, and existing competencies need to be used and practiced.

Eventually, Alzheimer's disease disrupts judgment, memory, motor skills, and the ability to learn from experience. Thus, safety decisions cannot be left

Photo 7.3.
Many older adults continue to lead active, productive lives. This 75-year-old man enjoys outdoor work with his 18-year-old grandson.

solely to the client. Some families have difficulties recognizing and support-ing the person's intact cognitive skills, while other families discover they cannot independently limit a loved one's freedom. At this stage, families may benefit from assistance in developing plans and methods for preventing falls, wandering, forgetting to eat, and hazardous behaviors such as leaving open flames and burners unattended or going outdoors in extreme weather without appropriate clothing. As the client's memory and judgment fade, stepping outside, closing the door, and having neither a house key nor coat is a real possibility. Some Alzheimer's clients may find it impossible to resolve such a problem, while others will neither look for a solution nor become emotionally distressed. For these individuals, Alzheimer's disease has destroyed awareness and knowledge about hazardous weather and ability to feel or notice when they are exposed to extremely hot and cold tempera-tures. They can become either hypo- or hypersensitive to pain and discom-fort.

In order to prevent roaming and other dangerous acts, families are forced to install locks to stop the individual from opening doors or having access to dangerous tools, kitchen knifes, and poisons. In some cases, fami-lies have to remove knobs for turning on stoves, food blenders, and other electrical devices. For many, restricting the freedom of a loved one creates sadness, self-doubt, and ambivalence, which, in turn, stops or slows them from taking appropriate action. When this occurs, family members need reas-surance and specific information from professionals. Families cannot be expected to take on new roles and a higher level of vigilance without accu-rate information.

Alzheimer's disease and other neurodegenerative problems can also place clients at risk for victimization. Therefore, social workers must be pre-pared to screen and assess hidden and obvious signs of physical and mental neglect, physical and sexual assault, and financial theft. Forrest (1997) states that one indication of possible victimization is when an Alzheimer's client expresses stark fear that cannot be explained. Determining whether abuse has occurred can be extremely difficult because an individual with a deter-iorating mind can believe that abuse is occurring when, in actuality, no vic-timization has taken place.

Additionally, Alzheimer's disease can cause individuals to develop behav-iors in conflict with their moral values. Children who are unable to deter-mine when and how to call for help or youths who are unable to defend themselves from molestation should not be left alone with a family member suffering from Alzheimer's disease (Forrest, 1997). Families can be helped to understand the importance of ensuring the entire family's safety through ongoing education and individual counseling. The probability that Alzheimer's disease will cause an individual to become a sexual predator is rather low but it is a possibility that must be periodically examined by adult family members. Learning that Alzheimer's disease has the potential for causing sexual or violent behaviors totally uncharacteristic of the person's moral values and history can stir emotions, concerns, and questions for family members. To resolve highly charged issues, social workers may, in addition to education, offer family members individual counseling or the opportunity to meet other families who have experienced similar problems with a loved one with Alzheimer's disease and who have changed or redirected the disturbing behaviors in a satisfactory manner.

Factors such as anxiety, fear, grief, cognitive dysfunctions, false beliefs, depression, delusions, or hallucinations can cause a person with Alzheimer's disease to experience a severe psychological crisis (Sano & Weber, 2003; Wise, Gray, & Seltzer, 1999). When chaotic uncontrolled behaviors, emotions, or accusations stemming from delusions occur, it is helpful for social workers to mobilize family members and service providers quickly to develop an intervention plan and assess whether the client is at risk for suicide or committing violence to others.

Well-conceived, professionally presented activities may not improve functioning but may help Alzheimer's clients pass time in a more pleasant and productive manner. Additionally, systematic social and cognitive interventions may assuage the family's feelings of grief and guilt even though they receive no relief from daily caretaking responsibilities. Psychosocial interventions for caregivers can significantly reduce psychological distress, increase knowledge, and improve coping skills but do not decrease the burden of care (Brodaty et al., 2003). In addition, there is little doubt that in the early stages of Alzheimer's disease difficult behavioral symptoms respond positively to psychotherapy, support, and cognitive reminders posted systematically in key locations (Sano & Weber, 2003). In addition, psychosocial interventions can delay the need for nursing home admission (Brodaty et al., 2003).

Each stage of Alzheimer's disease brings new challenges that affect caretakers differently. It is difficult to know when supports for a family or client will be most needed and effective. One critical period for families and clients is during the end stage of the disorder when death is nearing. By the final stage of Alzheimer's disease, the client's personality, behavior, and emotional reactions have changed drastically. The person known and loved by family and friends seems to have disappeared. This can frighten, upset, and trigger severe grief reactions from family members. The pain can be so great that they completely stop visiting the ill family member. Many times patients' reduced reasoning, abstraction, and memory skills prevent them from observing and understanding that they are being avoided. For others, however, islands of reality remain intact and the person experiences feelings of emotional abandonment and chronic loneliness (Forrest, 1997).

Newer medications are successfully slowing the rate of neurodeterioration but currently cannot reverse or cure Alzheimer's disease. It is predictable that as treatment extends the early stages of this illness, clients and their families will benefit from social work case management that organizes home health services, transportation, adjustment to illness counseling, and family problem-solving therapies. In the later stages of Alzheimer's disease, cognitive disabilities force many patients into assisted living and nursing home facilities. Since the decision to move clients into a care facility almost always falls on family members, making this decision causes major emotion-

---

BOX 7.7 PRACTICE STORY AND ADVICE FROM THE FIELD

Tonya M., medical social worker:
"We're standing with the client on the shore and a big wave is coming."

Tonya M. practiced as a medical social worker for 20 years in diverse settings including hospitals, nursing homes, and hospice care (Note: Hospice care refers to palliative care for the terminally ill that focuses on providing physical and emotional comfort to the client and his/her loved ones). Tonya's favorite setting is the hospital, where she advocated for and supported clients and their families through the challenges of medical illness. She related, "When you work in a hospital it's short term, 4 or 5 days, so you are referring. You are trying to equip that client with something to hold onto—trying to keep them from being overwhelmed. I always visualize it like standing on the shore with a big wave coming and part of what a medical social worker does is have clients step back so that they can move ahead and deal with [their medical condition]." For the past 10 years Tonya has worked as a clinical professor, passing along her wisdom and passion for the field to beginning medical social workers.

Practice Story

A lot of medical social work also has to do with dealing with the medical team. You are forever explaining clients to the doctors or to the nurses. They [members of the medical team] have a different mind-set. Not that social work has a better mind-set, just different. So you go to a hospital and a physician, they have in mind a medical model. A patient comes in with a medical problem. They want to fix it. I think probably the most difficult thing for a medical social worker is that they work in what I term a host environment. You don't go to a hospital to see a social worker—you go to get your medical problem fixed. So a medical social worker is kind of an odd man out. You have to be able to see many different viewpoints and respect those viewpoints. You have to be able to work in a team environment and to command respect—respect for your skills and your profession. And that does not always happen—if you can't think on your feet, if you can't be comfortable with people criticizing you, medical social work is not for you.

A new social work intern talked about the physician who came in while she was sitting doing paper work and he told her to get up. He told her that he was going to be charting, so he wanted her to move. And I said, "Really? What did you do?" She said, "I got up and felt bad about it ever since." So we role-played on how you can handle that a little differently. There is a hierarchy in a hospital, and you need to learn to smile and say, "There is an extra chair over there, Doc." This same intern was told that she needed to go clean up a mess—a patient had vomited, and that she needed to go in and do that. At that point she did laugh and say, "You know, that's really not my job." But I was afraid when she started telling that story!

Advice

Cultivate flexibility.   One of the exciting things about working in a hospital as a medical social worker is that you don't know what your day will be like. I used to walk in, as I am coming into work walking from the parking lot, I would turn on my beeper and be thinking about the things I would be doing that day, and it was all very logical in my mind. Generally speaking before I got to the hospital door, I was being paged, sometimes I was being paged overhead, to come to ICU STAT. So there was no rhyme or reason to what the day might be like.

Become comfortable with strong emotion. When you are working in medical social work, you deal a lot with crisis. One of the things that I enjoyed most was working in trauma, but that is only one aspect of the crisis. You know there is always a crisis in peoples' lives when they are faced with loss. And that can be loss of life, it can be loss of function, it can be loss of role, but those losses are a turning point in the client's life and in their family's life. So you are forever working in a crisis situation.

Become comfortable—as comfortable as you can—with death. Issues surrounding death are a big thing with medical social workers. Death is symbolic as well as real and when people see that it is true that the person that they love is going to die and will be gone—then there is a lot of denial. The medical team can't understand why, when I have told them their mother has less than 6 months to live, why they are asking about a lung transplant. For heaven's sake, she has lung cancer, what do they expect?

Be comfortable with emotion. The hospital is a place of high emotion. And medical social workers need to be comfortable with people who have not always expressed emotion. So they may bear the brunt of anger. That's a very common thing, to bear the brunt of someone's anger because you walked in the door. Or because you said that the doctor asked me to come and talk with you about when you are discharged from the hospital. That's very common.

Develop good communication skills. What you are doing then, so much of it is in promoting communication. When you are in a health-care setting, they talk a different language. So many times a social worker will go in with the physician while they talk with the patient. And then the physician will go in and he will say, "Mrs. Smith, your results came back, it's malignant. I do not want you to be too upset about this. We're going to provide you with palliative care and I am sure the social worker here can explain things for you." And then he leaves. And the social worker learns to ask that person, "What do you understand that the doctor said?" And you discover that they have no idea what "palliative" means—that it means comfort care. They are not sure what "malignant" means, because if it was cancer, the doctor would surely have said "cancer." So you know the explanation comes many times from the social worker.

In turn, the social worker is working with that medical team, to help them understand, first of all, why you cannot send this patient home and expect the husband to give the injections. The husband is in early stage of dementia and she is the caregiver for him; we have to get some more services in. You also are always explaining to physicians, although nurses can be bad on this too, why you have to go ahead and allow this person to make their own decisions, even if the decision is wrong, even if its going to be a dangerous one. So you have frail elderly people, and the physician will say to send them to the nursing home. Your job is to go in there and find, first of all, what does that patient want, and then tell them the pros and cons of their decision. So if they say, "I want to go home. I am not going to a nursing home. I want to go home." So you need to explain to them, "Okay, do you understand you have been falling and you live alone and you could fall, not be discovered, and die?" And if they understand, then you facilitate that decision.

Sometimes you are the only one that the patient can really talk to who understands what they are going through, and that's no exaggeration. Depends on what the problem is. Sometimes you will have families that come in and they raise Cain with medical staff. "Mom isn't getting her medicine on time, I want more people in here, I don't believe the diagnosis." And then you are working with that family to find out exactly what's going on there. That's what I call the "Daughter from California syndrome." She swoops in and says, "Hey, you are not going to send my mother to a nursing home. What's going on here? I don't care what the plans are, I demand this . . . this . . . and this." This throws the medical team into a tizzy, but you find out that the daughter is kind of guilty because she has been away.

A medical social worker needs to be appropriately assertive and to learn how to spend their brownie points. You have to learn when to advocate and when to save your brownie points. You have to have good judgment. I have known social workers—a new social worker once stopped the vice president of the hospital in the corridor and demanded that he provide more staff because they weren't getting patients' needs met. She felt that it was a very appropriate thing [to do], and he thought that social workers are some kind of nut cases or something.

Be comfortable with being a token. You are a token, and as such you bear much more responsibility than if there are a lot of you. Because the rest of the team will remember for years that strange social worker that did this strange thing. They will also remember for years where some social worker has been able to save the day. So you bear an extra responsibility because you are a token. You are a token.

Learn medical terminology and ask questions. If I could tell students one thing to do before they go into medical social work, it would be to take a medical terminology course. They need to know the language to interpret for the client, and also so they know what's going on. I relate to my students the first team meeting that I sat in on as a bachelors [degree] intern. When they talked about the pulmonary function of the cardiac patient—that it was such and such, and the something or other was so and so—and we needed to be sure and relate the situation to the family. I concentrated on keeping my face absolutely blank because I didn't know if it was good news or bad news. I had no idea. When the nurse told me that they put in a pig valve, I asked why they called it a pig valve. And she said, "Because it's from a pig!" "Really, a pig?" So there are a lot of things that you don't know, and if you take medical terminology, you know more, but you also need to be comfortable about asking questions. We don't train nor should we be training medical social workers to understand all the procedures in medicine; that's not their job. But they do need to understand enough, and the only way to learn is when they get in the field being comfortable with asking questions.

Become culturally sensitive. Medical social workers need to be as culturally informed and sensitive as they can possibly be. And what they don't know, they need to be able to go and find out. We don't equip students to walk out of here and be comfortable with all of the cultural values of African Americans, Hispanics, Mongs, and others. It can't be done, it's impossible. But they will be the ones who will speak up for being culturally sensitive. And in the health-care setting, 30% to 40% of the people now utilize alternative medicine. And particularly in some cultures this is very common and can have a great impact on the doctor's prescribing. They need to be able to talk with those clients and hear in a nonjudgmental why they are using traditional healing practices or unusual healing practices. They need to be comfortable hearing that and not be judgmental. And find how that can go ahead and fit in with what Western medicine has prescribed, or how it can be explained to people from a different culture or religion. You know you have certain religions that say no blood products, and [believers] are willing to literally put their lives on the line. That's a very difficult situation for the health-care team to stand and watch a person die, because they are refusing blood products. So sometimes you end up being a counselor for the medical team. Sometimes you feel like an octopus, where people are tugging on all of your tentacles.

al and economic costs for the client and family. Social workers can help to ease the pain of placement by aiding the family in locating facilities that provide humane care and individual treatment plans and incorporate the latest evidence-based medical and social interventions. It also becomes the social worker's job to help families remain focused on the realities of Alzheimer's disease and not be misled by false hopes, which can happen when activities designed to increase a client's quality of life are either inadvertently presented by the staff or perceived by the family as methods for healing. That is, movement, art, cognitive exercises, and other active interventions may reduce stress or depression and usher in short-term improvements in memory and other skills, but the onward destruction of Alzheimer's disease has not been arrested.

SUMMARY

In this chapter we have focused on medical social work with older adults. Later adulthood is a developmental period that may be characterized by a sense of fulfillment, meaningful relationships, and continued curiosity about the world. It is also a period in which all individuals eventually will experience significant loss and death. Some older adults will experience chronic and debilitating diseases. In this chapter, we have presented a developmental-ecological approach to understanding Alzheimer's disease. As the world's population continues to age, medical social workers increasingly will face clients and family members who need assistance in coping with this devastating disease. Medical social workers can function as part of a team of health-care professionals to provide support and education for individuals and families suffering from Alzheimer's disease. Box 7.7 contains a practice story and advice from an experienced medical social worker.

Study and Discussion Questions

1. What are some of the common physical, psychological, and social changes that occur during late adulthood?

2. Loss and related issues are major emotional challenges for older adults. Describe some common sources of loss in late adulthood.

3. What are some of the emotions and conflicts that a well spouse caring for an ill spouse may experience? What can a community do to support a person who has lost a spouse?

4. That are some of the physical and psychological characteristics of dying? How might the social and cultural context of dying affect the individual and his/her loved ones?

5. Those who work with older people need to be aware of the various types of dementia, including Alzheimer's disease. What are the causes of Alzheimer's disease, how is it manifested and treated, and what are the implications for families?

6. What are some implications of a developmental-ecological model for social work intervention with individuals living with Alzheimer's disease and their families?

7. What might be some factors associated with more "successful" aging?

8. Ageism is discriminatory treatment based on age. How pervasive is it in our culture? Provide examples.

9. To return to our opening example, what are some of the possible strategies for engaging Mrs. P. and her husband in services as their dementia progresses? How might Mrs. P.'s adult son be involved?

Resources

For students interested in learning more about Alzheimer's disease, a good source is: Lichtenberg, Murman, & Mellow (2003). An excellent first-person account of the experience of Alzheimer's was written by DeBaggio (2002) during the initial stages of his disease. For those interested in learning about aging and health care, we recommend the following sources: Kane (2003); Lunney, Lynn, Foley, Lipson, and Guralnik (2003); and Staudinger, Bluck, and Herzberg (2003). To learn more about death, dying, and bereavement, see Bonanno and Kaltman, (1999); De Spelder and Strickland, (2002); Lindstrøm (2002); and Stroebe (2001).

Students also can supplement this chapter with a number of Web-based resources.

The Alzheimer's Association provides peer and professionally led support groups for caregivers and a wealth of educational materials on topics related to Alzheimer's disease. Available at: http://www.alz.org/Services/overview.asp

The U.S. Government's Department of Human Services, Agency on Aging provides a wide range of practical information for helping older adults and their families make informed decisions and understand their rights. Available at: http://www.aoa.gov

Students interested in international issues of aging will find information at: http://www.aoa.gov/prof/international/international.asp

AARP provides an overview of resources for aging clients including job, retirement, and health benefits. Available at: http://www.aarp.org/internetresources

AARP provides information on how older adults can check on important benefits, including drug prescription assistance, and suggestions for help with rent, property taxes, heating bills, meals and other needs. Available at: http://www.benefitscheckup.org

The CDC's National Center for Health Statistics provides an overview of research findings about aging as well as a power point presentation that teaches steps for healthy living during the senior years. Available at: http://www.cdc.gov/nchs/agingact.htm

An important academic resource for students and clinicians is the American Psychological Association's journal, *The Psychology of Aging*. Information about the journal and sample articles available at: http://www.apa.org/journals/pag

References

Alzheimer's Association. (2006) *We're here for you.* Retrieved June 15, 2005, from www.alz.org/Services/overview.asp

American Association of Retired People. (2000). *Census number and percentage change since 1990: Children under 18 living in grandparent-headed households.* Retrieved May 2005 from http://www.aarp.org/grandparents

American Psychiatric Association. (2000). Practice guidelines for the treatment of psychiatric disorders. *Diagnostic and statistical manual of mental disorders* (Text revision). Washington, DC: Author.

Ball, K., Berch, D. B., Helmers, K. F., Jobe, J. B., Leveck, M. D., Marsiske, M., et al. (2002). Effects of cognitive training interventions with older adults: A randomized controlled trial. *Journal of the American Medical Association, 288,* 2271-2281.

Beason-Held, L. L., & Horwitz, B. (2002). Aging brain. In V. S. Ramachandran (Ed.), *Encyclopedia of the human brain* (Vol. 1, pp. 43-57). San Diego, CA: Academic Press.

Beautrais, A. L. (2002). A case control of suicide and attempted suicide in older adults. *Suicide and Life-Threatening Behavior, 32,* 1-9.

Berger, G., Bemhardt, T., Schramm, U., Muller, R., Landsiedel-Anders, S., Peters, J., et al. (2004). No effect of a combination of caregivers support group and memory training/music therapy in dementia patients from a memory clinic population. *International Journal of Geriatric Psychiatry, 19,* 223-231.

Berk, L. (2001). *Development through the lifespan* (2nd ed.). Boston: Allyn & Bacon.

Blazer, D. (1999). Geriatric psychiatry. In R. E. Hales, S. C. Yudofsky, & J. A. Talbott

(Eds.), *The American psychiatric press textbook of psychiatry* (pp.1447–1462).Washington, DC:American Psychiatric Press.

Bonanno, G. A., & Kaltman, K. (1999). Toward an integrative perspective on bereavement. *Psychological Bulletin, 125,* 760–776.

Bonanno, G. A., Keltner, D., Holen, A., & Horowitz, M. J. (1995). When avoiding unpleasant emotion might not be such a bad thing:Verbal-autonomic response dissociation and midlife conjugal bereavement. *Journal of Personality and Social Psychology, 46,* 975–989.

Brodaty, H., Fracp, F., Green, A., & Koshera, A. Meta-analysis of psychosocial interventions for caregivers of people with dementia.*Journal of the American Geriatrics Society, 51,* 657–664.

Carmelli, D., Swan, G. E., Reed,T.,Wolf, P.A., Miller, B. L., & DeCarli, C. (1999). Midlife cardiovascular risk factors and brain morphology in identical older male twins. *Neurology, 52,* 1119–1124.

Carstensen, L. (1997, August). Psychology and the aging revolution. Paper presented at the annual meeting of the American Psychological Association, Chicago.

Carter, J. (2000). The virtues of aging. In D. Sattler, G. Kramer, V. Shabatay, & D. Bernstein (Eds.), *Lifespan development in context: Voices and perspectives* (pp. 187–190). New York: Houghton Mifflin.

Centers for Disease Control and Prevention. (2003). *Healthy aging: Preventing disease and improving quality of life among older Americans.* Atlanta: National Center for Chronic Disease Prevention. Retrieved May 20, 2005, from http://www.cdc.gov/nccdphp/aag_aging.htm

Convit, A., Wolf, O. T., Tarshish, C., & de Leon, M. J. (2003). Reduced glucose tolerance is associated with poor memory performance and hippocampal atrophy among normal elderly. *Neuroscience, 100,* 2019–2022.

Cook, I.A., et al. (2002). Cognitive and physiologic correlates of subclinical structural brain disease in elderly normal controls. *Archives of Neurology, 59,* 1612–1620.

Cummings, J. L., & Mega, M. S. (2003). *Neuropsychiatry and behavioral neuroscience* (pp. 146–171). New York: Oxford University Press.

DeBaggio,T. (2002). *Losing my mind:An intimate look at life with Alzheimer's.* New York: Free Press.

DePaulo, R. J. (2002). *Understanding depression: What we know and what you can do about it.* New York:Wiley.

DeSpelder, L.A., & Strickland,A. L. (2002). *The last dance: Encountering death and dying* (6th ed.). Boston: McGraw-Hill.

Dubowitz, H., Feigelman, S., Harrington, D., Starr, R., Zuravin, S., & Sawyer, R. (1994). Children in kinship care: How do they fare? *Children and Youth Services Review, 16,* 85–106.

Duchek, J. M., Hunt, L., Roe, C. M., Xiong, C., Shah, K., & Morris, J. C. (2003). Longitudinal driving performance in early-stage dementia of the Alzheimer type.*Journal of the American Geriatrics Society, 10,* 1342–1347.

Forrest, D. V. (1997). Psychotherapy for patients with neuropsychiatric disorders. In S. C.Yudofsky & R. E. Hales (Eds.), *The American psychiatric press textbook of neuropsychiatry* (3rd ed., pp. 983–1018). Washington, DC: American Psychiatric Press.

Gibson, P.A. (1999). African American grandmothers: New mothers again. *Affilia, 14,* 329–343.

Gibson, P. A. (2002). African American grandmothers as caregivers: Answering the call to help their grandchildren. *Families in Society: The Journal of Contemporary Human Services, 83,* 35–43.

Gibson, P. A., & Lum, T. (2003). *Informal kinship care in Minnesota: A pilot study* (Final Report, pp.1–52). Minneapolis, MN: Minnesota Kinship Care Association.

Grim, C. W. (2002). *Elder health is family health* (pp. 1–3). Paper presented at the National Indian Council on Aging Conference, Albuquerque, NM.

Jamison, K. R. (1999). *Night falls fast.* New York: Vintage Books.

Kane, R. L. (2003). The contribution of geriatric health research to successful aging. *Annals of Internal Medicine, 139,* 460–462.

Kaplan, K. (1996). End-of-life decisions. In R. L. Edwards (Ed.), *Encyclopedia of social work* (Vol. 2). Washington, DC: NASW Press.

Kaufer, D. I., & Dekosky, S. T. (2004). Diagnostic classifications: Relationship to the neurobiology of dementia. In D. S. Charney, & E. J. Nestler (Eds.), *Neurobiology of mental illness* (2nd ed., pp. 771–782). New York: Oxford University Press.

Kennedy, G. E. (1990). College students' expectations of grandparents and grandchild behaviors. *The Gerontologist, 30,* 43–48.

Kinsella, K., & Velkoff, V. (2001). *An aging world: 2001.* U.S. Census Bureau (Publication No. P95/01-1). Washington, DC: U.S. Government Printing Office.

Kubler-Ross, E. (1969). *On death and dying.* New York: Macmillan.

Leaper, S. A., Murray, A. D., Staff, R. T., & Whalley, L. J. (2003). Cerebral white matter abnormalities and lifetime cognitive change: A 67-year follow-up of the Scottish mental survey of 1932. *Psychology and Aging, 18,* 140–148.

Lichtenberg, P. A., Murman, D. L., & Mellow, A. M. (Eds.). (2003). *Handbook of dementia: Psychological, neurological, and psychiatric perspectives.* New York: Wiley.

Lindstrøm, T. C. (2002). "It ain't necessarily so". . . Challenging mainstream thinking about bereavement. *Family Community Health, 25,* 11–21.

Lunney, J. R., Lynn, J., Foley, D. J., Lipson, S., & Guralnik, J. M. (2003). Patterns of functional decline at the end of life. *Journal of American Medical Association, 289,* 2387–2392.

Morris, P. L. P., Robinson, R. G., Andrzejewski, P., Samuels, J., & Price, T. R. (1993). Association of depression with 10-year poststroke mortality. *American Journal of Psychiatry, 150,* 124–129.

National Council on Aging, Inc. (2002). *American perceptions of aging in the 21st century. The NCOA's continuing study of the myths and realities of aging* (pp.1–16). Washington, DC: Author.

Neugarten, B.L. (1974). Age groups in American society and the rise of the young-old. *Annals of the American Academy of Political and Social Science,* 187–198.

Powers, D. V., Thompson, L., Futterman, A., & Gallagher-Thompson, D. (2002). Depression in later life epidemiology, assessment, impact, and treatment. In I. H. Gotlib & C. L. Hammen (Eds.), *Handbook of depression* (pp.560–580). New York: Guilford.

Raz, N. (2002). Cognitive aging. In V. S. Ramachandran (Ed.), *Encyclopedia of the human brain* (Vol. 1, pp. 829–838). San Diego, CA: Academic Press.

Rudolph, J. L., & Marcantonio, E. R. (2003). Diagnosing and preventing delirium. *Geriatrics and Aging, 6,* 14–19.

Sano, M., & Weber, C. (2003). Psychological evaluation and nonpharmacologic treatment of Alzheimer's disease. In P. A. Lichtenberg, D. L. Murman, & A. M. Mellow (Eds.), *Handbook of dementia* (pp.25–27). New York: Wiley.

Santrock, J. W. (2002). *Life-span development.* Boston: McGraw-Hill.

Seifert, K. L., Hoffnung, R. J., & Hoffnung, M. (2000). *Lifespan development.* New York: Houghton Mifflin.

Smith, I. M. (2003) *Bodies begin to show wear and tear at 30.* University of Iowa Virtual Hospital. Retrieved May 20, 2005, from http://www.vh.org/ adult/patieth /internalmedicine/aba30/1992/aging.html

Staudinger, U. M., Bluck, S., & Herzberg, P. Y. (2003). Looking back and looking ahead: Adult age differences in consistency of diachronous ratings of subjective well-being. *Psychology and Aging, 18,* 13–24.

Stroebe, M. (2001). Bereavement research and theory: Retrospective and prospective. *American Behavioral Scientist, 44,* 854–865.

Swenson, C. R. (2004). Dementia diary: A personal and professional journal. *Social Work, 49*(3), 451–460.

Szanto, K. (2003). Suicide behavior in the elderly. *Psychiatric Times, 20,* 1–6.

Taylor, E. H. (2002). Manic-depressive illness. In V. S. Ramachandran (Ed.), *Encyclopedia of the human brain* (Vol. 2, pp. 745–757). San Diego, CA: Academic Press.

Taylor, E. H. (2003). Practice methods for working with children who have biological based mental disorders: A bioecological model. *Families in Society: The Journal of Contemporary Human Services, 84,* 39–50.

Tobin, S. S. (1997). Aging: Alzheimer's disease and other disabilities. In R. L. Edwards (Ed.), *Encyclopedia of social work* (Supplement, 19th ed., pp. 15–25). Washington, DC: NASW Press.

Turner, S. R. (2003). Neurologic aspects of Alzheimer's disease. In P. A. Lichtenberg, D. L. Murman, & A. M. Mellow (Eds.), *Handbook of dementia* (pp.1–24). New York: Wiley.

U.S. Census Bureau International Database. (2004). *Midyear population, by age and sex* (Table 094). Retrieved May 10, 2005, from http://www.census.gov/pop ulation/wwwprojects/natdet-D1A.html

U.S. Department of Health and Human Services. (1999). *Centenarians in the United States* (CPR Publication No. P23-199RV). Washington, DC: U.S. Government Printing Office.

U.S. Indian Health Service. (2001). *Heritage and health.* Retrieved May 2005 from http://info.ihs.gov

U.S. Indian Health Service. (2002, September). *Facts on Indian health disparities* (pp. 1–2). Washington, DC: Author.

Williamson, G. R., Shaffer, D. R., & Parmalee, P. R. (Eds.). (2000). *Physical illness and depression in older adults.* New York: Kluwer Academic/Plenum.

Wise M. G., Gray K. F., & Seltzer, B. (1999). Delirium, dementia and amnestic disorders. In R. E. Hales, S. Yudofsky, & J. A. Talbott (Eds.), *The American psychiatric press textbook of psychiatry* (3rd ed., pp. 317–362). Washington, DC: American Psychiatric Press.

World Health Organization. (2002). *Deaths by cause, sex and mortality stratum in WHO regions, estimates for 2001* (World Health Report 2002, Annex Table 2, pp.186–191). Geneva, Switzerland: Author.

Wortman, C. B., & Silver, R. C. (1989). The myths of coping with loss. *Journal of Consulting and Clinical Psychology, 57,* 349–357.

Figure 8.1. Social workers consider how the issues they confront affect entire families. This adolescent's physical and cognitive disabilities affect not only his life, but those of his mother and infant sister.

8

CONCLUSION

Throughout the book, we have presented the perspectives of social workers interpreting social scientific research or commenting upon and describing professional practice. We conclude with a narrative written by an adolescent who experienced social work practice as a client in the child welfare system. Before entering the child welfare system, Summer spent her early childhood with her birth mother, who was alcoholic. Like many children of substance-abusing parents, Summer cared for younger siblings, experienced maltreatment, and frequently did not have adequate food or shelter. She also felt love and loyalty toward her birth mother and siblings.

At 6 years of age I went, along with my five brothers and sisters, into the foster care system. I was partnered up with my little sister to go through the process. The previous night was terrifying because of a fight between my birth mother's drunken boyfriend and their friends. And now this total change of lifestyle was confusing and scary. My sister and I were put into a group home where we spent the first Christmas. I can remember there were a lot of boys and girls and it felt like we were all shuffled around. It was strange and all so new to me, but I was glad that we had shelter and food.

Out of everything that happened, I remember specifically the care of one social worker, Wanda, who impacted my life greatly. On one particular occasion she took my sister and I out [from the foster home where the girls were placed after their stay in the group home] to our favorite burger place for one of our regular visits. I had something to tell her, but I could not do it in front of my sister. On the way out the door to go out for lunch, my foster father had told me to watch what I said. At that moment I knew something was wrong. So, I waited for my sister to go play in the playground. While sitting there I confided everything that pressed on my mind. My social worker made a difficult conversation easy by coming down to my level when I was trying so hard to reach hers.

We never went back to that foster home. Wanda took us and drove for what seemed an eternity. I cried once. With the wind blowing in my face, I thought she would not notice, but somehow, I think she did. I was very scared about the new fate that lay before my sister and me. There was so much I did not know. What was going to happen to us now?

I see now that my social worker was already coming up with a plan. She was thinking of a family that already had one of my little brothers. Within a short period of time my little sister and I were in a family that would bring us up the way a family should. That is not all, though! Before we knew it, two more of my brothers were being adopted by this family.

> Mom and dad took in six kids on top of their four. All six of us shared a common social worker who apparently had good judgment, character, and some love for us. I could have never dreamed up a more perfect family to be a part of.

As 17-year-old Summer's story illustrates, social workers can play pivotal roles in the lives of their clients. Summer's social worker helped place her on her current positive developmental trajectory: she listened when Summer described problems in her foster home, took the psychological burden of care of her younger siblings from her, and eventually placed her and her four younger siblings with a stable, loving foster family who eventually adopted them all. In this book we have emphasized the characteristics of successful social workers. The outcome of any particular case, however, also is influenced by characteristics of the client and available resources. Despite her difficult early childhood, Summer entered foster care as a bright, attractive child who was a physically and mentally healthy. She had the stamina and inner strength to cope with her significant losses, trusted and confided in an adult, responded to the help offered, and adapted to a family very different from the one in which she had been reared. Despite the widespread shortage of quality foster homes, Summer and her siblings were fortunate to be placed in a family with considerable emotional and social resources, and adequate physical resources to care for six additional children with many complex needs.

This story also helps to shift our focus from the perspective of social workers and social science researchers to social work clients. A continuing exercise and challenge faced by social workers is to imagine and then work from the perspective of the client. The clients with whom social workers practice are diverse and complex. Much of this book has focused on generalizations from empirical research. Information about social science research is critical for social workers in order to request needed resources and to plan and develop programs. The consideration of client characteristics and context also is critical. A major challenge faced by social workers is to take research-based knowledge about a group and apply it to a specific individual within a specific setting. Social workers must integrate generalized information from social science research with knowledge of a particular client or setting. Summer's very difficult early life and middle childhood put her at risk for various developmental and mental health challenges, and her social worker needed to be aware of those risks. These early experiences did not determine Summer's developmental outcomes. In supporting Summer, her social worker also was aware of Summer's unique characteristics and strengths, for example, her intelligence, adaptability, and artistic talents. Now aged 17, Summer is poised and talented, living a meaningful life, and prepared to make positive contributions to society. Ten years after entering foster care, Summer has traveled to Africa with her church group to work and study, is finishing high school, works part-time, and plans to attend college. She has her struggles, but she dispels the stereotype of the victimized, at-risk child.

Summer's story also illustrates the interaction of the social work issues presented in this book through boxes on violence, poverty, and substance abuse. Summer's birth mother is an alcoholic living in poverty and with violence. These multiple risk factors operate not independently, but together and over time to compound already-difficult circumstances. For example, impairment from substance abuse makes steady employment impossible, which, in turn, worsens poverty. Poverty may make it necessary to double-up, to live with friends and relatives who themselves may have substance-abuse problems. When violence fueled by substance abuse erupts, Summer's mother may believe that she has no alternative but to endure it. Finally, poverty, substance abuse, and violence profoundly affect not only adults, but their children and grandchildren as well. Witnessing violence between adults is a form of traumatic stress for children. In the absence of intervention, violence, substance abuse, and poverty may continue into future generations.

It is useful to draw out several themes that are developed throughout the book.

DEVELOPMENTAL-ECOLOGICAL FRAMEWORK GUIDES PROBLEM SOLVING IN SOCIAL WORK

A developmental-ecological framework facilitates social work assessment and intervention in a range of practice settings such as schools, mental health, child welfare, and social work education. In this book we have presented a developmental-ecological framework for understanding the complex lives of social workers and their clients. During human development, biological, psychological, and social factors interact over time in highly complex, mutually influential processes within particular cultural and historical contexts.

The developmental-ecological framework draws upon and integrates empirical research from biological, psychological, social, and cultural-historical perspectives. Human beings are shaped both by nature and nurture; that is, they are shaped by biology within the cultural-historical contexts into which they are born. Girls reared in both Victorian England and the twentieth century United States integrated a new sexualized component of their self-concept when they reached puberty. Possibly because of differences in diet and health, Victorian girls entered puberty at a later age and were less exposed to sexualized images of young girls than U.S. girls are exposed to in modern media. Furthermore, individual girls in Victorian England and the twentieth-century United States respond to puberty in various ways, for example, welcoming or resisting their change in status. Thus, the experience and meaning of puberty has both universal and culturally variable aspects resulting from an interaction of biological and psychological factors within specific cultural-historical contexts.

The example of girls' responses to puberty also underscores that individuals are active in their own development. In chapter 1, we saw how Clara Brown, the nineteenth-century African American pioneer, worked actively to use the resources presented to her within Central City and to avoid the risks associated with racism and sexism. She used nature and nurture to create a fit between her own considerable strengths and her environment.

A developmental-ecological framework views development as scaffolded by culture including systems of language, mathematics, religion, music, and so forth developed over centuries and interpreted and practiced by individuals living in specific communities. Children are not lone scientists out to discover the universe from scratch, nor are they unaided in this quest. Parents, teachers, social workers, older siblings, peers, and family and community members support children's emerging competencies. In the case of Summer, she was helped to understand her mother's illness by her social worker and foster parents, who helped her to interpret her early experiences in a way that allowed for her positive development. This family drew upon Christian beliefs to find forgiveness, to accept the past, and to move into the future secure in a belief in the inherent worth of each individual.

MODERN SOCIAL WORK IS EVIDENCE BASED

An evidence-based approach is necessary to professional social work practice and policy. The empirically based knowledge of modern social work is one of its most important distinguishing features from moralistic attempts at intervention that characterized nineteenth-century predecessors. It is our ethical responsibility as social workers to offer interventions that have been rigorously scrutinized and shown to be effective and not to cause harm or be wasteful of scarce resources. Reliance on popular opinion and limited personal experience is simply unprofessional and unethical.

Our in-depth discussions in each chapter are based on systematic quantitative and qualitative research. We encourage students to read critically, to ask themselves: Upon what is this claim or recommendation based: personal opinion, popular consensus, empirical research, practice experience? We also encourage students to practice the critical thinking model in empirical research to challenge existing practice and policy. We encourage students to ask: What are the alternative interpretations or explanations for the success (or lack thereof) of a given practice or policy? We remind ourselves that even the most effective intervention or policy is imperfect. To improve our profession, we must continuously access the limitations, as well as the strengths of our practice, by holding them up to the most rigorous scrutiny.

Figure 8.2.
Happy, well-functioning families come in diverse forms. This single mother is raising her biological and adopted children.

We recognize the limitations of empirical research and the important place of practice experience. First, empirical research is limited in scope. For many of the complex issues that social workers face every day, there are multiple valid perspectives is interpretations of human behavior. The child welfare worker must consider the legitimate, but often conflicting, perspectives of the state, the parent, and the child. Such complexity of experience and perspective is not often adequately represented in empirical research. Second, objectivity in research is never perfect. Objectivity is a goal toward which we strive. Bias, however, enters into research at multiple levels including the very questions asked, and the projects that are funded. In research, some compelling questions, such as the role of religion in human development, have been inadequately addressed, although other questions less central to understanding human behavior in the social environment receive more attention and research dollars. Next, quality empirical research is time-consuming and expensive. The reality is that social workers urgently need answers to address emerging social problems, for example, the impact of parent methamphetamine abuse in children and the child welfare system. Funding and conducting the research necessary to address such complex and pressing social issues can take years. In teaching human behavior in the social environment, we constantly challenge our students to consider the following questions: What questions does this body of research leave unanswered or inadequately addressed? What are the limitations, as well as strengths, of this empirical evidence? Despite the limitations of empirical research, we are committed to empirical research as the best current strategy for fairly and rigorously examining the quality of social work practice and policy in order to enhance our effectiveness.

At the same time, social workers must balance knowledge of research with knowledge of individual clients and settings. Any empirical body of research must be applied to particular clients or settings. Social workers must use their professional knowledge and practice experience to apply research about the general population, or a specific community, to their own particular clients or community. We encourage students to ask: How might empirical research inform my practice with this individual client or policy within this particular community? In the case of Summer, her social worker was aware of research indicating the mental health risks of trauma experienced early in life. Summer, however, was adjusting well within a family living in a remote, rural area. Rather than insist that the family travel long distances to seek treatment, the social worker educated Summer's foster parents regarding children's response to trauma. Further, the family was provided with referrals for mental health care should Summer require counseling in the future.

SOCIAL WORK ISSUES AFFECT MULTIPLE INTERACTING SYSTEMS

Throughout the book, we have concentrated on the individual as the focal system, but most social work issues affect multiple systems. Any given social work case is likely to involve many individuals at varying points in the life span, and many systems. Not only do these other individuals and systems have their own needs and resources, but they may serve as important sources of support (or risk) for the social work client. The placement of a child in foster care affects not only that child, but also that child's parent, who may be struggling with issues in early or middle adulthood and who has complex needs of her own, for example, for health, mental health, substance abuse, or domestic violence intervention. It also may affect older siblings, for example, adolescent siblings struggling to develop an identity apart from the family, and yet still very dependent on and identified with that family unit disrupted by foster placement of a younger sibling. The placement of a child in foster care also may affect extended family, for example, grandparents who must deal with their own child's struggles, such as addiction, violence, poverty, and failure as a parent. Grandparents also may be called upon to help raise their grandchild at a time in life when they are anticipating retirement. The issue of an individual child placed in foster care also affects multiple systems, including families, schools, and communities. For example, the child may need to change schools in midyear or go to live in another community.

In addition, any of the issues discussed in this book can affect an individual at varying levels of context. In the case of Summer (the focal system), she was affected by her strong physical and mental health, the microsystem (e.g., her foster parents built a positive and supportive relationship with her) the mesosystem (e.g., her social worker and foster parents built relationships with one another to support Summer), the ecosystem (e.g., Summer's foster father's employer encouraged him to take family time from work to help his new foster child adjust to her new home), and the macrosystem (e.g., social workers advocated for policy changes to facilitate adequate health and mental health funding for foster children and substance abuse intervention for their parents).

SOCIAL WORK ISSUES AFFECT INDIVIDUALS ACROSS THE LIFE SPAN

For the purposes of analysis, we have presented in-depth discussions of specific social work issues at various phases of the life cycle. Many issues addressed by social workers, however, affect individuals throughout the life span. Adults organize attachment relationships with aging parents, partners, spouses, close friends, and children throughout their lives. Similarly, issues of spirituality, relationships with individuals further along in life (mentors), mental and physical illness, and even death can occur at any point in the life cycle.

The issues of poverty, substance abuse, and violence presented in boxes throughout the book illustrate how social work issues affect individuals and communities over time. Poverty affects individuals from conception to death. A pregnant woman's poverty can undermine her prenatal care. The location of prenatal clinics, availability of transportation, work requirements, and fear of losing a job for taking time off can prevent low-income mothers from using free or nearly free prenatal care. In infancy and early childhood, poverty can affects low-income mothers' access to health care and quality day care.

By middle childhood, poverty can affect schooling. School funding is often based on property taxes; therefore, middle-income districts can receive a greater amount of discretionary school funding than low-income districts. Some states and local governments do not support preschool or require kindergarten attendance. This may result in children from poorer neighborhoods entering first grade unprepared and unaware of how to fit into the classroom. Children growing up in poverty-stricken areas may have few role models who were successful in school, and parents may lack the experience and skills to teach children effective study skills. The interactions among poor school preparation, large chaotic classrooms, ineffective home study supervision, a need to earn money, and a neighborhood culture of academic underachievement can literally push all but the most exceptional children out of school.

Poverty also effects the development of adults. Young adults who have grown up in low-income families and failed to achieve in school may see little hope of working their way into the middle class and may be more easily recruited into crime or use of street drugs and alcohol. Some young women from low-income families believe that marriage, especially a lasting marriage, may never be obtained. In order to maintain a sense of family and purpose, some young women who live in poverty choose to have children outside of traditional marriage. Children may be highly valued and represent a cultural and life goal that can be achieved.

Older low-income adults often lack critical medical care, proper nutrition, and social support. Without financial security, aging people can become isolated and forgotten. As illustrated in the chapter on aging, far too many individuals, particularly minority people, are forced to continue working, even though they are in poor health, or to survive on Social Security alone. Because of our Western idealization of youth, many older people have difficulty finding employment and experience a devaluation of their years of life experience. Illness for the aged person can be extremely frightening. Not only is death near, but inability to recover from illness may force the older adult into a nursing home. Because nursing homes are rarely fully funded by private or public health insurance, older adults fear that a lengthy nursing home stay will deplete their life savings.

A GLOBAL PERSPECTIVE IS NECESSARY TO SOCIAL WORK IN THE TWENTY-FIRST CENTURY

The main focus of this book has been on social work in the United States. As the world grows smaller, social workers and social agencies must become more globally minded and responsive—world poverty can no longer be overlooked. Because the poorest nations are unable to compete in world markets, their governments and health organizations are unable to cope with epidemics of HIV-AIDS, tuberculosis, and other diseases. As social workers, we are concerned because a substantial number of human beings are living in substandard conditions and dying unnecessarily. From a self-survival perspective, world poverty is a threat to industrialized nations. Revolutions, terrorism, and disease grow as desperation and hopelessness increase. The resettlement of refugees and increased illegal immigration expose citizens of industrialized nations to new and old communicable diseases. Simplistic policies such as closing borders or not aiding politically oppressed and poor immigrants are bound to fail. Unless world poverty is attacked in an organized global manner, Western nations will continue to experience an increase in illegal immigration and terrorist violence. Social workers must prepare to work more closely with relief organizations, refugee programs, and legal and illegal immigrants.

GLOSSARY

Acquisition Developmental process through which an individual actively interprets, responds to, and ultimately embraces, rejects, or elaborates upon the social patterns to which the individual is exposed.

Alzheimer's disease The most common and well-known type of dementia. It is characterized by progressive impairment of memory and cognitive function and may lead to a completely vegetative state and death after anywhere from three to twenty years. Neuropathologic indicators are neurofibrillary tangles and senile plaques.

Annual Program Meeting (APM) The largest national conference of undergraduate and graduate social work educators.

Anomia Impaired comprehension in which the principal deficit is naming persons and objects seen, heard, or felt; due to lesions in various portions of the language area of the brain.

Attachment Close, enduring, affective bonds that develop throughout the life span, for example, between infants and their caregivers.

Attention deficit hyperactivity disorder (ADHD) A behavioral syndrome consisting of short attention span, hyperkinetic physical behavior, and learning problems. Attention deficit disorder (ADD) presents without hyperkinetic physical behavior.

Autism A neurological disorder characterized by severely abnormal development of social skills and verbal and nonverbal communication. Affected individuals may follow rigid rituals, have a narrow range of interest, and activities, appear unable to understand others' feelings, and become upset with any changes in their environment.

Behavior modification The use of operant conditioning models (i.e., positive and negative reinforcement) to change behavior.

Bio-psycho-social-spiritual perspective An interdisciplinary framework embraced by social work that focuses on the well-being of the whole person physically, mentally, socially, and spiritually.

Bipolar disorder (Manic-depression) A psychiatric disorder characterized by episodes of mania. Individuals experience unusually high levels of exuberance, grandiosity, feelings of invulnerability, and extremely fast thinking.

Child welfare The government-organized formal service delivery system designed to assist children from birth through adolescence who have been abused or neglected, or whose well-being is at risk.

Classical conditioning The learning process by which an organism makes a connection between a neutral stimulus (such as a sound) when paired with an unconditioned stimulus (such as food) that results in an unconditioned response (such as salivation).

Clinical assumption Part of the assessment process in which certain facts are accepted with little or no challenge.

Clinical hypothesis Part of the assessment process that explains an observed behavior, problem, or social interaction.

Code of ethics The most visible compilation of the profession's ethical standards, for example the National Association of Social Workers' Code of Ethics.

Cognitive development Intellectual growth.

Constructivist theories of human development Developmental perspective that emphasizes the mutual impact of biological and psychological factors, as well as the individual's active role in shaping or constructing his/her own reality. Illustrated in the theory and research of Jean Piaget.

Contextual validity In the context of clinical assessments, contextual validity refers to the appropriateness of a clinical hypothesis drawn, in part, from theory, to the individual case under analysis. In the context of research, contextual validity refers to the appropriateness of the research methods to the sociocultural context under study.

Crisis nursery services Provision of temporary emergency care for children.

Cultural-historical theories of human development The theoretical framework that views the cultural and historical context as a critical third factor in development through which biology and experience interact. Illustrated in the theory and research of Lev Vygotsky.

Culture The physical objects, activities, values, and patterns of living and meaning that are shaped by the experiences of earlier generations and elaborated by later generations.

Dementia An umbrella term that covers a group of diseases that affect the brain in middle to late adult life. It is characterized by a progressive loss of cognitive and intellectual functions, which includes the diminishing of short-term memory, judgment, and language.

Developmental-ecological theory The analytic perspective that examines biological, psychological, and social characteristics of the individual as they are shaped over time within cultural and historical contexts. Related to the theory and research of Urie Bronfenbrenner.

Developmental relationship Term used in the research on mentoring to refer to relationships where mentor's goals and expectations vary over time in relation to the adolescent's changing needs.

Disorganized/disoriented attachment A type of attachment relationship in which children do not use caregivers as a secure base or employ any other coherent behavioral strategy to cope with stress. Rather, they show a range of responses to the "strange situation" procedure atypical of children in secure or insecure attachment relationships

Domestic violence Deliberate harming of a family member or intimate partner through physical, emotional, or sexual abuse.

Dual relationship Fulfilling a psychological need of the professional, and hence shifting the focus of the helping relationship from the client's needs.

Echolalia A neurological disorder characterized by a person's involuntary parrotlike repetition of words spoken by another person.

Ecology Branch of science that deals with the interrelationships of organisms with their environment.

Ethnographic methods Ethnography is a branch of anthropology that studies the beliefs, values, and practices of a specific social or cultural group within the cultural context. Ethnographic methods include interviews, direct observation, and review of records such as local newspapers and historic sources.

Exosystem From an ecological perspective, the exosystem is that level of context that consists of one or more settings that do not involve the person as an active participant, but in which events occur that do affect the person; for example, a husband may have no contact with his wife's workplace, but the stress she experiences there can affect the marital relationship.

Experience-dependent developmental process Developmental process evolved to make adaptive use of experience that can be "expected" at a particular time and in adequate quality for nearly all juveniles of a species, for example, visual stimulation and social contact. Experiences that are impoverished or distorted may have lasting detrimental effects on brain development.

Experience-expectant developmental process Developmental process encompassing several forms of lifelong neural plasticity that allow for some modification of earlier brain development, for example, learning of particular vocabulary, spatial information, and social relationships. Occurs through new synaptic connections.

Focal system The analytic vantage point of the ecological analysis, the perspective from which related systems are viewed (microsystems, mesosystems, exosystems, macrosystems).

Folk theories Informal understanding of human behavior and development. Includes values, beliefs, and explanations for how the social world works acquired within the family and community.

Human development The sequence of changes that begins after conception and continues throughout life.

Individual education plan (IEP) Formal plan to address difficulties a student may be experiencing in school.

Information processing A computer metaphor used to explain how humans process, store, and retrieve information.

Insecure/avoidant attachment Type of relationship reflected in the "strange situation" procedure in which infants remain more distant from their caregivers in times of stress when compared to securely attached infants.

Insecure/resistant attachment Type of relationship reflected in the "strange situation" procedure in which infants expend relatively more energy than do securely attached infants monitoring the whereabouts of their caregivers but are not readily comforted by their nearness.

Learning disorder/disability/difference Neurologically based substandard cognitive functioning which can challenge learning in certain contexts, especially school, for individuals with average to above-average intelligence.

Learning theory Explanation of behavioral changes as a result of experiencing the positive and negative consequences of behavior, as well as observing and imitating others. Associated with the theory and research of B. F. Skinner and J. B. Watson.

Macrosystem From an ecological perspective, the level of context that consists of the cultural patterns of the larger society in which other systems are embedded. It includes widespread societal values such as individual freedom, major institutions such as government and education, and economic structures.

Major depression Biochemical mental disorder characterized by sustained depression of mood, sleep and appetite disturbances, and feelings of guilt, worthlessness, and hopelessness. Precipitating life events do not adequately account for the degree of depression. It may occur at any age and tends to recur throughout life. It is biologically based (family history). Usually responds to antidepressants or electroconvulsive therapy.

Manic-depression See bipolar disorder.

Medical social work A social work specialization that focuses on the impact of disease and disability on individuals of all ages, their families, and communities.

Menopause Permanent cessation of ovulation and menstruation in women. Because of a decrease in ovarian function, the woman has not experienced a period for at least one year and is no longer able to become pregnant.

Mentor An older, more experienced adult who has a relationship with an unrelated younger person in which the adult provides ongoing guidance, instruction, and encouragement.

Mesosystem From an ecological perspective, the level of context that consists of the set of interrelationships between two or more microsystems; for example, a child's parent takes her to kindergarten and meets the teacher, thereby forming a new home-school mesosystem.

Microsystem From an ecological perspective, the level of context that consists of the immediate social environment, the day-to-day reality of the focal system, which includes those settings in which people have face-to-face, sustained, and significant relationships with others, such as families, peer groups, schools, workplaces, and churches.

Mutism Organic or functional absence of the faculty of speech. May indicate trauma or stress

National Council on Social Work Education (CSWE) Established in 1946 for the purpose of accreditation, which involves monitoring the performance of social work educational programs to deliver quality standardized curriculum.

Neuron Nerve cell; the basic unit of the nervous system.

Neurotransmitter Any specific chemical agent present at synapses or neuromuscular junctions that are capable of transmitting an electrical impulse by binding to their cognate receptor, thus enabling communication between brain cells.

Operant conditioning Changes in behavior shaped by the consequences of that behavior.

Oral history Historical information that is collected during interviews of individuals who have led significant lives.

Palilalia Neurological deterioration resulting in a person's repeating over and over his or her own words.

Physical ecology Includes climate, plant and animal life, and human artifacts.

Prefrontal cortex The anterior portion of each cerebral hemisphere of the brain. Functions include emotion, imagining, controlling attention, memory, forming explicit plans, and making decisions.

Prescriptive relationship Type of relationship in which adults rather than the youth prioritize their goals for the mentoring relationship and set the goals and ground rules for the relationship.

Pretend play A form of play associated with early childhood in which actions, objects, and persons are transformed or treated nonliterally.

Punishment From the perspective of learning theory, punishment is consequences of behavior that reduce the probability that the behavior will reoccur.

Reactive depression "Secondary" depression that occurs in response to real-life events, such as grief, illness, loss of job, family problems. It is characterized by depression, anxiety, bodily complaints, tension, and guilt. It may respond spontaneously or to a variety of ministrations. Accounts for more than 60 percent of all depressions.

Reinforcement From the perspective of learning theory, reinforcement (or rewards) are consequences of behavior that increase the probability that the behavior will reoccur.

Religion A system of symbols, beliefs, rituals, and texts shared by a community of believers. It provides a collective framework for expressing spirituality.

Resilience The ability of people to find meaning in their lives even in the face of extraordinary hardship.

Schizophrenia Neuropsychiatric disorder characterized by abnormalities of perception, content of thought, and thought processes (hallucinations and delusions), and by extensive withdrawal of interest from other people and the outside world with excessive focusing on one's own mental life.

School social work Social work specialization that blends the fields of social work and education to support the well-being and academic achievement of children and youth in schools.

Secondary trauma Guilt, overwhelming emotions, rescue motifs, nightmares, social isolation, and persistent sadness experienced from exposure to the trauma of others.

Securely attached Type of relationship assessed in the "strange situation" procedure in which children use caregivers as secure bases to which they may return in times of stress.

Self-report The systematic collection of individuals' own reports of their behavior or psychological processes.

Social developmental study Report by school social worker considering the child's developmental history in context including prenatal and family history.

Social ecology The range of situations in which people interact, including the people with whom they interact, roles they play, what they do together, how they interact, and the dynamics of social groups.

Socialization The process by which experts structure the social environment and display patterned meanings for the novice; for example, parents teach children.

Social learning theory Framework designed to explain how learning occurs when we observe and imitate or model others. Associated with the research and theory of A. Bandura.

Social science theory Formal, explicit framework designed to understand, explain, and predict the social world. Developed through empirical research and logic.

Spirituality The direct personal experience of the sacred; the awareness of a higher power, a causal force beyond the material or rational, that operates in all aspects of existence.

Strange situation A procedure designed by Mary Ainsworth to evaluate young children's responses to a friendly female stranger in the company of their mothers, when they are left alone, and when they are reunited with their mothers that allows observation of parent-child interaction during gradually escalating, low-level, relatively common, and nontraumatic stressors.

Strengths-based practice Perspective in social work that emphasizes the utilization of clients' strengths and resources in addressing problems.

Synapse The functional membrane-to-membrane contact of the nerve cell with another nerve cell; the connection between neurons.

Systematic observations of behavior Research method that involves the direct observation of the behavior of interest, for example, parenting practices, often through use of videotaping or audiotaping. May occur in the real-world settings of participants' lives, or more structured settings.

Teratogen A drug or other external agent, for example, a chemical, virus, or ionizing radiation, that interrupts or alters the normal development of a fetus with results that are evident at birth.

Transdisciplinary research team The team of scholars with specializations ranging from the biological to the social sciences working together to solve complex problems.

INDEX

Abuse
  alcohol, during pregnancy, 42
  child, poverty and, 85
  elder, 200–201
  parent methamphetamine, 87
Accidental deaths, adolescents and, 120
Acquisition, 15
Addiction, animal studies of, 149
Adolescence
  developmental-ecological analysis of
    biological factors, 116–117
    cultural-historical factors, 124
    psychological factors, 118–119
    social factors, 119–123
  development highlights of, 114–124
  economic transitions of, 122
  religious experiences in, 89
Adolescents
  accidental deaths and, 120
  bullying and, 120
  causes of hospitalization for, 116
  guns and, 119
  homicide and, 120
  homosexuality and, 117
  implications of developmental-ecological analysis of mentoring with, 131–135
  mentoring programs for, 112–114
  mentoring relationships and, 124–131
  overview of, 109–110
  paid work and, 122
  parents and, 119, 121–122
  puberty and, 122–123
  risk factors for violent behavior for, 121
  school drop-out rates for, 118
  school social work with, 110–114
  school violence and, 120
  sexual orientation and, 117
  substance abuse by, 125
  suicide and, 120
  violence and, 119–120
  as volunteers, 122
Adoption and Safe Families Act (1997), 37
Affilia-Journal of Women and Social Work, 25
African American church, 90
African American culture, storytelling in, 90–91
African American religion, features of, 90
Age, poverty rates by, 16. *See also* Older adulthood; Older adults
Aggressive behavior, chronic, 12
Ainsworth, Mary, 51–52
Alaska Native households, poverty and, 170
Alcohol
  abuse, during pregnancy, 42
  prenatal exposure to, 41
Alcoholism
  cost of, 148
  suicide and, 148

Alzheimer's Association, 218–219
  interventions for, 219–226
Alzheimer's disease, 199–200. *See also* Older adults
  depression and, 217
  developmental-ecological analysis of
    biological factors, 217
    cultural factors, 218
    psychological factors, 217–218
    social factors, 218
  overview of, 215–216
  stages of, 217–218
American Indian households, poverty and, 172
Animal studies of addiction, 149
Annual Program Meeting, 157
Anomia, 217
Antisocial personality disorder, 173
Applied social science research, 24–27
  methods used in, 25–27
Assessment process, 185–186
Attachment relationships, 38–39
  categories of, 52
  child welfare workers and, 49
  developmental-ecological analysis of, 50–58
    biological factors, 50–51
    cultural-historical factors, 56–58
    psychological factors, 51–55
    social factors, 51–55
  development and organization of, 47–58
  with foster infants, 39–40
  implications of developmental-ecological analysis of, 58–66
  insecure, 52
  physical ecology and, 57–58
  secure, 52–54
  sensitivity parenting and, 53
  social competence and, 54
  Type D, 54–55
Attention deficit disorder, 110
Attention deficit disorder with hyperactivity, 110
Autism, 6
Autobiography of a Face (Grealy), 85
Avoidant/insecure relationships, 52

Baby blues, 149–150
Beauvoir, Simone de, 214
Becoming a Doctor: A Journey of Initiation in Medical School (Konner), 152
Behavior, systematic observations of, 26
Behavior modification, 10
Biological factors. *See also* Developmental-ecological analysis
  of adolescence, 116–117
  affecting social work students, 154
  of Alzheimer's disease, 217
  of attachment relationships, 50–51
  of development and organization of attachment relationships in infants

and young children, 50–51
of late adulthood, 209–210
of major clinical depression, 185–187
of mentoring relationships, 126
of middle adulthood, 177–181
of midlife depression, 185–187
of older adulthood, 209–210
of young adulthood, 147
Biological theories, 5–6
Bipolar disorder, 6, 185, 191
Black, Janet, 156
Bronfenbrenner, Urie, 21
Brown, Clara, 1–3, 238
Bullying, adolescents and, 120

Cabot, Richard, 205
Cannon, Ida, 205
Carter, Jimmy, 200
Charity Organization Society, 88
Child abuse, poverty and, 85
Child and Youth Services Review, 25
Childbearing, young adulthood and,
    149–150
Children with learning disorders, adult
    outcomes for, 83–84
Child welfare
    infants and young children and, 37–40
    in Japan, 38
    social workers in, 37
    in United States, 37–38
Child Welfare, 25
Child welfare social workers. *See also*
    Social workers
    attachment relationships and, 49
    implications of developmental-ecologi-
        cal analysis of attachment relation-
        ships for, 58–66
Chronic aggressive behavior, 12
Clark, Cindy Dell, 44–45
Classical conditioning, 9
Clinical depression. *See* Major clinical
    depression
Code of Ethics, NASW, 153
Cognitive development, 10–11
Cole, Robert, 89
Community, 99
Constructivist theories, 10–12
Council on Social Work Education
    (CSWE), 145, 157
Crisis nurseries, 48–49
Cultural-historical factors. *See also*
    Developmental-ecological analysis
    of adolescence, 123–124
    of Alzheimer's disease, 218
    of attachment relationships, 56–58
    of development and organization of
        attachment relationships in infants
        and young children, 56–58
    of late adulthood, 214–215
    of major clinical depression, 191
    of mentoring relationships, 129–131
    of middle adulthood, 182–183
    of midlife depression, 191
    of young adulthood, 150–152

Cultural-historical theories, 14–18
Culture, defined, 14

Deaths, accidental, adolescents and, 120.
    See also Dying
Dementia, 199, 216. *See also* Alzheimer's
    disease; Older adults
Demographics, U.S., 204–205
Dental care, middle childhood and, 81
Depression, 183
    Alzheimer's disease and, 217, 218
    bipolar disorder and, 185
    major clinical. *See* Major clinical
        depression
    reactive, 176
Development. *See* Human development
Developmental-ecological analysis, 2–3
    of adolescent development, 116–124
    of Alzheimer's disease, 216–219
    of attachment relationships in infants
        and young children, 47–58
    biological factors in. *See* Biological
        factors
    cultural-historical factors in. *See*
        Cultural-historical factors
    implications of, for child welfare
        workers, 58–66
    of late adulthood, 209–215
    of mentoring relationships, 124–131
    of multicultural social work education,
        161–163
    overview using, 185–186
    problem solving in social work and,
        237–238
    psychological factors in. *See*
        Psychological factors
    social factors in. *See* Social factors
    of social work issues, 4–5
    of social work students, 154–157
    of spiritual development in middle
        childhood, 88–98
Developmental mentoring relationships,
    128
Disorganized/disoriented (Type D) attach-
    ment relationships, 54–55
Domestic violence, infants and young chil-
    dren and, 36
Drop-out rates, school, for adolescents,
    118
Dual relationships, 154, 155
Dying. *See also* Late adulthood
    depersonalization of, 214–215
    global perspectives of, 215
    process of, 209–210
    psychological aspects of, 210–211

Early adulthood. *See* Young adulthood
Ecological perspectives, in school social
    work, 112. *See also* Developmental-
    ecological analysis
Ecology, 3
    physical, 19
    social, 19–24
Education, social work, 158–161. *See also*

Social work students
 multicultural, 161–163
Elderly. *See* Late adulthood
Elder mistreatment and abuse, 200–201
Environment, role of, in human develop-
 ment, 5–6
Erikson, Eric, 148–149, 181
Ethical values, in social work, 153
Ethnographic methods, 26
Evidence-based social work, 238–240.
 See also Social work
Exosystems, 22–23
Experience-dependent developmental
 processes, 51
Experience-expectant developmental
 processes, 51

Families. *See* Parents
Fetal alcohol effects (FAE), 41
Fetal alcohol syndrome (FAS), 41, 42
First Baptist Church, study of
 adult-child relationships at, 95–96
 community involvement at, 93–94
 individual worth at, 94–95
 intervention for children at, 97–98
 Mother Edith Hudley's oral history of,
  92–93
 overview of, 91–92
 social work implications of, 98–99
 spiritual development at, 93–97
 spirituality at, 93
 storytelling at, 96–97
Focal system, 21
Folk theories, 4
Formal learning, 81–84
Foster care, 39–40
Foster youth, mentoring relationships and,
 129
Freud, Sigmund, 7, 43
Friendly visitors, 1

Gesell, Arnold, 5
Goal-corrected partnership, 47, 49
Grealy, Lucy, 85
Grief counseling, 213–214
Guns, adolescents and, 119

Hall, G. Stanley, 109
Heart attacks, warning signs for, 179
HIV-AIDS prevention, in India, 144
Homicide, adolescents and, 120
Homosexual couples, 150
Homosexuality, adolescents and, 117
Hospice care, 222
Hospitalization, causes of, for adolescents,
 116
Houston, Annie, 156
Hudley, Edith, 89, 92–93, 200
Human behavior
 folk theories of, 4
 social science theories of, 4–5
Human development, 3
 biological theories of, 5–6
 constructivist theories of, 10–11
 cultural-historical theories of, 14–18

ecological-systems perspectives of,
 18–24
psychodynamic theory and, 7–8
psychological and social theories of,
 7–14
role of environment in, 5–6

Immunization, of U.S. children, 45
India, HIV-AIDS prevention efforts in, 144
Individual education plans (IEPs), 110
Infant mortality rates, 44
Infants and young children
 attachment relationships and, 38–39
 child welfare and, 37–40
 development and organization of
  attachment behavior in, 47–58
   biological factors of, 50–51
   cultural-historical factors of, 56–58
   social-psychological factors of, 51–55
 development highlights of, 40–47
 domestic violence and, 36
 foster care and, 39–40
 health development of, 43
 immunization of U.S., 45
 mobility of, 46
 mortality rates of, 44
Informal learning, 81
Informal mentoring relationships, 112–113
Information-processing theory, 9
Insecure attachment, 52
Insecure/avoidant relationships, 52
Insecure/resistant relationships, 52–53
Intelligence
 alternative frameworks for, 10
 triarchic model of, 10

James, William, 41
Japan, child welfare in, 38
Jewish communal services, 88
Journal of Social Work Education, 157,
 159
Journals, professional, 25
Juvenile prostitution, in Taiwan, 115

Konner, Melvin, 152
Kubler-Ross, Elisabeth, 210–211

Labouvie-Vief, Gisella, 147
Language, 14
Late adulthood. *See also* Dying; Older
 adulthood
 developmental-ecological analysis of
  biological factors, 209–210
  cultural-historical factors, 214–215
  psychological factors, 210–214
  social factors, 210–214
 overview of development in, 208–209
Learning
 formal, 81–84
 informal, 81
 storytelling for, 99
Learning differences, 6
Learning disorders, children with, 84
 adult outcomes for, 83–84
Learning theory, 9–10

Macrosystems, 23
Major clinical depression, 173–178
   biological factors of, 185–187
   cultural-historical context of, 191
   developmental-ecological analysis of,
     183–185
   psychological factors of, 187–190
   social factors of, 190
   social workers and, 191–192
   suicide and, 184
   symptoms of, 183
   treating, 184
Manic-depressive disorder. *See* Bipolar
   disorder
Marijuana, adolescents and, 125
Maternal mortality rates, 44
Medical social work
   with older adults, 205–208
   practice story and programs
     for adolescents, 112–114
   formal, 113–114
Mentoring relationships
   biological factors of, 126
   cultural-historical factors of, 129–131
   developmental, 128
   development of, 124–131
   foster youth and, 128
   informal, 112–113
   prescriptive, 128
   psychological factors of, 126–127
   school social work and, 131–135
   social factors of, 127–129
   TALKS, 131
   types of, 128
Mentors, 112–113
   for adolescents, 122
   for adolescents experiencing puberty,
     117
   for girls during Victorian period,
     123–124
   psychological development of adoles-
     cents and, 118–119
   for sexual minorities, 117
Mesosystems, 22
Methamphetamine abuse, parent, 87
Microsystems, 21–22
Middle adulthood
   developmental-ecological analysis of
     biological factors, 177–181
     cultural-historical factors, 182–183
     psychological factors, 181–182
     social factors, 181–182
   developmental-ecological analysis of
     depression in, 183–191
     biological factors, 185–187
     cultural-historical factors, 191
     psychological factors, 187–190
     social factors, 190
   development highlights of, 177–183
   mental health care and, 170–177
Middle childhood, 77–79. *See also* Infants
   and young children
   cognitive competencies in, 80–81
   dental care and, 81
   development highlights during, 79–88

   guidelines for social workers for, 98–99
   mastering learning in school and,
     81–82
   parent relationships and, 85–86
   peer relationships and, 84–85
   planning and, 80–81
   poverty and health during, 80
   religious experiences in, 89
   spiritual development in, 88–98
Midlife adults, 169–170
   mental health care with, 170–177
Midlife crisis, 181
Miller, Joshua, 155
Moos, Rudolf, 23
Mortality rates
   infant, 44
   maternal, 44
Moskovitz, Sarah, 89
Multicultural social work education,
   161–163

National Alliance for Mental Illness
   (NAMI), 190
National Association of Social Workers
   (NASW) Code of Ethics, 153
National Council on Social Work
   Education (CSWE), 145
National Elder Abuse Incidence Study, 201
Neighborhood violence, 13
Neurotransmitters, 50, 186–187
Norton, D., 21

Older adulthood. *See also* Late adulthood
   biological factors of, 209–210
   cultural-historical context of, 214–215
   physical problems of, 209
   psychological factors of, 210–214
   social factors of, 210–214
Older adults. *See also* Alzheimer's disease;
   Late adulthood
   elder abuse and, 200–201
   medical social work with, 205–208
   "middle-old," 208
   "old-old," 208
   poverty and, 203
   prescription and over-the-counter drug
     abuse by, 202–203
   social workers and, 203
   "young-old," 208
On Death and Dying (Kubler-Ross),
   210–211
Operant conditioning, 9
Over-the-counter drug abuse, 202–203

Paid work, adolescents and, 122
Parenting
   middle childhood and, 85–87
   sensitivity, 53
Parenting assessment teams, 69
Parent methamphetamine abuse, 87
Parents
   adolescents and, 119, 121–122
   attachment relationships and, 53–54
   mentoring relationships and, 130–131
Pavlov, Ivan, 9

Peer relationships, 84-85
Physical ecology, 19
    attachment behaviors and, 57-58
Piaget, Jean, 10-11, 43
Planning, middle childhood and, 80-81
Play, 34, 43
    pretend, 43-46
Popper, Karl, 4
Postpartum depression, 150, 151
Poverty
    by age, 16
    Alaska Native households and, 170
    American Indian households and, 170
    child abuse and, 85
    children's health and, 80
    older Americans and, 203
    prenatal development and, 42
    rates of, by race, 16
    in United States, 16, 147, 170
    world-wide, 17
Practice stories and advice
    of child welfare work, 62-66
    of medical social worker, 222-226
    of mental health social worker,
        188-189
    of school social work, 132-135
    of social policy, 100-102
    for social work education, 159-161
Prefrontal cortex, 79-80
Prescription drug abuse, 202-203
Prescriptive mentoring relationships, 128
Pretend play, 43-46
Professional journals, 25
Psychodynamic theory, 7-8
Psychological factors. *See also*
        Developmental-ecological analysis
    of adolescence, 118-119
    affecting social work students, 154-155
    of Alzheimer's disease, 217-218
    of attachment relationships, 51-55
    of development and organization of
        attachment relationships in infants
        and young children, 51-55
    of late adulthood, 210-214
    of major clinical depression, 187-190
    of mentoring relationships, 126-127
    of middle adulthood, 181-182
    of midlife depression, 187-190
    of older adulthood, 210-214
    of young adulthood, 147-150
Puberty, 112, 116-117
    adolescents and, 122-123
Punishment, 9

Race, poverty rates by, 16
Raise Up a Child (Hudley), 89
Ratcliff, Donald, 89
Reactive depression, 176
Reinforcement (rewards), 9
Religion, defined, 88
Research
    applied social science, 24-27
    methods used in, 25-27
Research on Social Work Practice, 25
Resilience, spirituality and, 89

Resistant/insecure relationships, 52-53
Respite services, 48-49
Rewards (reinforcement), 9
Rhodes, Jean, 124, 129
Rogoff, Barbara, 15-17
Rosengren, Karl, 89
Rousseau, Jean-Jacques, 109

Scaffolding, 15
Schaie, K. Warner, 147
Schizophrenia, 6
School-aged children. *See* Middle child-
        hood; Young adulthood
School drop-out rates, 118
School learning, 81-84
School social work. *See also* Social work
        with adolescents, 110-114
    ecological perspectives in, 112
    implications of developmental-ecologi-
        cal analysis of mentoring for,
        131-135
    mentoring programs and, 131-135
    practice stories and advice for,
        132-135
School social workers, 110. *See also* Social
        workers
    adolescents and, 124
    tasks of, 110-111
School violence, adolescents and, 120
Secure attached attachment relationships,
        52-54
Self-report methods, 25-26
Sensitivity parenting, 53
Settlement House movement, 88
Sexual minorities, mentors for, 117
Sexual orientation, adolescents and, 117
Skinner, B. F., 9
Sleeping patterns, 177-178
Social activities, 19-20
Social climate, 23-24
Social competence, attachment relation-
        ships and, 54
Social composition, 19
Social developmental studies, 15
Social ecology, 19-24
    social activities and, 19-20
    social climate and, 23-24
    social composition and, 19
    social interactions and, 20
    social system dynamics and, 20-23
Social factors. *See also* Developmental-
        ecological analysis
    of adolescence, 119-123
    affecting social work students, 155-156
    of Alzheimer's disease, 218-219
    of development and organization of
        attachment relationships in infants
        and young children, 51-55
    of late adulthood, 210-214
    of major clinical depression, 190
    of mentoring relationships, 127-129
    of middle adulthood, 181-182
    of midlife depression, 190
    of older adulthood, 210-214
    of young adulthood, 147-150

Social interactions, 20
Socialization, 15
Social learning theorists, 9
Social-psychological factors, of attachment relationships, 51–55
Social science research, applied, 24–27
    methods used in, 25–27
Social Science Review, 25
Social science theories, 4–5
Social Security, 204
Social system dynamics, 20–23
Social systems
    components of, 20
    interacting levels of, 21–23
    self-preservation and, 20–21
    stability of, 21
Social work. *See also* Child welfare
    across life span of individuals, 241–242
    applied social science research and, 24–27
    developmental-ecological analysis for problem solving in, 237–238
    ethical values in, 153
    evidence-based, 238–240
    global perspective need to, 240
    knowledge base of, 1
    medical. *See* Medical social work
    multiple interacting systems and, 240–241
    psychodynamic theory and, 8
    school. *See* School social work
Social Work, 25
Social work education, 158–161. *See also* Social work students
    multicultural, 161–163
Social Work Education, 25, 157, 159
Social workers. *See also* Child welfare social workers; Mental health social workers; School social workers
    challenges facing, 1
    in child welfare practice, 37
    commitments to social justice by, 1
    counseling clients facing death and, 211–214
    influence of, 235–236
    medical. *See* Medical social workers
    older adults and, 203
    practice stories of. *See* Practice stories and advice
    professional journals for, 25
    religion and spirituality issues and, 88
    school-aged children and their families and, 98–99
Social work practice, impact of constructivist theories on, 11–12
Social work programs, 145
Social work students. *See also* Social work education
    developmental-ecological analysis of
        biological factors affecting, 154
        cultural-historical context affecting, 156–157
        psychological factors affecting, 154–155

    social factors affecting, 155–156
    education of, 158–161
    ethical values and, 153–154
    facilitating professional development of, 152–157
    multicultural education of, 161–163
Social work values, 153
Sperry, Doug, 91
Sperry, Linda, 91
Spiritual development, in middle childhood, 88–98
Spirituality, 99
    defined, 88
    resilience and, 89
The Spiritual Life of Children (Cole), 89
Sternberg, Robert, 10
Storytelling, 99
    in African American culture, 90–91
    at First Baptist Church, 96–97
Strange situation, 52
Strengths-based practice, religion and spirituality and, 89
Stress, parent sensitivity and, 53
Students. *See* Social work students
Substance abuse
    adolescents and, 125
    prescription and over-the-counter drug abuse, 202–203
Substance dependence
    defined, 7
    gene-environment interaction and, 171
    of parents, 86–87
    risk factors for, 9
Substance use, in United States, 8
Suicide
    adolescents and, 120
    alcoholism and, 148
    major clinical depression and, 184
    making assessments for, 191–192
    risk factors for, 184
Swenson, Carol, 218
Systematic observations of behavior, 25–26

Taiwan, juvenile prostitution in, 115
TALKS mentoring program, 131
Taylor, Jill McLean, 23
Teen pregnancy, 111
Teens. *See* Adolescents
Teratogens, 41, 42
Thomas, James, 218
Thorndike, Edward Lee, 9
Transdisciplinary research teams, 26–27
Type D (disorganized/disoriented) attachment relationships, 54–55

United States
    Alzheimer's disease in, 216–217
    American Indian and Alaska Native median income in, 170
    changing demographics in, 204–205
    child welfare system in, 37–38
    domestic violence in, 36
    immunization of children in, 45
    infant mortality rates in, 44

older Americans and poverty in, 203
poverty rate in, 16, 147, 171
school drop-out rates in, 118
substance use in, 8
suicide in, 185
teen pregnancy in, 111

Values, ethical, social work, 153
Van Wormer, Katherine, 156-157
Violence
    adolescent, 119-120
    adolescents and, 119-120
    domestic, infants and young children
        and, 36
    neighborhood, 13
    school, 120
Violent behavior, risk factors for, adoles-
    cents and, 121
Volunteers, adolescents as, 122
Vygotsky, Lev, 15, 43, 118

Watson, John B., 9
Wechsler intelligence scales, 9-10
Work, paid, adolescents and, 122
Wyatt, Richard Jed, 83-84

Young adulthood
    childbearing and, 149-150
    development highlights of, 146-152
        biological factors of, 147
        cultural-historical factors of,
        150-152
        psychological factors of, 147-150
        social factors of, 147-150
    social work and, 143
Young children. *See* Infants and young
    children